The Joy is in the Journey

A Woman's Guide Through Crisis and Change

by

Betty Hill Crowson

1663 Liberty Drive, Suite 200
Bloomington, Indiana 47403
(800) 839-8640
www.AuthorHouse.com

First published by AuthorHouse 04/18/05

ISBN: 1-4208-2297-7 (sc)

Library of Congress Control Number: 2004195563

Printed in the United States of America
Bloomington, Indiana

This book is printed on acid-free paper.

Acknowledgments

Just as it takes a village to raise a child, it takes an enclave of family and friends to write a book. That said, I thank each and every one of you who have encouraged me to stay faithful to the writing, and who have prayed for me to do so.

I would especially like to mention my dear friend Jane Militello who has been an active listener, reader, and supporter of *The Joy is in the Journey* since its inception in June of 1998. There were many days when I might have burned the manuscript page by page had it not been for Jane's calming wisdom, her ever-present faith in the value of and necessity for this book, and her undying support for me as a writer and teacher.

In June of 2001, God blessed me with an angel by the name of Marilynn Pysher. Since that time, Marilynn has been tireless in her efforts at proofreading, editing, creating graphics, and scrawling an occasional "huh?" over sections of my writing. She has encouraged me almost daily with her humor, love, and unfailing belief in my capabilities as an author and presenter. Her words of, "You go girl!" upheld me more times than even she could imagine. My gratitude is profound.

I am also extremely grateful for the many women who were generous enough to share both their trials and their triumphs to be used as the glue that binds this book together. As these stories support the principles and concepts of the text, they are invaluable to the integrity of this body of work. Thank you. I could never have written this book without you.

I would also like to thank Sister Maureen Kervick who enabled me to begin retreat ministry several years ago; The Reverend Dr. Steven Crowson for keeping a roof over our heads; our son Robert for sharing me with the computer a lot longer than either of us ever thought possible; Ashala Gabriel for introducing me to the foreign world of proposals and platforms, and stretching me far beyond my comfort zone; Dr. Christiane Northrup for her wonderful endorsement that encouraged me to stay faithful to the writing at a time when I needed it most; my sister Judith Parks for her willingness to drop everything to proofread over and over again; all of the friends of Bill Wilson who have supported me since 1978 to walk tall in my own truth; and, especially, the women that I have coached and who have attended my many week-end retreats over the years. I thank all of you "women of dignity and honor" for always reaching out to widen the circle of love, support, and wisdom.

It is with great gratitude and thanksgiving that I dedicate *The Joy is in the Journey: A Woman's Guide Through Crisis and Change* to all the women who have gone before me and to those who walk beside me. It is my sincere hope that this book will enable other women to not only find their authentic path, but also discover the joy that is in the journey.

Table of Contents

A Message to the Reader

There are many reasons to read *The Joy is in the Journey: A Woman's Guide Through Crisis and Change.* Whether you have recently experienced a change in circumstances, feel consumed by emotional excesses, have a desire to make significant changes in a lifestyle that no longer fulfills or gratifies you, or simply wish to follow through with a decision you have already made, this is the book for you. There is no mistake that it has found its way into your hands.

The chapters ahead outline specific "Solutions" that focus on helping you transition successfully. They work concurrently, providing the necessary tools for you to cope with the present conditions in your life, while promoting a deeper self-learning and spiritual awareness. The chapter arrangement is such that the work contained within each chapter prepares you for the next. The chapters flow one into another, with the last bringing you back again to the first. It can be guaranteed that each time you go through the Solutions, you will discover something you missed the time before. The nature of this process is that as you evolve and grow by putting these Solutions into action, you will understand the content - and yourself - at a deeper and more meaningful level.

At the same time, there is no need to get confused or mired in the work of any one chapter. If the specific suggestions seem irrelevant at the time, or the concepts too difficult to grasp or put into action, do not worry. It is not necessary to do this work perfectly or all at once. However, let there be no doubt - this book *does* involve work. The more open-minded you can be, and the more willing to follow suggestions to the best of your ability on a consistent basis, the greater your chances of not only successfully surviving this critical or transitional period, but also of experiencing the true meaning and the authentic joy that is contained within the journey of your life.

Introduction

One Woman's Journey into Wholeness

I was born feet first -- and lived much of my life the same way, with my feet either jumping in, or dragging me through all kinds of situations, relationships, and transitions, long before the rest of me had a prayer of catching up. I never went looking for change. It contained too much of the unknown to suit me. Yet, despite my efforts at avoidance, crisis and change have had a way of lurking in the shadows, waiting for me around every bend in the road.

Raised on a Maine dairy farm, my early memories are dim ones, more like faded snapshots of cows, chickens, crops, kids, and chaos. My parents were extraordinary people who were extraordinarily busy most of the time. As a child, I hardly knew them. My mother's time and energy were consumed with the physical demands created by several children, (seven of us in all), while my father was a handsome, shadowy stranger who moved quietly between the barn and fields.

According to the stories told, I was an inquisitive and energetic child, extremely attached to my younger brother, Bobby, with whom I shared the same age for one week each year. We were inseparable from the beginning, much like twins. In fact, they affectionately referred to us as "double trouble." For a few short years, life felt happy, safe and predictable.

There was absolutely no way any of us could have been prepared for the tragic drowning death of this wonderful little boy on a hot summer's day when he was seven years old. In an instant, life as we knew it ceased to be. We became a family in crisis, a family who knew only one way to cope with this devastating loss; to try and put it behind us by acting as if it had not happened at all.

When we don't know what to do, we tend to do what we know. My busy parents got even busier. And Bobby's life, as well as his death, became a subject that we kids knew not to mention. Instead, feelings were buried beneath layers of busyness, the clothes were packed away, and the memories tucked within. The place in our family previously occupied by Bobby was now filled with a huge, oppressive presence. Grief moved in with us on that hot August afternoon – and everyone tiptoed around it, unable to acknowledge it or call it by name.

At eight years old, I instantly lost all previous sense of security and predictability. The silence surrounding this crisis only added to my confusion and apprehension. I became consumed with feelings for which I had no knowledge or experience, and, hence, no solution. So I did what I thought I was supposed to -- I pretended they weren't there. Little did I know the damaging effect that unresolved and unexpressed feelings have on a little girl's inner sense of self and of feeling safe. By pushing these feelings underground, they proceeded to cast a dark shadow across my self-confidence and self-esteem, distorting my every perception and emotion.

As I drifted into middle childhood, I became a "grey" child, one who experiences the world as somewhat flat and colorless. No longer curious and energetic, I felt overwhelmed, exhausted, and inwardly frightened. My emotional life mimicked a game of musical chairs. I was constantly afraid that the music would suddenly stop, fearful that I wouldn't be able to find a seat. This was the state in which I entered adolescence. Although I managed to do well scholastically during high school, emotionally, I muddled through. My SAT marks were high enough to get into any school I wanted. Yet, I became a waitress and bartender, while my friends went off to college.

The next twelve years of my life were spent in making wrong turns on what I now know as the right road. During this time, I developed a dependent and debilitating love affair with alcohol, a relationship that fueled every wrong decision and bad choice I made. And, believe me, I made many. Within a decade, I married and divorced, started and quit college, ran and lost a business, bought and lost a couple of houses. I had several car accidents, my license revoked, and I was hospitalized for a half-hearted but potentially fatal suicide attempt. I drank to overcome my fears and anxieties, and had greater ones in return. I drank to get rid of my discomfort, and felt even more self-conscious. The more I drank, the more I failed, and the more I failed, the more I drank. I became caught in a vicious cycle that led in one direction -- downward. During these years, I was a lost soul in every sense of the word -- a young girl/ woman who was emotionally and spiritually bankrupt.

I have a lot of compassion today for the girl I used to be. It is nothing short of miraculous that I have lived to tell the story. But at age 26, a wonderful gift came into my life that helped change the direction in which I was heading. His name was Robert. He was a friend of my boss, a kind, gentle soul whose unconditional love played a huge part in my eventually coming to realize that I had a problem with alcohol.

Robert and I enjoyed a long-distance relationship for five years before eventually marrying, shortly after my 31st birthday. It was a few weeks later that, (through the Grace of God), I was to take my last drink. This was definitely good luck on every front! I was happily married and had entered a spiritual program of recovery. Rather than lost, I finally felt found. For the first time ever, I had genuine hope, a newfound optimism that I was going to be okay.

Yet, despite my happiness at this time, I kept having an uncanny premonition that something awful would happen to Robert. I remember lying awake at night, watching him in his sleep, terrified that he might die from a brain tumor or something. I have no idea where these thoughts came from. I used to think it was because I was basically a negative and fearful thinker.

One of the very saddest parts of my story is that my husband did die of a brain tumor -- one month after our first wedding anniversary. He became ill shortly before Christmas that year, complaining of a "weird" headache. I'll remember forever the moment I discovered how seriously ill he really was. We were in a hospital room, awaiting the results of several tests he had undergone. Robert was sitting quietly on the examining table, the doctor left the room for a phone call, and I picked up the chart. For one endless moment, the world ceased to exist. There was no hospital room, there was no sun, there was not even a breath of air. The words MALIGNANT NEOPLASM were so huge that there was no room left in the universe for anything else.

During the four months of his progressive illness, I tried to prepare for the eventuality the best I could. But when the end finally came, I was completely undone. Standing there beside his bed in the room on the 8th floor, all I could think was, "Please God, don't let me jump out of the window." Life had presented a crisis for which I felt totally unequipped to cope.

As if the grief wasn't bad enough, my many phobias and fears became heightened during this time of insecurity and trauma, making themselves known in a multitude of situations. Driving, shopping, being in crowded spaces, even standing in a grocery line, could put me into a cold sweat or bring about an anxiety attack. Without a doubt, it was the most difficult period of my life.

And yet, looking back from my vantage point of time and recovery, I can see how in many ways, Robert's death was a major catalyst in my becoming an earnest spiritual seeker. I wanted answers. I couldn't understand why my husband had to die at a time when I was just beginning to get my act together, even beginning to develop a relationship with a Higher Power. At first I was baffled, confused, and angry. It didn't make sense. How could God have allowed this to happen, especially when I was finally doing everything "right?" I will be forever grateful to my best friend, Kathy, who reassured and comforted me during this painful time, with four of the most important words I have ever heard. "Betty," she would say, "God cries with you."

After Robert's death, I felt totally confused about what to do next. Should I stay where I was, or should I move back to New Hampshire? Where did I fit without my husband? How was I going to make a living? What would I do? And how would I ever get through the pain? Once again, I was led to find the answers.

During the months I had spent in the hospital with my husband, I had experienced first-hand the lack of emotional support for the terminally ill and their families. This was at a time when the Hospice Movement was still in its infancy, and holistic doctors like Bernie Siegel were looked upon with skepticism. Because of my own ordeal, I felt consumed with the desire to work with people facing life-threatening diseases. This propelled me, despite my overwhelming anxiety, to start and finish college.

These college years were a learning experience in every sense of the word, providing me with more opportunities than I would have chosen in which to face, work through, and overcome my many fears and phobias. It was during these years that, a day at a time, I learned to put one foot in front of the other, to act "as if" regardless of how I felt, and to suit up and show up, even when I felt certain that I couldn't. I graduated Summa Cum Laude, ultimately becoming a licensed social worker.

As the years went by, I dated once again, and eventually met and married a man who was and is an Episcopalian priest. This required another move to a different community. Professionally, after spending a brief heart-wrenching period of working with the terminally ill, I switched hats to take a job in the field of addictive behaviors. At the same time, I became very interested in the holistic health movement, using every opportunity to attend workshops, seminars, and retreats that focused on the relationship between mind, body, and soul. I took up running, joined women's groups and, in general, got very busy with my life. Yet, even though I was doing everything right, and even though things on the outside looked good, I continued to carry within me an inner sense of a sad little girl. Mornings would find me overwhelmed, exhausted rather than enthusiastic, much as I had felt in adolescence. "What is wrong with me?" I wondered.

Driven by desperation, I finally got into therapy with a woman who immediately recognized that I was in delayed mourning. With her help and guidance, I began the long-postponed process of grieving the loss of my husband Robert, as well as the loss of my brother Bobby so many years before. But I didn't stay in therapy long. After all, with my history of moving on "feet first and fast," it seemed too self-centered to focus for any length of time on my own problems.

At age 40, I had the good fortune of becoming pregnant. I was delighted at the prospect of becoming a mom. Due to my age, the doctor recommended amniocentesis during the fourth month in order to rule out the possibility of Downs Syndrome, or to detect any potential abnormalities. Eager to see my baby on the ultrasound screen, I was in no way prepared for the doctor to tell me that the baby had no heartbeat. It was a girl, and she had died, probably a week earlier. I was devastated.

With more painful misfortune, my next pregnancy ended in miscarriage. Finally, gratefully, even though I was now over forty, I became pregnant once more. When I found out it was going to be a boy, I knew immediately that I wanted to name him Robert after my brother and my late husband. As the pregnancy progressed, however, I began to have misgivings about this name. Would naming him Robert be a jinx? Would this be the third Robert that I would lose? I mentioned this, once again, to Kathy. Her reply was immediate. "Betty", she said. "That's superstition. And you are a woman of faith."

I brought my son Robert home from the hospital on August 5th, 1989 -- my fifth wedding anniversary, and, coincidentally, the same day my brother had drowned. Aside from gifts I couldn't begin to enumerate, Robert's birth served to reinforce my belief that we have choices in life. We can let our tragedies make us or break us. My son is living proof on a daily basis that life and love go on, provided we allow them to.

During this little boy's early years, there was much stress in our home. Due to a precancerous condition, it became necessary for me to undergo a hysterectomy when he was a year old. When I was recovering from this, my husband developed a heart problem, requiring angioplasty. While in the critical care unit, his kidneys shut down due to a bad reaction to the dye. He finally recovered from both of these, only to have a huge schism occur in the parish where he was priest. Stress was piled upon stress.

I did my best to hold it all together. In the process, once again, I fell asleep to myself. Trying to be all things to all people, my personal sense of balance and self-care were put on the back burner. I began giving from my core rather than from any surplus. This doesn't work well for anyone.

As the months went by, I intuitively sensed that something was physically wrong with me. I voiced these concerns to my internist, who ran blood tests and took x-rays. Everything looked okay. But the fact that I had an intuition caused me to begin renewing my efforts at self-care. I planned a week-end get-away with girlfriends, became more involved in my women's groups, began exercising more often, and started doing a daily healing meditation.

Months later, a routine mammogram was to reveal the unthinkable -- I had breast cancer. As shocked as I was, I was not surprised. And even when the doctor told me, "This doesn't look good," I somehow believed that the breast cancer had not spread because of the healing meditation I had been practicing for over six months. Fortunately, this was the case. Following surgery, I "only" needed radiation treatments. They began the same day my little boy started preschool.

As terrified as I was to have cancer, I remember saying to a close friend at the time, "There must be a gift in here somewhere." I'm happy to say that there were gifts galore. One of the biggest was the fact that coincidentally, just one month prior to my diagnosis, I had started therapy with a Jungian therapist by the name of Dr. Eckles. I believe that this wise and wonderful man was put in my path deliberately. For three years, we met on a regular basis. He helped me as I worked through my feelings of being betrayed by my body. We spoke about the cancer and its treatment, about the many challenges of my marriage, and about my fears of raising a child. Typical of Jungian therapy, we discussed my dreams in depth, as we addressed my unresolved pain of the past. We spoke about God, about love, about soulfulness, and faith.

During this period, God also put other people in my life, loving friends who were supportive and accepting of me and my process. Over time, with much effort and the help of many, my inner pain and grief finally began to dissolve. When they did, a strange thing happened -- my heart, mind, and spirit caught up to my feet. After years of running and feeling fragmented, I began to feel centered, whole, and integrated.

This was not a fast, nor an easy process. Hours were spent in which I struggled to make sense out of that which didn't make sense. For days on end, I would attempt to find some means of putting my life into a framework where I could understand it, and therefore have some control over it. Always, just as I would think I had arrived at the magical answer, Dr. Eckles would lean towards me and calmly say, "Well, it remains to be seen."

It has now been several years since I last saw Dr. Eckles. Yet the time I spent in his office continues to benefit and support me as my life evolves in ways I never could have imagined.

To begin with, even though I had told my husband on numerous occasions that I could never move and leave my friends and family, one day I read about a church on a little island in New York that was looking for a new priest. I had never heard of the place, yet strangely enough, I felt called. The next day, I asked my husband to consider applying for the position. I immediately began preparing for the move, months before they even replied to my husband's application. Needless to say, he did get the job.

It was at this point that I also decided to make major changes in the work I did. With many years of continuing education in the field of holistic health, my dissatisfaction with conventional social work had increased. Over and over again, I would see living proof of the futility of attempting to treat one part of a problem without addressing the whole person -- mental, behavioral, physical, and spiritual. So, upon moving, I made a conscious decision to only do work that reflected a commitment to living in the solution, rather than focusing on the problem.

Once again, God put the right people and the right circumstances in my life so that I could use my education, gifts, and talents in ways to benefit others. Over the past several years, I am and have been a woman with irons in many congruent fires. As a retreat director, I develop and present week-end spiritual retreats for women on such universal themes as healing, letting go, making right choices, getting unstuck, and finding God in the ordinary as well as the extraordinary. As a speaker, I give talks to companies, organizations and groups on subjects of balance, spiritual awareness, and connection. I am a guest preacher at area churches. From the barroom to the pulpit: if that's not proof enough of the existence of God, I don't know what is.

At the same time, I have developed a spiritually based Life Coaching practice that helps individuals to clarify their values and priorities, achieve specific goals, work through their transitional or critical times, make realities out of good ideas, and find ways to stay balanced and become spiritually conscious. I am also a writer, spending the last six plus years working on the contents of this book.

Regardless of the particular nature of my work – whether directing retreats, preaching, writing, or coaching – it all begins with the same simple prayer: "God help me, to help You, to help us all." *The Joy is in the Journey* was written in direct response to this prayer. It has but one primary purpose: to help women take whatever life gives and use it as a catalyst for becoming usefully whole and serenely content. This is achieved through a guide of practical solutions and underlying principles based upon my education, personal trial and error, years of working with women, and my willingness to continue to grow along spiritual lines.

This willingness has given me a completely new perspective on life. Rather than feel like a victim because of life circumstances, I have come to consider myself a student, with my every need becoming an opportunity for deeper spiritual growth. In fact, I am convinced that it is not in spite of my crises and changes, but *because* of them, that I am who I am today -- a woman of dignity and honor; a woman of substance and self-knowledge; a woman who has journeyed through the dark night of the soul to finally find herself and become whole in the process; a woman who has come to believe from experience, that the many "coincidences" in her life have all been part of a Master plan.

The Basic Nature of Change

To be alive is to be vulnerable to the winds of change. This is especially true for women of today. We are constantly and continuously in flux, experiencing crises, changes, and transitions for which we are seldom prepared. How could it be otherwise? To think, of the many things we women have been taught to do, nowhere have we been given directions on how to *successfully* maneuver through the transitional periods of our lives.

Yet, the only constant thing in life *is* change. It happens with and without our permission. Some changes we desire, some we dread, while still others devastate us. Some are big, some seem insignificant. Often, our changes overlap, with one following right on the heels of another. Or they happen in clusters, when several unrelated events coincidentally take place within the same time period. Even when we've chosen our change, we don't necessarily escape the consequences. Because, regardless of its particular nature, all change has the ability to:

- Negatively impact how we feel about ourselves
- Upset the status quo and throw us off balance
- Require us to let go of something or somebody
- Create emotional responses and/or a need for healing
- Cause us to question ourselves
- Challenge everything we have previously believed
- Generate confusion and indecision
- Bring up old, unresolved issues

These responses to a critical or transitional period are normal, natural, and predictable. Yet few of us have the resources and know-how to effectively and successfully deal with them. Because we don't know what to do when change happens, we respond in typical ways: we do what we know, we do what we think we're supposed to, or we do what has been modeled to us by others. Unfortunately, this often means that we deny, ignore, try to control, isolate, anesthetize, stay chronically busy, get sick, or move on far too quickly. Many of these less-than-optimal responses are reinforced by a culture that values and validates the quick-fix mentality. We needn't look far to be encouraged to pop a pill, have a drink, smoke a joint, jump into a new relationship, or go on a spending spree as ways to cope with our transitional angst. While some of these so-called solutions may initially appear to work, time usually proves otherwise when the long-term effects of our shortsighted responses catch up to us, causing us to feel even more restless, anxious, unfulfilled, and alone.

We have become so accustomed to living with these feelings, we think they are normal; they are not. They are symptomatic of the fact that, even though we manage to muddle through our crises and changes, we really don't know how to successfully adjust to them, learn from them, and use them as the stepping stones to those things which we truly seek – fulfillment, connection, and inner peace.

Probably the biggest reason we experience such difficulty with change is because we've never been given directions on how to go through it successfully. We lack "transitional know-how," and so rather than value and embrace change, we react to it from our primal fight or flight response. This fear-based orientation causes us to take a narrow view of life and life changes. In an attempt to gain a sense of predictability and safety, we consider our lives as a series of events that occur in a chronological and linear fashion. We even go one step further by compartmentalizing these life events in two distinct and separate categories – hellos and goodbyes, beginnings and endings.

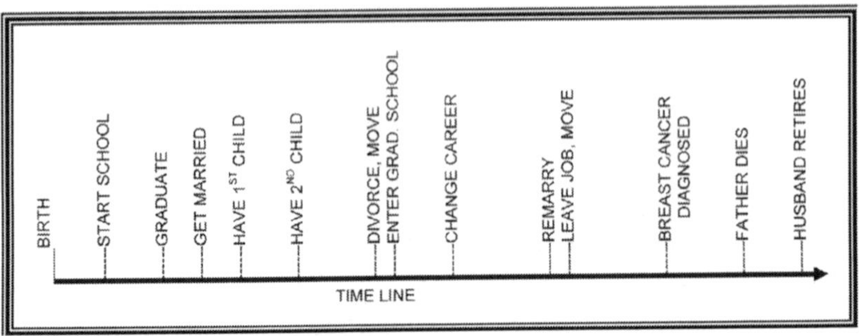

Linear Perspective of Life Events

This linear perspective causes us to miss a crucial point: *As important as the events of our lives are, it is what happens before, between, and after the events that determines the quality of our lives.* Simply put, all change includes a necessary and critical period of adjustment during which there are certain things we can do that will better ensure the direction our lives will go, and how *whole* we will be in the process. This work includes redefining and accepting who we are under changed circumstances; getting our feet back under us; learning how to let go; grieving our losses, the old as well as the new; honing our ability for discernment; paying attention to guard against falling into old, or creating new, ruts of dysfunctional or destructive behaviors; finding ways to live in the divine discomfort of the waiting period; and taking right action to promote healing, wholeness, and fulfillment. This work is not only pivotal to our ability to grow and evolve authentically, but when we fail to acknowledge, value, and do it, we suffer adverse consequences:

- We find it difficult to move into the next hello because we are overly-attached to, or stuck in our goodbyes.
- We continue to haul yesterday's stuff (feelings, attitudes, emotions, fears) into every new situation.
- We think that was then and it shouldn't affect us now. When it does, we blame and shame ourselves by thinking, "I shouldn't be feeling like this!"
- We respond and react on automatic pilot rather than make deliberate and conscious choices and decisions.

- We stay aligned with old dreams and desires that may not be in our own best interest (or anyone else's).
- We jump too quickly into the next hello, ending up with the same old, same old, cleverly disguised.
- We feel fragmented instead of whole.

Rather than promote fulfillment and joy, these responses leave us empty and anxious. They compromise our ability to evolve and move forward into new beginnings that are more in keeping with our innermost desires, wishes, and values. The truth is, in most cases, we can do better. We can feel better. But not without first understanding the basic nature of change.

1. *Change is a process, not an event.* One of our biggest difficulties stems from the fact that we over-identify with and give far too much time and attention to the *specifics* of our lives. By putting the lion's share of our energies on the individual hello and goodbye "events," we fail to give credence to the importance of the underlying "process."

2. *The process of change includes an essential and crucial period of adjustment.* All of our beginnings and endings require some period of adjustment either before, between, or after them. Although in some cases we do give ourselves permission and time to adjust -- for instance, when we're grieving the painful loss of a loved one — for the most part we deny, minimize, or ignore the fact that *all* change, even the smaller ones, requires an adjustment period.

3. *It is during the adjustment period that the critical and potentially transforming work-of-living takes place.* The pivotal work of life takes place in the spaces before, after, and between our goodbyes and our new beginnings. It is within these spaces that we have the opportunity to learn more about who we really are, and what we wish to become. During these periods of adjustment is where we learn to let go, heal, self-examine, discern, take right action, and most importantly, pay attention to our spiritual cries for attention. The work of the adjustment period could be summed up to

> that of "*getting over our false sense of selves in order to find our authentic and best selves.*" In other words, this is where we undertake the critical and potentially transforming work of moving through and beyond our inner layers of defenses, pain, grief, or fear that have previously kept us a stranger to ourselves and others.

It is seldom the events of our lives that make or break us. What really determines whether we remain survivors, or whether we learn to thrive in the face of almost anything, is how we choose to *respond* to these life events. We can allow our crises and changes to cripple, paralyze, or destroy us, or we can use them to transform us into the women we most want and are meant to be. The deciding factor is our willingness to do the work of adjusting to our life changes. Doing this work is what enables us to eventually integrate all of our crises and changes into one marvelous and usefully whole woman. At the same time, learning to adequately adjust to our beginnings and endings moves us beyond the constraints of our linear lunacy, so that we can relax and allow our lives to unfold and unfurl in an ongoing, ever-changing cycle.

Transitional periods provide pivotal opportunities for us to change directions and take an entirely new road. Perhaps a recent situation has caused us to hit rock bottom, at the same time propelling us into a sincere desire to make different choices for our future than we have for our past. Maybe it has even been so traumatic or timely that we are prepared to make the *huge* shift from what has always appeared important, to what really is.

The Joy is in the Journey: A Woman's Guide Through Crisis and Change has been written to help us get from here to there. It will not only give us practical suggestions and directions to navigate through the outer challenges and complexities of our critical periods, but at the same time, it will also guide us into a deeper connection with our authentic selves, the significant others in our lives, and with an ongoing, ever-present spirituality that works. And the more willing we can become to put the following Solutions and Principles into daily action, the greater our chances of enjoying the benefits. If we take the suggestions as outlined in the chapters, it can be guaranteed that with repeated effort, time, and the help of our Higher Power, the following will take place:

- We will develop a greater compassion for the women we were and a deeper love for the woman we are.
- We will experience a sense of security that doesn't depend on the outer circumstances of our lives.
- Rather than stay paralyzed by the fear of the unknown, we will know how to cope with our insecurities as they arise.
- Our relationship with ourselves will deepen, and our relationships with others will take on new meaning.
- We will feel less isolated and alone.
- Our doing will become an extension of our being, rather than the other way around.
- We will live our lives purposefully rather than randomly.
- Our energy will be focused on the solution, rather than consumed by the problem.
- We will come to experience how our need can become God's opportunity.

The more we follow the guide of *The Joy is in the Journey,* the more we will peel away the inner layers that have previously kept us hidden from ourselves and unavailable to others. In the process, we will begin to appreciate that life is far more than a series of beginnings and endings. Rather than hello and goodbye events, we will come to experience life as the marvelous, multi-level, many dimensional, complex helix that it truly is. Not linear, but spiraling and comfortably okay – an ongoing cycle, a dance in a whirlwind.

Once we learn the best steps for this dance, something magical will happen to us. We will become graceful and confident players in the ongoing musical of our lives, empowered as never before to take whatever life presents and use it as an opportunity to continually grow and evolve into women who feel useful, connected, and joyous -- women who are fully alive and completely engaged in the greatest God-given transition of all –

life!

The First Solution: *Practice Self-Acceptance*

Underlying Principle: Self-Acceptance is the first positive step through crisis or change.

One of the first challenges women must face during a period of change is that of self-acceptance. Even under the best of conditions, our inner self-esteem is tenuous and often conditional. Given a transitional period, this self-esteem becomes even more fragile, compromising our ability to accept ourselves, and draining our energy in the process. This is not our fault. Today's self-acceptance is greatly influenced by yesterday's childhood experiences that determined our self-worth. If this early self-perception was one of "not enough," many of us have compensated for this over the years by developing and maintaining specific external conditions in which we could feel okay, at least for some periods of time. Unfortunately, a crisis or change usually rearranges or removes these external conditions, thus exposing the fraudulent nature of our self-esteem underneath and leaving us feeling increasingly naked, vulnerable, and "less than." Rather than accept ourselves in this fragile state, we do the opposite: we beat ourselves up mentally and emotionally just for being human, using the same energy that we might otherwise use to grow and evolve. The First Solution addresses this debilitating issue. It shows us why we are who we are, and gives us tools to reduce the self-defeating influence of our negative inner critic.

To begin practicing self-acceptance at the starting point of our journey through crisis and change will be a real stretch for many of us. However, it is the only place we can begin if we hope to transition successfully. Self-acceptance makes everything else possible, from coping with our multitude of transitional feelings, to making wise choices and decisions for our future. And although some of the concepts in this chapter may initially seem difficult, the First Solution only makes a beginning on our ability to accept ourselves; each of the following Solutions will increase our potential to do so.

We begin with self-acceptance because our lack of it has a tremendous negative impact on our ability to cope with and move through any crisis or change. For one thing, when we don't accept who we are and where we are, our mental and emotional energy begin to work against us rather than for us. Instead of moving forward into changes that are transforming and fulfilling, we get stuck spinning our wheels in our lack of self-acceptance. As a result, our choices and decisions reflect this inner self-doubt, as do the negative feelings we try to hide and/or manage.

For many women, our ability to accept ourselves has been tied in closely with the circumstances of our lives. When everything is status quo, we are able to convince ourselves that we feel okay. Then we get hit with a transition or an unexpected crisis, and all bets are off. Our old insecurities – those we thought were way behind us -- come screaming to the foreground. When this occurs, our self-acceptance can seem to evaporate in an instant, thus adding to our transitional angst.

Why does this happen? Why do we fall into self-doubt at a time that is already loaded with stress? Why, when we really need understanding and compassion, do we fail to give these to ourselves? In fact, why do we do the opposite by emotionally beating ourselves up when we feel so vulnerable to begin with?

Although this chapter addresses the long answer to these questions, the short answer can be summed up in just a few words: "We are who we are for reasons long past." In other words, there are reasons we fail to accept ourselves at a time when we really could use some self-acceptance. For many of us, self-rejection is as familiar as an old shoe. Even though we may not have tried it on for a while, it is one we've been carrying around within us, perhaps for a lifetime.

Few of us really understand the connection between our current inability to accept ourselves as we are and the inner self-perception that we developed a long time ago. Indeed, if we were to really examine this core issue of self-esteem, we would probably find that our weak to poor self-image developed in us when we were mere children, undoubtedly due to causes and conditions beyond our control. However, we learned to adapt along the way. Often, this meant finding ways to outwardly compensate for our lack of self-esteem by hiding it underneath a security blanket of external contingencies. In other words, if conditions were such that we grew up believing that we were not good enough *as is,* we managed to develop certain outer criteria by which we could consider ourselves acceptable. As time passed, this form of "contingent" self-esteem, rather than being based on internal convictions, began to depend more and more upon things outside of ourselves: where we live, who we live with, our bank account, what we do, the salary we make, our position in the company, our ability to keep everyone happy, or even our physical appearance.

Unfortunately, self-esteem which depends on something that can walk out the door, die, grow old, change, or be affected by the stock market, is really no genuine self-esteem at all. So when a crisis or change rearranges the exterior landscapes of our lives, as it so frequently does, it removes this blanket of contingencies and exposes the frightened, confused, sad, woman/child underneath. It leaves us feeling,

- I'm nobody now.
- I don't belong anywhere.
- I'm lost and confused.
- I'll never be happy again.
- Everything's wrong.
- Why am I so afraid?

As if having our blanket of contingencies ripped off isn't enough, we also tend to forget that most things are beyond our control, and we consequently blame ourselves for what is happening or not happening in our lives. Even after giving something our supreme effort, if the results aren't what we had hoped for, rather than take credit for trying, we attack ourselves with such accusations as:

- I should have been able to prevent this.
- I should never have said what I did.
- Why couldn't I have just let well enough alone?
- I should have tried harder.
- If only I had done something sooner.

Even when we make *positive* changes such as landing a new job, moving to a great new place, or getting married, a period of adjustment occurs. After all, *every* change causes upheaval that requires time before things feel comfortable again. Yet, for some strange reason, we think this should not be the case with those changes we have chosen. So when we experience self-doubt and insecurity after consciously choosing a change, instead of assuming these feelings to be normal and predictable responses to something new, we, once again, put ourselves down by thinking,

- I should be happier.
- I shouldn't be feeling so insecure and vulnerable.
- I feel so inadequate.
- I probably made another mistake.
- What's the matter with me?

For many of us, it is an age old scenario that gets set in motion the moment a crisis or change creates a shift in the status quo. Losing the familiar causes us to feel an increased vulnerability and insecurity. In return, not feeling on top of our game throws us into the opposite extreme of feeling like we're at the bottom of the pile. Then, rather than accept ourselves in the midst of our transitional insecurities, we think something is drastically wrong with us instead. We become our own worst critic at a time when we really need to be our own best friend.

The only way we can begin to stop this negative and debilitating cycle is by understanding that *we are who we are for reasons long past.* The truth is, most of our current feelings about self have more to do with yesterday than with today. Therefore, in order to examine the origin of our present self-perceptions, the first step we must take is a backwards one.

The Birth of Self-Perception

Our core impression of who we are was developed early in life and, for better or worse, remains within us throughout our lifetime. Genetics and early environmental circumstances both play crucial roles in this early imprinting. Not only does our DNA give us unique characteristics, abilities, talents and looks, but we also are born into unique family systems with specific cultural, social, and financial differences. Both factors influence our inner feelings of self-worth from which we get our ability to accept ourselves.

When we are born, our primary and immediate needs are centered around one basic instinct -- survival. Provided we receive air, water, food and warmth, we can stay alive. We can survive. Yet, in order to do more than survive, we have additional needs; ones that are not as obvious, but every bit as essential. These refer to our emotional needs for attention, affection and approval. These needs are not neurotic, nor a sign of being overly-dependent. Scientific studies have proven that being held, cuddled, comforted, and loved are crucial to a baby's physical development and emotional well-being. When these things are withheld or missing, children suffer adverse consequences. They fail to gain weight, are intellectually compromised, have little or no emotional affect, and sometimes even die.

As infants, we believe ourselves to be an actual physical part of our primary caretakers. It is only gradually that we grow into the awareness that we are, indeed, separate. As we do this, we begin to determine who we are and what we are worth through the reactions of those around us. In other words, because we have no developed ability for reasoning, the manner in which our primary caretakers treat us, and even each other, determines what we think about ourselves. The way they respond and react to us becomes the mirror from which we decide on a deep, inner level how worthy and lovable we are or are not.

The impact of these early responses and environmental experiences is far more powerful than we can imagine. It can be compared to putting a newborn kitten in with a litter of puppies to be raised. Because the other puppies are the predominant reflection for the kitten, she will grow up acting like and thinking she is a dog. The same is true for an infant. Not only is self-perception formed during the early months and years of life, the degree to which it is healthy or distorted is largely dependent on the attitude of those around us.

Therefore, little girls who receive unconditional love, support, consistency, and opportunities to succeed as well as to fail, are likely to become women who are confident, self-loving, and able to make mistakes. Those who grow up in an atmosphere of approval and affection have a good chance of giving these same things to themselves as they go through life. When the principal mirrors reflect love and respect, little girls usually grow up with a certain feeling of "all right-ness." Living in predictable and safe environments increases their chances of becoming women who feel secure within themselves. Under favorable circumstances such as these, most little girls will develop a healthy self-acceptance that will remain intact *even through life's difficult and insecure moments.*

A great example of this positive reflection of self is portrayed in Connie's story of going to breakfast one morning at a local restaurant. There, sitting at a table in the corner, was a very little girl with her father who was a giant of a man. He was just sitting, watching his young daughter as she toyed with her food, talking to him practically non-stop, and periodically getting up and walking around before returning to her breakfast.

Through it all, the man remained attentively focused on her every word and movement. Finally, she told her father that she was finished and ready to leave. Her father took her coat off the back of his chair and tenderly put it on her, gently smiling while taking care to button each tiny, little button with his big giant hands.

"Imagine how good that little girl will grow up to feel about herself," Connie exclaimed. "Being that small and having the ability to make a giant wait!"

Unfortunately, this positive reinforcement of who we are has not been the experience for many of us. For reasons beyond our control, some of us encountered and lived through early childhood experiences that, rather than promote a healthy self-image, caused it to be damaged, wounded, or distorted.

Children who are raised in the inconsistency of caretakers who are alcoholic or mentally ill can grow up feeling as if their life mirrors a game of musical chairs. They are always on guard for the music to stop, hyper-vigilant as to where the chairs are placed. Little girls who suffer early childhood trauma, loss, or abandonment can grow up viewing the world as a mine field, a fearful and unsafe place to be. If we were brought up in an environment of anger, criticism, or contempt, those internalized voices may continue to repeat the same damaging messages of our past. Children who grow up seeing their parents fight continually, or their mother physically/emotionally abused, may not only blame themselves, but either adopt the poor coping habits of the victim or abuser, or spend their lives trying to fix everything.

If we were denied love, attention, and affirmation as a little girl, we may have grown to consider ourselves as unimportant, less-than, even unlovable. If we received only superficial responses from those who reflected back our self-worth, our self-image may be a shallow or substance-less one. If our family systems had no healthy language to identify and resolve feelings, we may have felt "wrong" for even having feelings in the first place.

The roots of "not good enough" may have been planted in an early childhood environment that demanded unrealistic and unattainable perfection. If we were told time after time that "You can't do anything right," "You should have been a boy," or that, "You're stupid," chances are that we grew to believe it. If the feedback we received from families or institutions was such that it instilled guilt or shame, we have probably grown to internalize and repeat those same negative messages to ourselves.

Some of our less-than-favorable childhood experiences may have compromised our present ability to give and receive love by making it difficult for us to set appropriate boundaries. Perhaps our caretakers emotionally suffocated us by their over-affection or control, resulting in our closing down our hearts and feelings in an attempt to protect ourselves. Or, if we grew up feeling basically unlovable, we may tend to become enmeshed or overly involved in our relationships, taking loved ones hostage for fear that they will leave us. In either case, intimacy doesn't feel safe, and so we continually sabotage it.

Although there are usually exceptions to every rule, deprivation, degradation, neglect, or abuse of any kind have an extremely negative impact on a little girl's self-image. And because we have internalized so many of these early messages and experiences, our self-image doesn't get better on its own. On the contrary, as we begin to grow and develop, our inner committee continues to feed us the same distorted convictions regarding our self-worth. The discomfort caused by this distortion makes it absolutely necessary for us to develop outer conditions on which to counteract our inner perceptions. Because we're convinced inwardly that we're not okay, we find external ways to make ourselves *appear* acceptable, not only to others, but to ourselves.

Some of these ways include being driven to over-achieve, maintaining a particular "role" in life, having the status of living or working in a certain place, owning the right house, driving the right car, living in the right neighborhood, having the right credentials, being married to the right man, having the perfect kids, the perfect hairdo, the perfect body, the perfect wardrobe. Although some of us may go in the opposite direction by developing self-destructive behaviors that support our inner conviction that we're not enough, most of us will attempt to find some desirable conditions on which we qualify to be acceptable. Of course, some women manage to do both; we abuse ourselves behind closed doors, while maintaining the illusion of having it all together.

When our self-esteem is "conditional" on outer circumstances, even if these conditions appear to work for us, the bottom line is that our self-esteem is not genuine. When things shift and change, and we lose our requisite conditions, we can get thrown head-first into the paralysis of our negative self-images and feelings. In the past, aside from causing us to lose any semblance of self-acceptance, this renewed insecurity and lack of self-worth has confused, baffled, and overwhelmed us. That need no longer be the case, provided we become willing to examine this underlying dynamic in our own lives.

Guilty For Being Alive

The following stories are to help us understand the enormous influence of yesterday's circumstances on today's ability for self-acceptance. The more we can comprehend that *we are who we are for reasons long past,* the greater our chances for developing true compassion and genuine self-acceptance, two attributes that will not only support us through this transitional period, but also enable us to make healthier choices for the future. We'll begin by looking at Susan's story.

As an only child of two alcoholic parents, Susan's early childhood did little to foster a healthy self-esteem, confidence, or a feeling of safety and well-being. For one thing, she never knew what to expect when she got home from school. One moment her father would be loving and kind, only to fly into a rage the next. Her mother could also become a screaming maniac on a moment's notice. This inconsistency of her parent's moods and affection was confusing and terrifying. Unfortunately, but not surprisingly, Susan married a man just like her parents.

Susan first sought counseling when her marriage of twenty-one years was falling apart. She was 46 years old and her husband had just moved out, leaving her with their sixteen-year-old daughter and Susan's aging mother. Susan had also recently gained a significant amount of weight, further compromising her already fragile self-image.

It wasn't easy for Susan to talk. She had learned many years ago how to keep silent about what was *really* going on. However, her present pain and anguish were so great that they compelled her to open up. She began by speaking of her childhood.

"From the time I was little, I knew my mother drank a lot of beer. I also knew it was something you never talked about. I remember the first time I found an open beer bottle hidden inside a kitchen cabinet while she was cooking dinner. She was furious and told me to get out of the kitchen. She never seemed to want me around, so I always felt like I must have done something wrong; that, for some reason, she didn't like me.

"Things got really bad when I was a teenager. My mom's drinking was so awful I didn't dare bring anyone home after school. I could never predict what mood she might be in. Once when I did bring some friends home, my mother was so giddy, I was mortified! Nobody seemed to notice, at least they didn't mention it; but I'll never forget how ashamed I felt. As if it was somehow my fault! The thing I remember most about those years is feeling anxious all the time. I couldn't concentrate and I couldn't relax. The year I turned sixteen was the worst in my life. My grades went from all A's to C's and I gained 40 pounds in the process!

"I was hoping never to feel like that again. But here I am – thirty years later, feeling abandoned and rejected, *again.* And gaining weight, *again.* The thing that really depresses me is that, for some reason, I feel like it's my fault! Even though I've done everything within my power to keep this marriage together, I feel guilty that it didn't work out. As if I were to blame! Isn't it bad enough that I have to get separated without feeling guilty, too?"

Even though Susan had managed to live the semblance of a normal, satisfying life for many years, when she encountered the crisis of having her marriage fall apart, it brought up all the old guilt, shame and rejection she had felt as a child.

It is important to remember that when we are children, we are totally egocentric. In other words, we think that we are responsible for the things that happen in our lives and the way in which the significant others in our lives respond to us. At a young age, we don't have the ability to reason. We are unable to think, "Gee, my mother must be acting this way because she's an alcoholic", or "I'm sure the only reason he's saying those things is because of his mental illness," or "I know he felt he had no other choice but to leave." Whether we are one, five, ten, or fifteen years old, when something happens around us that isn't right, we think that we have somehow caused or contributed to it. Regardless of the situation, our first thought is, "What am I doing wrong?"

Unfortunately, even as we age, this continues to be our initial thought through many of our subsequent life challenges. When a crisis or change takes place in our lives, we quickly fall back into the old feelings of being responsible, wrong, or less-than. Any semblance of self-acceptance gets lost in the process, and our ability to transition successfully becomes greatly compromised.

Many of us have also grown up assuming a tremendous amount of responsibility for the people and the situations in our lives. It is no mistake that we are the fixers of the world, both within our families and circle of friends, as well as professionally. We waste a lot of our energy trying to make everything right. We find it difficult to say "no" under the best of conditions. We are chronic givers -- human doings rather than human beings. While we could certainly argue the point that there are lots of things in life that need to be done, there is a whole population of us who do things primarily because we feel guilty if we don't.

Where does this guilt come from? Once again, most of it has been learned and internalized from our early childhood, from our families, institutions, culture, and through our life experiences. And, even though guilt has its positive aspects (causing discomfort when behavior is inappropriate or malicious), most of our guilt was picked up long ago and serves no good purpose whatsoever.

My sister Judy was twelve when my brother Bobby drowned – right before her eyes. As the oldest of the then six of us, she already assumed a great deal of responsibility for a young girl. What made things even worse on that horrible day was that she had challenged the kids to a race across the river, one that we had waded across many times. She had no way of knowing that recent rains and an extremely fast current had dramatically altered the bottom of the riverbed. Where the water used to be only a couple of feet deep, an enormous river channel had been tunneled out. It was into this hole that Bobby stepped and immediately disappeared. None of us knew how to swim.

Our lives are not so much influenced by what happens to us, but by how these situations are responded to. Bobby's death was so traumatic that nobody in the family could speak of it. The silence surrounding this tragedy reinforced my sister's feelings of guilt and responsibility. It would have been so much better if someone - minister, neighbor or family friend - could have helped our family address our devastating grief. As it was, Judy spent many years blaming herself for something far beyond the control of a little girl.

This inner guilt doesn't go away on its own or as we grow up. In most cases, we learn to function in spite of it. But when a crisis or change challenges our sense of self or our security, we can instantly be thrown right back into the feeling that we've done something very, very wrong in our lives.

Some early childhood situations leave us full of shame as well as guilt. This is especially true for women who have been victims of incest or other forms of sexual abuse. For some crazy reason, we think we should have been powerful enough to change what happened, even though we were children.

Maria was six years old when she was sexually molested by her older brother. "For years, I thought it was just a bad dream. The scene is crystal clear: the pink vinyl couch, the cluttered, musty basement, the shade-less rectangular window, the loud hum of the refrigerator in the corner. Even when I became a teenager, I tried to push the reality out of my head, convincing myself that this ugly nightmare was just that, and not real. It was in my early twenties that I finally began to understand I was a victim of incest.

"I was the youngest of four, and the only girl. The brother closest to me in age was ten years older. They all thought I was spoiled. But that's not what I remember. I remember the fear, guilt, and shame that were always lurking one step behind me: fear that somebody would find out, guilt of being "dirty," shameful of my willingness to participate. For years, I wondered, did I have a choice? Or was I truly a victim of somebody older and bigger who forced me to perform sexual acts that an innocent, six-year-old girl shouldn't know anything about?"

The truth is, we are not responsible for the things that happen to us as children. We are victims of circumstance. And through no fault of our own, we learn to blame ourselves. When bad things happen to us as children, and nobody intervenes to tell us we are not to blame, we go through life feeling guilty and ashamed for circumstances over which we had absolutely no control. Even though we eventually grow up to be adults, we never outgrow these inner feelings without taking active measures to recover and/or heal, such as individual or group therapy.

Striving for Perfection

There is probably no area where our past feelings of "not quite measuring up" impact our ability to accept ourselves more than in our unrelenting pursuit of perfection. Perfectionism is the bane of modern women. For many of us, it has become our driving force. It awakens with us in the morning, dictates our behaviors and feelings about who we are, and leaves us tossing and turning throughout the night.

Perfectionism is not about trying to do a good job or even trying to do our best. It is about having an underlying need to get it perfect in order to feel okay about who we are. Even though we know intellectually that human perfection is an illusion, we still feel like we don't measure up when we cannot achieve and maintain this idealistic standard in our bodies, families, houses, relationships, jobs, emotional responses, and anything else we might be trying to make "perfect." This causes difficulty enough under normal circumstances; it becomes disastrous during a time of crisis and change when things often fall short of our ideals. With perfectionism as our standard, it becomes next to impossible to accept the woman looking back at us in the mirror.

Take Monica, for instance. Before she was ten years old, she had become more than familiar with the trauma of crisis and change. She had emigrated with her European family from North Africa to New York, leaving both her culture and extended family behind; she entered public school in Brooklyn not speaking a word of English; she returned to North Africa within one year to witness the illness and near-death of her younger sister; she moved to France where her father was unable to find work; and she finally re-settled in Brooklyn in a small apartment with her parents and grandparents where the tension was very high. Throughout these changes, the burden of holding things together fell on Monica's shoulders. She learned to be a caretaker, translator, and confidant to the adults around her.

"I always felt like I was the one who needed to take care of things," Monica confided at our first meeting. "My mother was prone to hysteria and mood swings. She started abusing prescription drugs when I was very young, including tranquilizers and sleeping pills. That was the only way she knew how to cope. When her father died, she sank into a deep depression and started to talk about suicide. She would faint and lie in a catatonic state for hours, while doctors maintained there was nothing physically wrong. By the time I was fifteen, she had already overdosed for the first time. Trying to kill herself became her habitual response to feeling depressed or overwhelmed."

Monica had a tremendous amount of responsibility while growing up. The stress of her young life was so intense and terrifying that perfectionism became her primary strategy for survival. Compulsive in the areas of organization, order, and discipline, Monica strived to be the "perfect" student, daughter, and sister. She would do such things as get up early in the mornings, straighten things up, and make breakfast for everyone in the family. On week-ends, she would become the mother, cleaning the apartment, trying to make everything right and nice. In school, she got all A's and spent most of her free time at the local library, immersed in books and stories of faraway places.

Keeping the outer conditions of her life "just so" became of critical importance for Monica to feel okay about herself. On the surface, she managed well for years. So well, in fact, that when her mother nearly succeeded in killing herself when Monica was nineteen years old, the whole family entered therapy. All except Monica, that is. Nobody thought she needed it.

While attending college on scholarships, Monica met her husband when they were both studying to become architects. They married when she was twenty-two and moved to Berkeley, where he continued his education. When they arrived in California there was a nation-wide recession, and Monica found it impossible to land a job in her field.

Without warning, all of the roles on which she had previously based her identity and self-worth were removed. No longer a student, an employee, or even her mother's caretaker, she became paralyzed with fear and insecurity. Who was she now? Where did she fit? What was she supposed to do? Her conditional self-esteem became replaced with self-doubt. Overwhelmed by anxiety, it is no coincidence that she considered suicide as an option. After all, since the time she was a young girl, this had been modeled as the solution to life's problems.

"I couldn't believe it!" she exclaimed. "Despite all those years of doing everything possible to be the opposite of my mother, I ended up in the same crazy place: an isolated, depressed housewife. And, just like my mother, I felt like killing myself!"

At the time, Monica had no knowledge of why she felt this way. So she did the only thing she knew -- she redoubled her efforts at perfectionism. By her mid-twenties, her life, once again, looked great on the outside. She and her husband had returned to New York, rented a loft apartment in the Flower District in Manhattan, and she was employed at a small architectural firm. Within three years, Monica and her husband were able to move out of the city and purchase a one bedroom co-op in a nice community near her family.

To all appearances, things were good. Monica had the right address, the right job, the right man, the right clothes, and the right social life. However, rather than enjoying her outward success and feeling good about herself, Monica became rigid, anxious and exhausted. Underneath all the outer trappings, she continued to carry the frightened, not-good-enough little girl around within her. When things didn't go just right, which frequently would happen, she felt inadequate, unworthy and afraid.

Living in the illusion of perfection takes a tremendous amount of effort and energy. It is also impossible to continue to fool yourself forever. So when Monica came home one day to find her husband in bed with another woman, her illusionary perfect world shattered. Not only did she want to kill herself, this time she actually tried to.

It was at this point that Monica hit an emotional bottom like none she had known before. Her desperate attempt at suicide made her realize the fragility of her self-esteem. "I thought there was something wrong with me. How could he do such a thing? But more importantly, why would I be willing to take my life over it? I was so afraid of my responses to this betrayal, I knew I needed professional help."

This was the beginning of a long, painful process for Monica. With the help of a therapist, a church, and membership in a 12 step program, Monica began reprogramming, re-parenting, and recovering herself. Slowly and steadily, she came face to face with the past reasons she had developed a self-acceptance and esteem that was contingent on things being just right. With the help of her therapist and others, she began to see how distorted this self-image really was. She was then able to take specific steps to begin changing it. It was timely because, over the next five years, she was to face many additional crises and changes, including the suicide of her mother.

For some of us, our need for perfection takes the exact opposite track from Monica's. Rather than strive to make everything look perfect, we become immobilized instead. In our fear of not being able to do it *perfectly*, we don't do it at all. "Nothing" becomes preferable to imperfection. In these cases, our inaction only serves to reinforce our inner conviction that we are not enough.

Still others of us, in our quest for the illusive perfection, make our self-acceptance contingent on something yet to come. Without even knowing it, we place the hidden conditions of 'when', 'if', 'provided', 'after', and 'as soon as' on our self-acceptance. We tell ourselves, "I'll accept myself *as soon as* I lose 10 pounds, *when* I get the right house (man, car, job), *if* I find the perfect outfit, *provided* they like the presentation. I'll accept myself *after* I get rid of this fear, *when* I don't feel so vulnerable, *as soon as* I lose this guilt and shame."

Sometimes we don't accept ourselves because of things that cannot be changed under any circumstance. This lack of self-acceptance is a total waste of our time and energy. Let's face it; we have several areas that are unalterable. We might not be able to carry a tune, we might not be mathematically oriented, and we may have no creative gifts. We cannot change the year we were born, and there is absolutely nothing we can do to change *anything* on the road behind us. We can take certain measures to process and resolve issues, but we cannot change the past. And the more energy we use to beat ourselves up over something that cannot be changed, the less energy we have to change something we can!

Not only is striving for perfection a waste of our energy, it also keeps us preoccupied and miles away from what is genuine. If this is our pattern, there is only one way we can change it – by removing perfection as our prerequisite to self-acceptance. Instead of constantly picking on ourselves for our human flaws, imperfections, and idiosyncrasies, we need to make a conscious decision to consider that we are "good enough" just as we are, right in this moment of time.

This concept of good enough is challenging for us women. After all, we have been coloring within the lines for a very long time. We know the appropriateness of dotting our i's, and crossing our t's. We have learned our lessons well, perhaps too well. Along the way, we've gotten confused by learning to equate our self-worth with how perfectly we could do it all. Since perfection is impossible, the end result was that we never felt like we quite measured up. It is time we stopped doing that. As simple as it may sound, considering ourselves as "good enough" is our solution.

Let's take a moment to examine "good enough" a little closer. To begin with, good enough does not refer to mediocrity. Nor is it about acting inappropriately in any way. If we are doing anything that goes against our innermost values, priorities, and belief systems, then we don't feel good enough for a reason. If we are harming ourselves or others in any way, we might need to exercise a little self-restraint in some areas of our lives. There are many occasions when an act of self-restraint will move us closer to feeling okay about ourselves.

Good enough is about having self-expectations that are not unrealistically high or self-deprecatorily low; expectations that are reasonable and balanced; ones that fall someplace in the middle between demanding too much, or expecting too little, *from ourselves*. Finding this middle ground will not be an overnight process, for sure. But we don't have to do it perfectly! We can make a good enough beginning just by lowering our expectations of what we should be doing and feeling *right now*. And we don't have to feel bad about being a perfectionist in the first place. After all, it is not our fault. We are who we are for reasons long past. The more we can understand this, the better our chances of "gentling" ourselves through this transitional time.

Just for this moment, we need to put our unrealistic expectations to the side and adopt a new attitude -- one in which we consider that we are "good enough" just as we are *right now,* in whatever circumstances we might find ourselves, *right now*. Whether we're overweight, broke, or unemployed, we are good enough. Even though our house needs cleaning, we didn't get the promotion, and our partner left us, we are good enough.

We are good enough even if we are hypersensitive, overly reactive, easy to anger, prone to depression, or full of anxiety. We are good enough in spite of what our family members might or might not be doing. We are good enough even if we must make choices that don't make us the most popular gal on the block. We are good enough just as we are, just where we are, at this beginning point in our journey.

This may seem like a cop-out to those of us who have spent a lifetime trying to be perfect; it is not. It is simply another tool, a most useful one, to help us stop preoccupying ourselves with the unrealistic and unrelenting pursuit of an illusionary perfection. After all, how many "perfect" people do we really know? In truth, how many would we want to know?

Regardless of what we might believe at the moment, it is our imperfections that make us uniquely us. When we can accept ourselves just for being who we are at this point in our journeys, we'll be much better able to do the work that lies ahead.

*Self-acceptance is the first positive step through crisis or change***.**

Practice Makes "Good Enough"

We are who we are for reasons long past. There is both good and bad news about this statement. The good news is, by recognizing that there are reasons we react and respond in certain ways, we can begin to understand that we are not defective, overly-needy, or crazy for feeling the ways we do. The not-so-good news, however, is that if we developed a negative self-image during our childhood, there is no way to completely undo it. Awareness may help us re-frame our perceptions, but there is nothing that will ever change the reality of our past. No amount of money, success, busyness, or even counseling can change what happened or didn't. Nothing we own, do, or say, can make things different.

Therefore, we must remain vigilant for our perfectionist tendencies that tend to rear their imperfect heads, especially during a transitional time. We must guard against trying to be all things to all people, and feeling guilty when we fail. We must begin to notice what pushes our low self-esteem buttons; to watch for our insecurities to arise, and then to take immediate action to counteract them. One of the actions we can take is to develop a *practice* of self-acceptance.

This practice of self-acceptance is not only possible but necessary, if we want to accept the woman in the mirror. Fortunately, we are not talking about jumping right into *unconditional* self-acceptance. We know that's not possible. Rather, we are referring to the *practice* of self-acceptance. Although it requires a commitment of time and energy in order to become habitual, it is not nearly as difficult as practicing the piano or learning a new sport. It also doesn't involve dexterity, physical coordination, spiritual conviction, or emotional readiness. It does not require us to fix anything, move anywhere, change ourselves, add something new to our lives, or figure anything out. And it has nothing at all to do with accepting the present circumstances of our life.

Regardless of what we might have previously believed, the practice of self-acceptance does not require healthy self-esteem. While it is true that women with good self-esteem generally have an easier time accepting themselves under any or all conditions, it is not a prerequisite. The self-acceptance we are going to work on embracing is based entirely on making a decision; a decision to accept ourselves just as we are, with whatever self-esteem we have or don't have.

All it takes to begin this practice is willingness – willingness to become *curious rather than critical*, about ourselves and how we think; willingness to stay vigilant for mental sabotage, and then to immediately counteract old negative thought-talk with positive self-reinforcement. This is called "thought changing," and even though it requires constant effort in the beginning, it gets easier with time.

This is how it works: when the old inner tapes start playing -- the ones that say we're too emotional, too anxious, too old, too lazy, too stupid, not good enough, etc -- instead of letting them play on and on, we make a decision to shift gears and to consciously change our inner dialogue. We may need to do this by talking out loud to ourselves, gently encouraging ourselves to let go of our self-defeating thoughts, and to replace them with more positive ones. We make a conscious effort to rewind these old tapes that don't work at all, delete the messages on them, and then record a new message, one that says, *"Just for today, I'm going to accept myself, just as I am. It doesn't matter how I feel, it doesn't matter how I look, it doesn't matter what's going on around me, it doesn't matter what other people are doing or not doing. Just for this moment in time, I'm okay just the way I am."*

Another technique for thought and attitude changing is to ask ourselves, "What's going well in my life today? What am *I* doing right?" When we feel ourselves slipping back into the old familiar role of feeling "less than," we can consciously switch our mental channel to a more positive station by asking, "What do I have to be grateful for today?" Gratitude is a great promoter of well-being and self-acceptance.

We also must remain *curious rather than critical* regarding our feelings and mood swings at this time. This is an area where we women often lack self-acceptance. Even though there are always strong feelings associated with transitions or crises, for some strange reason when we feel angry, overwhelmed, sad, or afraid, our first thought is, "I shouldn't be feeling like this!" We than compound our emotional difficulties by beating ourselves up just for feeling the way we do.

Where did we learn that feelings are wrong? Feelings aren't right or wrong, they just are. Rather than give them power that they don't deserve, all we need to do at this point is to accept them for exactly what they are. The Solutions that follow will help us move *through* these transitional feelings, but we can't do that until we first stop struggling with our non-acceptance of them.

Another common pitfall regarding our ability to accept ourselves is our tendency to compare our insides with somebody else's outsides. When we are in the middle of transitional angst and indecision, everybody's life can look ideal in comparison to ours. When our own self-esteem is low, the first thing we do is convince ourselves that everyone else has it so together.

This was certainly Patty's case. When going through her divorce, she felt certain that most women she knew or saw were happily married. There was one particular couple that she watched with envy every Sunday morning in her church. It was a second marriage for both. They were an older couple and only married for a year. Week after week, Patty would watch them standing together, always touching one another, obviously devoted and very much in love. It was even rumored that he brought her home a yellow rose every day. Oh, if only she could be like that, loved and adored by such a handsome and attentive husband. It was a shock to all who knew them, when one day at work, this man took his own life for no apparent reason.

Although this is an extreme example, the truth is, we never really know what's going on in another person's life. Therefore, we would do well to stop comparing.

Another suggestion for practicing self-acceptance is to begin putting some effort into our humor muscle. As women, we take ourselves and our lives so dang seriously. If we could learn to laugh more at our own idiosyncrasies and inconsistencies, we might begin to enjoy rather than criticize our basic humanness.

What would it take for us to lighten up, to loosen up, to develop a sense of the ridiculous, or wear the world like a loose garment instead of a girdle? Laughter stimulates and increases our endorphin level which, in turn, makes us feel better, heal quicker, and helps put our problems in perspective.

Self-acceptance is the first positive step through *successful* crisis and change. It is, in fact, what makes authentic change possible. All it requires is a decision and a willingness to practice the suggestions in this Solution. Doing so will enable us to take giant steps towards improving the quality of our lives. So why not do it? We're worth it.

Seeing Ourselves Clearly

A woman's life has often been compared to a tapestry, beautiful on one side, messy and chaotic on the other. If we look upon the back of the fabric, all we see are the loose threads, the knots, and the imperfections. It can be said that these fragments represent our life experiences -- the good, the bad, the ordinary, and the extraordinary. Try as we might, when we look from this perspective, it is difficult to make any sense out of the confusion of dangling threads and mismatched colors.

However, by turning the fabric over, we quickly get a different view - an "ah ha" moment where everything falls into its right place. Just by a simple change in perspective, the tapestry is revealed in all its glory, and the whole takes on new meaning; not simply a bunch of fragments, but a work in progress -- beautiful, complex, and magnificent.

In a similar fashion, if we can begin to appreciate that all of our life experiences have contributed to our being the women we are *right now* at this very moment, we will begin to change the ways we see ourselves. Rather than consider ourselves as "less than" or "not good enough," we will realize that we could never be the marvelous works of art we truly are without *everything* that has happened in our lives. Each situation, good, bad, and in-between, has played a pivotal part in contributing to who we are. And the more we come to understand that who we are is okay, the greater our chances of experiencing the freedom of having a self-acceptance that is not dependent on outer circumstances, but that comes from within.

One day, as a woman was looking in her make-up mirror, the sun hit it at just the right angle, giving her a good glance at her *real face.* Every line and wrinkle was accentuated in the enlarged reflection. Her first impulse was to feel bad about the fact that she was getting older and seemingly less attractive.

However, as she continued to look carefully into her own eyes, she was suddenly reminded of an early spring morning at a Boston Hospital. It was a year after her diagnosis of breast cancer. A recent mammogram had revealed suspicious calcifications on her other breast, requiring a biopsy. A dear friend had driven her to the hospital for this procedure.

According to instructions, she wore no make-up and, upon arriving, had to immediately don a less than flattering hospital gown. As she walked out of the dressing room, her friend looked up and said, "You look beautiful."

Remembering her feelings from hearing those loving words, she looked with increased compassion and gratitude at the face which stared back.

"You look beautiful," she said. And immediately felt better.

Self-acceptance is the first positive step through crisis and change.

Suggestions for Practicing Self-Acceptance

1. Buy a notebook. It doesn't need to be expensive or fancy, just something in which to record your thoughts and reflections on the several assignments in this book.

2. Begin by writing down three words that describe who you think you are. Do these words involve other people? Careers? Possessions? Try to think of three words that are not contingent on outer circumstances.

3. Find a baby picture of yourself. Look deeply into your infant eyes and see yourself for the bundle of potential and love that you really were and still are. Frame this picture and place it in a prominent place. Every time you walk past this picture, make a point of using your adult self to reflect back to this baby how incredibly beautiful, worthy, and lovable she is.

4. Can you understand how you may have internalized messages from yesterday that influence the way you feel about yourself today? Spend a few moments writing about how you are feeling at this moment. If these feelings include vulnerability, insecurity, or feeling not good enough, are you aware of any past experiences that may be contributing to this?

5. Being "curious rather than critical," notice how much energy you spend putting yourself down by thinking something about you isn't okay. When this happens, try to put your thought-changing practice into action.

6. Is your inner dialogue full of the "shoulds?" If so, whose voice is doing the talking? Can you distinguish between the voices within? In your journal, write in large print: *Just for today I will not "should" all over myself.*

Meditation on Self-Acceptance

Find a quiet space where you will not be disturbed for a period of about twenty minutes. It might be helpful to have soft, quiet music playing in the background. Make yourself as comfortable as possible, removing any restrictive clothing or shoes. Either sit or lie in a relaxed position.

Begin by taking some deep breaths, inhaling through the nose, and exhaling through the mouth. Spend about five minutes breathing this way, slowly bringing the air in through your nose, and letting it go completely out through your mouth. With every exhalation, say the word "relax" to yourself, or picture the word "relax" written on your forehead. Each time you say this word, feel your body getting heavier and heavier, sinking further into the floor, chair or bed. When thoughts come racing to the surface of your mind, simply float them away by bringing your attention back to the breath, back to the word "relax".

Once you begin to feel that your body is in a relaxed state, read the following words out loud to yourself:

> *"I am exactly who I am meant to be. Right here. Right now. Every step I have taken, every decision I have made, every person I have encountered, have all helped make me who I am. Each and every circumstance of my life, even those I think are negative, have somehow contributed to my worth, my substance and my wisdom. They are all part of the wonderful whole which is me. I am who I am for reasons. No matter how I feel today, regardless of what is going on in my life, I am absolutely good enough."*

Do this three times, slowly. Absorb the full implication of the message these words convey. Own them as being your truth. As you go through the day, whenever you feel tempted to fall back into old negative thinking about yourself, repeat the following words: *I am who I am for reasons. And I am good enough.*

The Second Solution: *Become Balanced*

Underlying Principle: Every situation is improved by self-care.

A woman's life is full of conflicting demands. Because we tend to minimize our own need for self-care, we are typically out of balance and live close to the emotional edge. Although this is difficult enough on a good day, our chances of really falling over the side sharply increase during a critical or transitional period. As we become consumed with taking care of business, we tend to ignore our self-care to an even greater extent. The more energy we put into "doing," the less balance we have, and the more we feel fragmented, anxious, resentful, and exhausted. The Second Solution gives us tools to counteract the potential for this downward spiral. By showing us how to recover, regroup, restore, and recharge our own batteries, we are empowered to get our feet safely back under us. Just as self-acceptance is the first positive step through crisis and change, balance is what determines how successfully we will be able to deal with the emotions and circumstances of today, as well as the uncertainty and the possibilities of tomorrow.

As modern "human-doings," we women seldom give much thought to the concept of balance. In fact, most of us are habitually out of kilter, without a clue what a balanced life looks or feels like. Physically, we operate at high speed and maximum capacity. We live with the chaos of daily agendas that are stretched to the outer limits. Our time and energy are consumed with taking care of the people, places, and the too many things in our lives. Sometimes, even our recreation feels like work!

Mentally and emotionally, we live in a whirlwind. The practice of having our head, heart, and feet in the same place at the same time is a lost art. Rather than being present in the moment, we are mentally far removed, either planning our next action, or trying to recover from the last one. We spend our mental and emotional energy lamenting over what's gone by, worrying about what might be, or plotting and scheming to "make things happen" according to our wishes. Addicted to our own adrenalin, our emotional imbalance is evidenced in our frequent mood swings and outbursts that may very well be exacerbated by present circumstances.

Spiritually, we are so far removed from our own Truth that the thought of connecting with and nurturing our inner spirit is inconceivable. Slowly and insidiously, we have allowed any spirituality we might have had go underground, displaced by our emphasis on security, achievement, or acquisition. In the hurry-up mentality of our everyday existence, we have lost any viable connection to a Higher Power or Higher Purpose.

Similar to our self-acceptance, when the circumstances of our lives appear to be going well, we convince ourselves that we are doing "just fine." But life has a way of presenting days that aren't so good, ones full of the unexpected, the unanticipated, and the undesired. When this happens, those of us who are way out of balance to begin with (most of us, most of the time), can be pushed right over the emotional edge in a nanosecond.

It is such a strange paradox: *Our need for balance is the greatest during a crisis or change. Yet, these are precisely the times when we are most prone to ignoring our efforts at self-care.* In other words, when change is afoot, rather than retreat, restore, and take care of ourselves, we become "justifiably" consumed with the busyness of fixing, controlling, keeping our financial head above water, and taking care of everyone else. At a time when we would greatly benefit by slowing down and becoming centered and sane, we speed up, redouble our efforts at control, or sink into a paralyzing depression. None of these works well.

Our failure to "retreat and regroup" during a transitional period causes more difficulty that we might think. It is the primary reason we become physically and emotionally burned out, or *more* burned out in the case of some. Being out of balance also causes us to "react" (rather than respond) in ways that may not be in our own best interest or in the best interest of others. At the same time, our lack of balance pours fuel on any insecurities that may arise and intensifies our feelings of depression, anger, fear, and confusion. This, in turn, contributes to our making decisions and choices that are fear-motivated rather than consciously thought-out and chosen. And this same propensity to plow ahead instead of taking care of ourselves, keeps us spinning our wheels in old familiar ruts, instead of moving on in directions that maximize our gifts and potential.

Just as we began to appreciate in the previous chapter that *we are who we are for reasons long past,* there are *reasons* we have become so out of balance, as well. We will look at these in greater depth during this Solution so that we can begin restoring some balance and sanity to our lives. It is important to remember that this is not at all about finding fault with ourselves; it is about increasing our awareness so that we can take action to change. After all, if we had known better or been shown better, we would have done better to begin with.

Balance 101

Before we go any further, it will help us to know exactly what balance implies; what it is, and what it isn't.

Simply put, balance is about being centered, whole, energized, and calm, rather than anxious and fragmented. A balanced life has a noticeable absence of extremes, excesses, or obsessions. It is a compromise between too much and too little -- a happy medium between work and play, giving and receiving, responsibility to others, as well as to self. Balance includes having downtime as well as busy-time, discipline as well as spontaneity. Balance gives us the potential to be present in the moment, and to feel and do the best we can under any given circumstance.

There is a direct relationship between balance and the practice of self-care. Yet, despite the fact that *every situation is improved by self-care*, this is not an idea that is reinforced or validated in our society or in our families. On the contrary, we are more likely to be affirmed for being out of balance. People applaud the woman who attempts to be all things to all people, even if she is falling apart behind closed doors. To be working on "self-care" is to be suspect, considered selfish and narcissistic.

Adding to the dilemma is the fact that few of our lifestyles promote balance and self-care. With overloaded schedules and calendars, we don't enjoy the luxury of time and opportunities for healthy self-care disciplines. It is also doubtful that friends and family have a habit of magically appearing on the doorsteps of our home or office, to offer, "Here, let me do that for you, so that you can have some extra time for yourself." In fact, usually, the opposite happens.

Take Margaret, for example. Her boss was a high-powered, type A personality who expected her to drop everything and pick up the slack each time he became over-extended. His tendency to leave things to the last minute routinely compromised Margaret's intentions to go home at a normal and reasonable hour. Night after night, as a direct result of his procrastination and poor planning, she would be asked to work later. Her entire family paid the consequences as, time and time again, she would arrive home late, hungry, hassled, and cranky.

It took a diagnosis of breast cancer for Margaret to realize that not only was her life way out of balance, but that by allowing her boss to make unreasonable demands, she had played a part in it. After all, his procrastination should not constitute her crisis! The good news is, her illness brought her face to face with what was really important in her life, and she began changing her behavior in response. She not only found her voice regarding her need for balance, she started using it.

One day, as she was preparing to leave work, her boss called her into his office to do another "rush" job. "I can't do it today," she replied. "I don't want to be late for my yoga class."

"Well, I'm glad you have *your* priorities straight," he replied sarcastically. He didn't even realize to what degree he had spoken the truth.

We, too, are challenged to not only get our self-care priorities into place, but also to stand up for them. Being assertive about our right to take the time to be balanced is not easy, but the bottom line is this: *any business we're trying to take care of becomes counterproductive if our mental, physical, emotional, or spiritual health suffers because of it.*

It is time we became empowered by making a conscious commitment to self-care. For some of us, this will be an entirely new undertaking. For all of us, it will require changing old behaviors in order to make new choices. And be forewarned: pursuing a balanced lifestyle will have its own set of consequences where others are concerned. Not everybody will want us to change, especially if we stop using all our energies to take care of them. Those closest to us may have great difficulty adjusting to our initial attempts at making "me-first" choices. We need to be prepared for this so that we don't let their reactions dissuade our efforts. Because, the truth is, if we can persevere in our attempts to achieve a balanced lifestyle, it will become increasingly evident that we will become better stewards of ourselves and everyone else in our lives.

Every situation is improved by self-care.

Life Without Balance: The Price We Pay

Similar to our lack of self-acceptance, our tendency to be out of balance was probably born many years ago as well. In fact, the two often go hand in hand, with one feeding the other. Many of us who lack self-esteem punish ourselves by being constantly out of balance. And when we are out of balance, we are usually far distant from self-acceptance. We have been this way for so long, we think this is how life is meant to be. Or, worse yet, we don't even think about it.

That was certainly true in Sally's life. Raised on a Long Island farm by two hard-working and emotionally distant parents, from the time she was seven, it was expected that she would do the physical labor of a hired hand. In this family of origin, the main emphasis was on long hours and hard work. Nobody ever asked Sally if she was tired, hungry, thirsty, or lonely.

Marrying at the early age of 18, she unconsciously chose a man just like her parents, one who believed in long days and hard work. Her husband, Paul, derived his self-worth through acquisition. Some would say he was obsessed with toys-- boats, riding lawn mowers (three to be exact), cars, and guns. From the beginning of their marriage, Paul made every decision, from the checkbook to which house they would build, buy, or sell. Similar to Sally's parents, he never asked her opinion about anything. And, of course, Sally would never have dreamed of telling him, or of even asking herself what she thought. After all, she had not been given opportunities in life to know or use her own voice.

At the age of 50, perhaps complicated by an out-of-balance lifestyle, Paul suffered a fatal heart attack on the way to work. Sally went into shock. Not knowing what to do next, she did the only thing she knew, the same thing she had been doing her entire life -- she went to work. She worked and worked and worked. Concepts like balance, self-care, or, God forbid, enjoyment, were as foreign to her as if they existed in another culture.

As the months went by, the consequences of Sally's workaholism made themselves known in a multitude of ways. Feeling chronically fatigued and depressed, everything felt like a struggle to Sally. With a mind that was constantly racing ahead to what needed to be done next, she was unable to be peacefully present in any given situation. Inside and out, she felt fragmented and disjointed, disconnected from everything and everyone, especially herself. She experienced first-hand what a life of quiet desperation was all about.

Charlotte was another woman who managed to survive without any balance in her life. She was only twenty-six years old when her husband left her and their two small boys for another woman who, coincidentally, had two small children of her own. He immediately bonded with his new family, leaving Charlotte to raise their boys pretty much on her own.

Because Charlotte had grown up with little affirmation or affection from her parents, her ultimate goal was that of making sure her sons had everything, materially and emotionally. From the time her husband left, Charlotte over-compensated for the fact that her children had an absentee father. In her attempts to be both parents, the pendulum swung far out of balance. Not only did she become emotionally enmeshed in her sons' lives, but also she lavished them with gifts galore on even the smallest of holidays, spending money she did not have. Of course, the one place she could cut corners was on her own needs. She had no idea how depleted she truly became over time.

The consequences for Charlotte's lack of self-care were spread out over everyone. For the boys, it was evidenced in the struggle they eventually had to go through in order to make the emotional separation necessary to become healthy adults. And by the time they finished college, Charlotte was consumed with debt, her house needed much in the way of repair, and, although her children had the straightest, whitest teeth, she was forced to get dentures at the age of 50 because she had neglected to spend money on her own dental care.

Maureen is another example of a woman who suffered the pangs of distress from being out of balance. After twenty years of marriage, she left her husband and two teen-age children for another man. When the relationship didn't last, she increasingly spent her time and energy obsessing about it, and trying to "make it happen." As it become clear that things weren't going to go in the direction she had hoped, she became consumed with rejection. She couldn't sleep or eat. Indeed, it felt as if she were falling apart. In an attempt to get relief from her feelings of distress, she grabbed hold of the wrong things. She took up smoking and began drinking more than usual. Both of these behaviors only served to exacerbate her emotional agitation; the more off-balance she became, the more frantic and anxious she felt. As her inappropriate behavior escalated, a painful situation became even more unbearable.

Many of us are like these three women. We have not known or been taught how to take good care of ourselves on a regular basis.

Even in those cases when we have, our first tendency during a period of crisis or transition is to put our own self-care practices on the back burner as we take care of the business at hand. Our self-neglect during these periods of change makes getting through them a lot harder than it might otherwise be.

This is what happened to Fran. A senior editor at a large publishing company in Manhattan, she enjoyed her job immensely even though working in a windowless office in the heart of Times Square drained her energy on a daily basis. Still, as a woman with healthy self-care instincts, she took active measures to recharge her personal batteries on a daily basis in order to counteract the negative effects of her working environment.

Her biggest commitment to herself was to not work longer than a certain time every day if at all possible. Even though it was difficult to leave unfinished manuscripts on her desk, she knew that the idea of "catching up" was an unrealistic one. So daily, she would set her timer for six o'clock, and when it went off, she would organize her work for the next day and then leave. Granted, this didn't make her too popular among her out of balance co-workers, but she was willing to pay the price.

Fran also bought fresh flowers for her office on a regular basis, and covered the walls with pictures of the things she loved dearly, such as plants and nature. She made frequent lunch dates with supportive and interesting friends, kept healthy snacks on her desk along with lots of water, and exercised everyday by walking to and from the subway, a good three miles altogether.

Eventually, motivated by her love of plants and gardens, Fran made the decision to leave her job in the city to pursue an advanced degree in landscape design. This was something she had dreamed of doing for years. The school she attended was in a small Massachusetts town. The move itself was a huge transition. Added to this was the difficulty and intensity of the course work into which she was thrown headfirst after being out of college for many years. Complicating matters further was the fact that Fran's underlying need for perfection came screaming to the surface, demanding all A's.

As Fran put all of her efforts into full-time study, she spent less and less time "refilling, recharging, and replenishing." Gradually but steadily, she became further and further removed from her center of balance. She paid the consequences for this by gaining weight and feeling isolated and lonely. And even though she excelled academically, her self-critic could not allow her to feel good about it.

Each of these women came from a different orientation regarding their relationship with self-care, yet they shared the same consequences for their lack of balance. By making themselves the low woman on their own totem pole, they ended up feeling that way. And whatever transition they were in became compromised as a result.

It is a spiritual axiom that when we don't take care of ourselves, we become less of who we really are, rather than more. Fortunately, the opposite is also true: when we begin to put time and effort into balance and self-care regardless of what's going on in our lives, we not only feel better about ourselves, but also become more empowered to handle the everyday circumstances of our lives. *Every situation is improved by self-care.*

Balancing Time and Energy

When the conditions in our lives change, how and where we spend our time and energy usually makes a shift as well. Situations pop up unexpectedly, and even those that are planned can add extra commitments to our otherwise busy agendas. When this happens, our first thought is seldom about how to make extra room to accommodate these additional time and energy consumers. Instead, we try to cram them into our already too-full days, getting more out of balance every moment that we do.

It might be helpful to think about our time and energy in the same way we think of a bank account. In financial terms, when we put more money in the bank than we withdraw, we experience the freedom of operating from a surplus. However, when more comes out than goes in, the hard facts are -- we've exhausted our funds.

This same premise holds true in terms of our time and energy. Provided we "regroup, restore, and replenish" on a regular basis, we can continue to expend our energy and feel good while doing so. But if our energy is constantly being depleted without getting refilled, we become physically, emotionally, and spiritually bankrupt. By not refilling the vessel, we have no surplus and are reduced to giving from our core. When we give from the core rather than the surplus, we become over-whelmed, under-appreciated, over-extended, resentful, and exhausted; in other words, less of who we really are.

Even when the changes in our lives are positive ones, too much is still too much. Many of us habitually operate with a pretty full plate, so when additional chores, responsibilities, or even pleasures are piled on, it can be more than we can handle. This is what happened in Jessica's life. Fifty-one years old, she had been divorced for many years, with two adult children who no longer lived at home. Jessica worked in the field of Human Services and was pursuing her Master's degree part-time. Both required a lot of time and energy.

Right in the middle of a very full life, Jessica met the man of her dreams and got married. Now, instead of living alone, she had a husband who had his own extended family as well as two very large dogs and one sailboat. Overnight, her commitments increased by leaps and bounds. Where before she had cooked only when and if she wanted, she was now shopping and cooking daily. The laundry had doubled, and because she didn't know how to ask for help, she was the one who always did it. Dinners with his grown children were frequent, to say nothing of having two dogs to care for. Her life not only felt unmanageable, it was! In fact, Jessica began feeling resentful at a time she expected to be happy.

Yet, she loved her husband and knew she wanted to be married. She also enjoyed cooking and caring for him. What she failed to understand, however, was that these things required extra time and energy for which she had not made any allowance. By not creating extra room for her marriage, she was unable to relish and take delight in the newness of her life; instead, she felt overwhelmed and burdened.

The stress of "too much" is all too familiar for women. In Jessica's case, it was created by a positive change. For many of us, however, the opposite is true. We encounter unwanted crises and changes that add extra work, extra people to care for, and additional appointments and commitments that we would just as soon not have. Rather than figure out how to fit these things in, we try to cram ten pounds of effort into a five-pound bag.

It is time we did things differently. Instead of continuing the same behavior while expecting different results, we need to step back, assess the situation, and ask ourselves some very important questions prior to taking on anything new:

- Am I already doing too much?
- Am I placing unrealistic expectations on what I "should" be able to accomplish in a day?
- Are other people placing unrealistic expectations on what I "should" do?
- Am I taking care of everyone else's needs, at the expense of my own? If so, why?
- When was the last time I had any fun?
- Where/how do I get my energy refilled?

It might help us answer these questions by taking an additional inventory to determine exactly where our time and energy does go. A very helpful tool to use is the Time Energy Assessment process. (TEA). This is done by drawing a vertical line down the middle of a blank piece of paper in order to separate it into two distinctive columns. On top of the left side, we write *outgoing energy*, and on the right, *incoming energy*.

We begin by looking at our outgoing energy. In other words, where is our time and energy being consumed? In Jessica's case, the days of her week were pretty well accounted for prior to getting married. Her pre-wedding list looked like this:

Outgoing Energy
40 plus hour a week job
additional night meetings
two courses for Master's degree, homework
travel to graduate school and back – 1 hour each way
active in a weekly woman's group
work out at the gym three times a week
spend time with grandchildren

By writing these things down, Jessica saw clearly that, prior to getting married, her weekly agenda didn't have any gaps that needed to be filled. In fact, it didn't have any extra time at all! Yet, she had attempted to squeeze in a new husband and lots of additional commitments involved with her new marital status. To make matters worse, because she didn't know how to ask for help, she was taking total responsibility for the household chores. Additionally, because we know that changes often happen in clusters, her father became critically ill at the same time. This created more demands on an already overloaded circuit.

When Jessica updated her Outgoing Energy list to include all the new time and energy commitments that had recently been added to her life, it expanded to the following:

Outgoing Energy
40 plus hour a week job
additional night meetings
two courses for Master's degree, homework
travel to graduate school and back – 1 hour each way
active in a weekly woman's group
work out at the gym three times a week
spend time with grandchildren
time devoted to husband/relationship
daily shopping, cooking/cleaning up, increased laundry
weekly dinners with husband's family
care-taking parent

As this completed list unfolded in front of her eyes, Jessica understood why her life felt so unmanageable – because it was!

No wonder her husband felt he wasn't getting enough of her attention! And no wonder she felt fragmented, hassled, and tired. It is exhausting to try and do more than you have time to do. Only by seeing the insanity of her life in black and 'write', could Jessica begin to make choices that not only gave her new marriage the time and energy it needed, but that gave her what she needed to grow and bloom at the same time.

Knowing that she would have to let go of *something*, she began by asking herself some serious questions. What was most important to her? What were her priorities? What did she absolutely need to do? And where did she prefer to spend her time and energy? By answering these questions honestly, she was able to do the necessary pruning to make her life more manageable and, therefore, much more enjoyable.

Her first decision was to drop one of her graduate courses. Next, she enlisted her new husband's help with the household chores. Together, they decided what was reasonable in terms of spending time with both of their extended families. Making their marriage a top priority, they designated certain nights as "theirs," not to be shared with anyone else. All of these decisions helped to make Jessica's life feel right-sized. The more balanced her life became, the happier and less anxious she felt. Rather than struggle to simply manage her days, she began feeling like an active and eager participant in them.

In order to get our own lives right-sized and enjoyable, we, too, can take this two-step outgoing energy analysis. First, we write down where and on what we spent our time and energy prior to our recent change. We then add our newly acquired commitments. The goal of this process is to help us identify exactly what we spend our time doing, so that we can see when we are doing too much.

As we look over our completed list, it might be good to ask ourselves some additional questions.

- Have I given up anything to accommodate something new?

- Am I still trying to stuff ten pounds of effort into a five-pound time slot?
- Am I doing something that somebody else could be helping me with?
- Am I doing for others what they need to be doing for themselves?
- Do I routinely get to the end of the day feeling as if I haven't had a moment to myself?
- If so, what can I let go of in order to change this?

Throughout this process, it is helpful to remind ourselves that *when we're over-extended, everything becomes a chore – even the pleasurable.*

Although many of our changes result in additional commitments, we must also recognize that some changes have the opposite effect. Instead of adding new people or responsibilities to our lives, they create a huge, empty gap in a once-full life. Although empty spaces can be a gift in disguise if we use them to our advantage, they can also be excruciating painful, awkward, and lonely. Often, in our discomfort, we want to fill these empty spaces quickly, using little discernment with our choices. Sometimes we take the opposite extreme by becoming emotionally paralyzed and doing nothing. Neither way promotes balance.

Regardless in what direction our energy scales are tipped – whether we are living with the stress of too much or the pain of too little – we need to find ways to take better care of ourselves. In other words, we must take active measures – despite our discomfort -- to replenish, recharge, and refill so that we can recover our equilibrium and get our feet back under us.

So let's go back to our sheet of paper and finish the T.E.A. process. After completing the left side – "outgoing energy" – we need to place our attention on the right side, that of "incoming energy." This is where we take an assessment of what promotes our energy reserve and what we can add to help this process. In other words, where do we replenish the well?

In Jessica's case, by pruning some of the commitments on the outgoing side, she immediately began feeling the positive effects. But even though she worked out and attended a woman's meeting, she was still challenged when it came to finding additional ways to refill, recharge, and replenish her vessel. Undoubtedly, that will be the case for most of us, but we need not worry. We are here to learn, and our next section on *Human Beings not Human Doings* gives us concrete and practical suggestions for becoming balanced, and for staying balanced.

Human Beings, not Human Doings

Over the years, we women have been subtly brainwashed into believing that our role in life is to take care of everything and everybody else. Unfortunately, we have often done this at the expense of our own self-care and well-being. On a regular basis, we have learned to put our own needs on the back burner, promising to attend to them as soon as we get caught up with the rest of our chores.

In our busyness, we fail to recognize the critical role that self-care plays in a woman's life and in our ability to serve others. After all, if we are overwhelmed, compromised or incapacitated, we can't be of much use to others, let alone ourselves. Think about it – even in an airplane, we are told to put on our own oxygen mask *first.* So despite what we might have been taught, or what we currently believe, taking care of our own needs is more than a good idea. It is a necessity if we want to transition successfully; that is, if we want to use this crisis or change to bring us closer into mental, physical and spiritual well-being, rather than further away from our own truth and essence.

Because most of us are neophytes in this area of self-care, we probably haven't a clue where to start. We might think of self-care as buying a new outfit or getting our nails manicured. While both of these are great ideas, self-care is far more than buying something new or having an occasional pamper. Self-care is a way of life, one that promotes the idea of us as human *beings,* rather than human *doings*. Although this may be a huge stretch for those of us who pride ourselves in being chronic doers, all wise women know that the most important thing to "do" is to "be." That said, our ability to stay calm and balanced in the midst of any transitional storm will be in direct proportion to how well we put the word "beings" into everyday action.

- B. - Breathe deeply
- E. - Examine eating habits
- I. - Incorporate regular exercise
- N. - Nurture self
- G. - Get adequate sleep/rest
- S. - Seek support

Let's look at these more in depth.

B. Breathe Deeply

Strange as it might seem, if we want to become balanced, serene, and sane, we needn't look beyond our very next breath. Just think about it. Our first reaction to fear, anxiety, excitement, or stress of any kind, is to unconsciously tighten up. Instead of slowing down and breathing deeply, we tense up. When this happens, it sends a message of impending doom to the rest of our body. This triggers our innate fight or flight response which, in turn, causes our breathing to become shallow and compromised, even to the point of creating such symptoms as trembling voice, shaky hands, cold sweats, and anxiety attacks. Our response to any of these symptoms is to tense up even more. This becomes a self-defeating cycle: the more we tense up, the shallower our breath becomes; the more we stop breathing correctly, the tenser we feel. As this cycle progresses, our feelings of vulnerability and discomfort become increasingly heightened. The only way we can begin to counteract these feelings is by bringing our focus back to the breath.

Dr. Andrew Weil, noted for his work in the field of holistic health, knows well the relationship between balance and the breath. In fact, he begins his workshops with a breathing technique called the "Centering Breath." This exercise can be done anywhere, anytime, and provides great benefits, especially during times of increased anxiety, impatience, anger or sadness.

Take a few moments and try Dr. Weil's Centered Breath. Begin by placing your tongue behind your front teeth. Now breathe in slowly through your nose to the count of 4. Hold your breath to the count of 8 and then slowly breathe out through your mouth for a count of 7. Do this four times in a row. (A note for the excessive: Just because four is good, doesn't mean that forty is better! This exercise only needs to be done four times in order to have a transforming effect).

Conscious breathing is integral to several relaxation and meditation disciplines as well. The practice of yoga is built around breathing techniques. One of these, "The Complete Breath," improves circulation, provides relief from both physical and mental fatigue, and revitalizes the whole body. It is accompanied by very simple movements that almost anyone can do.

1. Begin by standing with your feet several inches apart and arms at your sides, exhale deeply. As the breath is expelled, feel the lack of vitality in the body. Pay attention to how wilted and depleted the body feels. Contract the abdomen to assist in complete exhalation, while rounding your neck and shoulders over, keeping them limp.

2. Begin a very deep and slow inhalation. As you inhale, feel your abdomen become filled with air. At the same time, begin to stand taller, raising your arms, palms up, as you visualize a birth of activity in your body.

3. Continue to inhale slowly and deeply, and as you do, continue bringing your arms up over your head. Feel your chest expand as your palms meet overhead. Hold this pose and your breath for a count of five.

4. Now reverse the procedure by turning the palms outward, and bringing them back down to your sides as you slowly exhale through the nose. Return to the beginning pose,

with abdomen contracted, head and shoulders rounded over. Repeat without pause five times.

Another relaxation/breathing technique is called "Alternative Breathing." Like the others, it can be done at any time, and only takes a few moments.

1. Begin by sitting in a comfortable position with good posture.
2. Rest the index and third finger of your right hand on your forehead.
3. Close your right nostril with your thumb.
4. Inhale slowly and soundlessly through your left nostril.
5. Close your left nostril with your ring finger and simultaneously open your right nostril by removing your thumb.
6. Exhale slowly and soundlessly and as thoroughly as possible through your right nostril.
7. Inhale through your right nostril.
8. Close your right nostril with your thumb and open your left nostril.
9. Exhale through your left nostril.
10. Inhale through your left nostril. And so on and so forth.

You can begin this exercise by doing five cycles, gradually increasing the number to ten or even twenty-five. This breathing exercise requires a certain amount of focus that is extremely helpful in keeping our minds free from anxious thoughts and distractions.

Breathing is definitely the world's greatest natural tranquilizer. It is our first line of defense against the symptoms of stress, depression, and anxiety, and the truth is, these exercises work. They have been proven over and over again to provide instant relief and comfort when we have the willingness to give them a try. If balance is what we seek, breathing is where we begin. It energizes both body and mind, takes only a minute, and doesn't cost a cent!

E. Examine Eating Habits

All crises and changes have the ability to affect our appetite and/or the way we eat. Our emotional responses to the situations in our lives can cause us to lose our appetites completely, or to want to take comfort in food. Rather than nurture and nourish our body, we are vulnerable to either starving it, or fueling our emotions with the wrong things. For instance, we feed our depression sugar, give caffeine to our anxiety, or add alcohol to our despair. These things only make a difficult emotion worse.

Further compounding our problems is that many women suffer from trigger-happy insulin reactions. In other words, our blood sugars go up and down quickly and often. Both high and low blood sugars can create a chemical imbalance that, in turn, contributes to our mood swings. When we don't eat regularly and nutritiously, this chemical imbalance can make us feel cranky, nervous, fatigued, or depressed. While it is proven that a little bit of dark chocolate will raise our endorphin levels and make us feel better, the ingestion of large amounts of sugar and/or junk food does exactly the opposite. It floods our body with insulin, creating an emotional roller-coaster ride. And because what goes up must come down, when our blood sugar levels crash, our moods crash as well.

There is a direct relationship between our physical and emotional well-being. And even though emotions have a direct effect on how we feel physically, the opposite also holds true. So, when we feel an excess of any emotion, before we look everywhere else for the cause, we might take a quick inventory of how well we are eating.

Bearing in mind that change creates stress, and undergoing stress burns calories and nutrients more rapidly, it might be helpful for us to incorporate some of the following suggestions into our day:

- Eat six small meals throughout the day
- Drink large quantities of pure water
- Include at least five servings of vegetables and fruit per day
- Check with our health practitioner regarding increasing vitamins and/or minerals
- Limit sugar, caffeine, alcohol, and carbohydrates, especially if feeling depressed or anxious
- Monitor the use of fast foods

- Avoid eating in the car, in front of the television, or right before going to bed

Once we begin to identify the relationship between how we eat, how we feel, and how we respond, we'll be more likely to make the necessary adjustments in this area.

I. Incorporate Regular Exercise

Without a doubt, exercise is the best natural antidote to any kind of emotional excess or distress. We may not want to hear it, but if women exercised more, we would be much less likely to need anti-depressants, sedatives, or tranquilizers. Exercise increases our feelings of well-being by raising our endorphin levels. It also helps us to break any cycle of obsessive or negative thinking. *Move a muscle; change a thought.*

Contrary to how some of us may be rationalizing, we do not need to be young, fit, or even motivated, in order to start exercising. We also don't have to run a marathon, hike Mt. Everest, bike five hundred miles, or fit into a size four. There is a very simple philosophy regarding the use of exercise -- <u>if it can move, move it.</u>

Here are some suggestions for the novice, the unmotivated, or the unskilled.

- Find something you enjoy doing physically: bowling, skiing, running, walking, aerobics, biking, hiking, tai chi, yoga. Be willing to try something new. If you can't find something you enjoy, find something you can tolerate. And if you can't find something you can tolerate, just do it anyway, whether you like it or not.

- Make an investment. Buy a new pair of walking shoes; join a gym or indoor pool; sign up for a yoga class or tennis lessons; invest in a purple sweat suit.

- Find ways to be accountable. Get a tennis partner; join an exercise group; make plans with friends to walk around the mall; take a hike with your sister; obtain the services of a life coach who can help you help yourself.

- Think big, start small. Envision the end result, but begin with baby-steps: utilize an exercise video that is in keeping with your age and fitness level; take a simple walk around the block; lift soup cans while watching the news. You may not have the same stamina or shape that you had ten or twenty years ago, at least in the beginning, but you can still be physically fit.

- Commit to the process. Exercise will never fit into your day, so it needs to be planned for and committed to. In other words, give it the attention it deserves. Schedule it in; mark it on your calendar. Make an appointment to exercise and then keep it, just as if it were a doctor's appointment. (Which you'll have a lot less of once you commit to regular exercise).

- Understand that with any new behavior, the first three weeks are the hardest. So if you can persevere for this period of time, it will get easier. In fact, after three weeks of exercising, you won't feel right without it.

The benefits of exercise far outweigh the effort required. Exercise helps us feel stronger and more competent; it lifts our moods and changes our perspectives; it increases our self-esteem and confidence; and it empowers us at a time when we might otherwise be feeling powerless.

N. Nurture Self

Self-nurture is also pivotal in terms of a woman's balance and self-care. Contrary to what we might have previously believed, self-nurture is not about making pleasure or happiness our primary goal in life. Rather, it involves treating ourselves with kindness and gentleness, with respect and patience, the same way we would treat a good friend going through a similar experience. Self-nurture is about giving ourselves some extra TLC when we need it and even when we don't! It is about acknowledging ourselves as worthy of self-care, for better or worse, in sickness or in health, through crisis or change. Self-nurture is how we comfort ourselves amidst the chaos, the confusion, the difficult, or the unknown. There are a number of small, inexpensive ways to do this.

Mary's first steps towards self-care and nurture arose out of necessity. Her husband had fought a long battle with prostate cancer. During the last month of his life, he was confined to the hospital ward. Night after night, Mary would drive herself home to an empty house, weary after hours of leaning over his bed.

"By the time I got home at night," she said, "my body ached as much as my heart. The first thing I would do was to draw myself a hot bath, just as steaming as I could stand it. I'd put on relaxing music, light candles, and sit in the warmth of the tub. Between the hot water and quiet music, my muscles and my mind finally began to unwind and relax. I honestly don't think I could have kept going back to the hospital day after day without those nightly baths. They renewed me in a way that nothing else could have. They also helped me to sleep better at a time when I really needed my rest."

Self-nurture can be as simple as this – taking a hot bath with music and candlelight. But there are several other things it can include as well. For instance:

- making and eating homemade soup
- wearing comfortable clothing
- keeping our bedroom and car uncluttered
- reading with a good light

- climbing into a bed with clean sheets
- wearing a fleece robe and comfy slippers when it's cold outside
- maintaining friendships
- watching a good movie
- having an afternoon cup of tea with our feet up
- reading an inspirational book
- talking on the phone with good, supportive friends
- lowering our self-expectations – (just for now)
- spending time in prayer, meditation, or reflection

We won't always be in crisis, change, or transition. But while we're here, we can use this time to develop a more nurturing attitude towards ourselves, one that we will hopefully continue to practice throughout our lives. The fact of the matter is, the better we care for ourselves, the better we can care for others. The greater we feel about ourselves, the greater we will truly feel about others. Everyone benefits by our commitment to self-care.

G. Get Adequate Sleep/Rest

Handling the stress of change takes a tremendous amount of energy. Instead of less sleep and rest, we usually require more. Yet, it is difficult to make rest and relaxation a priority in a culture that is notoriously deprived in this area. Even though recent scientific data indicates that the average adult needs between seven and nine hours of sleep each night, how many of us come close to that on a good day, let alone during a crisis or change? The reality is, rather than take active measures to guard against getting fatigued, most of us tend to push ourselves even harder during these transitional times. This is especially true when we think we have something to prove or to make up for, either to ourselves or to others.

When we don't get enough rest, we become increasingly tired. And *nothing distorts our perception of reality more than fatigue.* It disguises the good and makes the bad seem worse. When we are tired, even the smallest things have a way of mushrooming. If we find that hard to believe, we need only spend some time with an over-tired child.

There is no self-care possible without taking the time to renew and replenish ourselves by resting. Maybe we need to lie down for an hour in the middle of the day, instead of throwing in an extra load of laundry. If taking care of young children, it may be prudent to rest when they rest, rather than washing the kitchen floor. In our places of employment, we can choose to periodically close the door and close our eyes for five minutes. These mini-breaks provide much benefit.

We also need our sleep. It is hard enough dealing with some of our days on a good night's sleep; it can be next to impossible to cope without it. But sometimes we just can't sleep. Our hearts are so heavy and our minds so busy that sleep is out of the question. How do we handle this dilemma of needing something that we seem unable to get?

In cases such as these, there are several things we can do:

- Keep the bedroom uncluttered and the bed made.
- Put ourselves in the proper place at the proper time. In other words, in bed at a reasonable hour.
- Soak in a hot tub or read a good book (or both) before retiring.
- Avoid falling asleep on the couch or in front of the television.
- Don't drink caffeine after a certain hour.
- Do some yoga stretching before retiring.
- Use a meditation tape to help relax.
- Absolutely, positively, don't watch the evening news right before going to bed.
- Rather than sleeping pills, drink herbal tea, or explore homeopathic remedies.

If lack of sleep continues to pose a problem, it may be necessary to seek professional help. It is important to remember, however, that sleeping prescriptions are not meant as a way of life, but as a bridge back to life.

S. Seek Support

There is no balance possible without moral support and encouragement. Most of us are very good at offering support to others, but when it comes to asking for help for ourselves, well, that's a horse of a different color. We don't like feeling vulnerable and we don't know how to ask for help when we do. Still, everybody needs somebody who is in their corner and who supports their efforts, whatever those efforts are. If we're in the midst of a devastating loss, we need help. If we are making an unfamiliar or critical change in our lives, we need those who will encourage us through it. Regardless of the nature of our crisis or change, support is paramount in our efforts to stay balanced. We not only need it, we're worthy of having it. But where and how do we get it?

Help may be closer at hand that we know. Some of our transitions actually come with built-in support systems if we are willing to utilize them. For women going through divorce or separation, there are support groups offered specifically for this. There are also bereavement groups, as well as support groups for living with cancer, diabetes, Alzheimer's, and heart disease. There is help available for those who care-take loved ones who have debilitating or terminal illnesses.

There are groups that support the unemployed, those who wish to change careers, or those desiring to start their own business. If we have recently moved, our transition can be made easier by the support of a church group or community woman's club. Information regarding all these groups can be found by checking local newspapers or calling area hospitals.

When it comes to moral support and encouragement, friends can be our greatest resource. Most of us have a close woman friend on whom we can rely. Yet, we can't assume that she will know how to help us or even that we need help, without our asking for it. And because we are sometimes confused ourselves regarding what exactly we might need, it would be beneficial to answer the following questions:

- What kind of support do I need right now?
- Do I need somebody that I can call at anytime of the day or night?
- Do I need physical support, help with child care or cooking?
- Do I need somebody to drive me to appointments?
- Do I need somebody to reinforce the fact that I can make this change?
- Do I need people who will give me an occasional hug? Or listen to my wild ranting and raving?
- Do I need somebody's shoulder to cry on?

Once we determine what we need, the hard work follows. This involves actually asking for support. This can be a real *stretch* for most of us. We're so afraid of being rejected, or of having somebody consider us needy, that we would rather limp along unaided than ask for what we need. Yet, everyone requires extra help now and then. Maybe we could take advantage of the fact that most women like to be of service. Just think of how willing we are to say "yes" when somebody else is in need! If we can begin to realize that our need gives somebody else the opportunity to be useful, it may make it easier to ask for help. We should not wait until we feel beyond help before we do this, either. In the cases where we can anticipate what our needs are going to be, we would do well to set up our support systems beforehand.

There are three things we need to remember about getting help for ourselves.

1. We cannot be balanced without support.
2. We deserve to be supported.
3. We are responsible for developing our own support systems.

Once we know these things, there are numerous places to garner the encouragement, love and support we need. Aside from those previously mentioned, we can find additional support through the services of a counselor or therapist, in our churches or other places of worship, through membership in twelve step programs, from friends and family members (when they are able), and from ourselves as we take the steps to create balance in the midst of crisis and change.

All of the aforementioned suggestions are meant to help us become more human beings than human doings. They give us some tangible means of balancing our Time/Energy Assessment chart. Belonging on the side entitled "Incoming Energy," they are the "how" of our ability to regroup, replenish, and recover from the stresses of this transitional period.

Our biggest challenge throughout this process will undoubtedly be that of learning to say "no" more often to others, and "yes" more often to ourselves; to say yes to our need for rest, for exercise, and for time alone; to say yes to opportunities to loosen up and have fun, to be with like-minded positive people, and to do what feels right, good, and joyous; to say yes to situations, circumstances, and choices that are more in keeping with our deepest wishes, desires, and goals; to say yes to *everyday a little play;* to say yes to our right to live a balanced and healthy lifestyle. Our chances of living in balance and self-care are infinitely increased when we stop trying to whip ourselves quickly into shape, but instead, "yes" ourselves patiently through our transitional period and into wholeness.

Every situation is improved by self-care.

Suggestions for Becoming Balanced

1. For one week, spend a few moments each morning doing one of the breathing exercises described on pages 43-44. Whenever you feel an excess of emotion during the day, make a conscious effort to stop and breathe deeply before taking action.

2. Create your own Time-Energy Awareness chart. Take a blank piece of paper and draw a vertical line down the center. On the left "Outgoing Energy" side, make a list of the things that presently consume your time and energy. Are some of these new, having been recently added due to a crisis or change? If so, what can you let go of in order to accommodate these new responsibilities? Could somebody else by doing some of these? Ask them.

3. On the right "Incoming Energy" side of your T.E.A. chart, write down the sources of your energy renewal. Where do you get refilled and replenished? How does this side of the chart stack up to the left side? Are the columns completely out of balance? Go back to the section on BEINGS and incorporate some healthy self-care practices into your day. As you do so, add these to this right side of the chart.

4. Devote an entire day to observe your body and your emotions. During times of emotional excess, ask yourself the following: "Am I hungry? When and what have I eaten today? Am I tired? Do I need to lie down for a few minutes? When was the last time my body enjoyed the benefits of exercise? What and who is supporting me during this time?" Use the suggestions outlined in this chapter to develop an exercise program and an ongoing support system.

5. Write in your journal: *Every situation is improved by self-care.*

Meditation on Following the Breath

Carve out some time when you will not be disturbed. Lie down on your back in a comfortable position. Bring your attention to your breathing. Feel your abdomen expand as you inhale, and contract as you let your breath go. Breathe deeply as you continue to focus on this expansion and contraction of your stomach area. If thoughts tend to crowd their way into your consciousness, don't struggle with them -- simply let them go and gently bring your attention back to the breath.

Now imagine this breath moving freely and effortlessly throughout your lower body. Follow it as it goes through your abdomen and into the muscles of your legs, calves, and feet. With every inhalation, feel your breath warming and relaxing all of these muscles. Each time you exhale, imagine the tension and stress flowing out of your body and into the floor beneath you. Spend a couple of minutes following the breath throughout this part of your body. Allow your body to feel heavier and more relaxed with every breath.

Now shift your attention to follow your breath as it goes upward and outward, moving through the back of your neck, into your shoulders, and down your arms. Breathe into these areas, feeling the tiredness leave your body and flow out through the tips of your fingers. Spend a few moments breathing relaxation and warmth into this upper area of your body.

Now bring your attention to the area of your back. Follow your breath as it travels throughout your upper and lower back, relaxing and softening all of the muscles along your spine, draining the tension and stress from these areas. Let the warmth of your breath soften this area as you sink deeper into the surface beneath you.

Now imagine your breath moving into the space that surrounds your heart. Breathe deeply into this area. With every inhalation, allow your heart to expand, soften, and open up. With each exhalation, let go of whatever has been keeping your heart closed and hardened.

Continue to follow your breath as it flows upwards into your head, scalp, and face. As you inhale, feel these areas softening and relaxing. As you exhale, imagine yourself letting go of the tension and stress that is so often carried in your head and face.

Spend a few moments following the breath as it travels throughout your entire body. Feel the warmth of your breath as it moves down, out, and through all of your weary bones and muscles. Focus on breathing relaxation into any places that continue to feel tension or stress. Allow these areas to relax, soften, and open.

As you continue to follow the breath, feel your energy become restored and replenished. Remind yourself that deep and focused breathing is the most efficient way to regain emotional, physical, and spiritual balance.

The Third Solution: *Grow Spiritually*

Underlying Principle: A Spiritual Connection is our greatest resource.

Transitional periods often exacerbate a woman's inner longing for more. When we are in the vulnerability and uncertainty of a crisis or change, our need to feel comfortable in our own skins, our desire to be fulfilled, and our inner yearning to feel connected to Something Greater than ourselves can make themselves viscerally felt. Because we haven't always known healthy or appropriate ways to get these inner needs of ours met in the past, many of us have spent a lifetime looking for answers in all the wrong places. This transitional period is the perfect opportunity for us to make a radical shift. Instead of continuing to put the lion's share of our efforts into the satisfaction of our every instinct, we can consider spirituality as being that for which we have been searching. The Third Solution will be our guide for making this organic change. By becoming spiritually attuned rather than fear-motivated, we will acquire the emotional stability necessary to cope with our present circumstances. At the same time, we will become empowered to do the work that lies ahead of us; the work of uncovering, recovering, and discovering our authentic selves.

Regardless of who we are, if we took a moment to look deeply into our souls, we would have to admit that long before this particular crisis or change occurred, our spiritual nature had been crying out for recognition. It has spoken to us in the language of "cosmic unrest," clamoring loud and often for our attention through the poignant longing of our hearts, the restlessness of our inner spirits, and in our chronic questioning, "Is this all there is?"

In the past, we have typically mistaken our feelings of inner discontent as symptomatic of something lacking or defective in the external and material circumstances of our lives. So we have focused both our energy and our time on the pursuit of outer acquisition, achievement, or external change. Even though some of our choices and actions may have momentarily satisfied our instincts, many of them have ended up contributing to our feeling unfulfilled, uncomfortable in our own skins, and distanced from our spiritual center.

Because a transitional period often exacerbates this "cosmic unrest," a crisis or change can be a pivotal catalyst for reversing our outward focus. Making this shift from the material to the spiritual is not as difficult as we might initially think. Regardless of what our present feelings or thoughts are regarding the concept of spirituality, down deep we all seek the same things: to feel useful and fulfilled, and to know that we are not alone. Spirituality is how we get to this point, and all that is required to journey on this path is a willingness to consider a different approach.

Just as parts of the first two Solutions were new and uncomfortable at first, the suggestions in this Solution may initially seem that way as well. Maybe we're in a crisis or change that makes the idea of seeking spirituality incomprehensible at the present moment. Or perhaps we have spirituality confused with old religious beliefs that haven't worked well for us in the past. It doesn't matter. Whatever our prior spiritual or religious orientation is or isn't, the spirituality advocated within these pages applies to all -- for it speaks of a woman's connection to her own inner spirit and the ability to bring that awareness into the relationships and circumstances of our lives.

At the same time, although this book neither endorses nor rejects any particular religious belief, it is based upon the conviction that there is, indeed, a Power Greater than ourselves. What we call this Power, whether Universal Force, Higher Purpose, Higher Consciousness, Jesus, Buddha, Allah, Mary, Holy Spirit, or Great Spirit, doesn't matter. Nor is it important what our understanding of this God is or isn't. Whether we have all the faith in the world, none at all, or even negative feelings regarding the concept of spirituality, the most important thing we can do is stay open to the possibility that spirituality is what we have always been seeking. For, in truth, spirituality is what will support, comfort, and bring us hope during a difficult or unfamiliar change. At the same time, it is the key that unlocks the many rooms inside of us that have so long waited to be discovered, opened, and celebrated.

A Spiritual Connection is our greatest resource.

The Basic Nature of Spirituality

As we begin to explore the idea of spirituality, it is important that we don't get bogged down trying to make it fit within certain parameters. The most wonderful thing about spirituality is that it cannot be defined, explained, or understood through mere intellect. It doesn't fit one particular mold or definition. The reason is because, quite simply, spirituality is far *more* than we human beings could ever dream of making it.

Spirituality is an all-encompassing experience of knowing ourselves as *more* than our physical bodies, our educated minds, our multitude of thoughts, or our emotional responses. It is about being aware of, and consistently in touch with, the true nature and essence of our *being* -- our "real" self which instinctively and intuitively knows the Truth; that same self from which we became separated and disconnected so long ago.

Choosing to walk upon a spiritual path allows us to recover and re-engage with this *spirit-self* which is and has always been within us. When we reunite with it, everything changes. We begin to understand ourselves and others on a whole new level. We are able to put things in better perspective, especially ourselves. By coming to recognize ourselves as spiritual in nature, we find it easier to accept those things about us that we have had difficulty with before. We begin to understand at a deep internal level that we are not the best, nor the worst; that we are magnificent, as well as insignificant.

This new perspective gives us the wherewithal to look beyond the self-centered "I" in order to relate to the world in a way which takes, once again, *more* than our individual selves into account.

Because we're no longer at the center of our own universe, we can dare to remove the many false masks we have become accustomed to wearing, and put all pretense aside; we can stop taking ourselves so seriously, and begin wearing the world a little more loosely.

More than all of this, when we become spirit-minded rather than material focused, our thinking becomes elevated to a Higher Consciousness. In most cases, we come to believe in Something Greater than ourselves, and thus begin to trust the circumstances of our lives to unfold naturally. Instead of constantly struggling to "make it happen," we can "let it happen" by taking responsibility for the effort, yet leaving the results up to God as we understand or don't understand God. There is no more need for urgency, hyper-vigilance, control, or manipulation. We can relax with confidence, knowing that regardless of how things might appear and feel in the present moment, we are right where we are supposed to be.

At the same time, growing in spiritual awareness renews our strength to cope with present circumstances, while giving us the hope to look beyond the moment. With God in our lives, we can appreciate that there is value in our suffering and worth in our pain. And even at those moments when we feel uniquely separate and all alone, we know that we are not. We are part of and connected to everything that ever was, everything that presently is, and to everything yet to come. In fact, we are *more.*

This is what choosing to grow along spiritual lines is all about -- *more.* It is about embarking upon a way of life that guarantees never to be dull or redundant. By becoming spiritually attuned, we become *more* in touch with ourselves and the world around us, never less. We also have *more* of a wisdom base to intuitively know when to say yes, and when to say no; when to work on acceptance or to initiate change; when to move on or bloom where we're planted; when to let go or attempt to hold on.

Growing spiritually empowers us to feel whole, peaceful, and unafraid in a world that often seems fragmented, chaotic, frightening, and confusing. "When I am at peace, the world is at peace." This peace doesn't come from having our ducks all in a row, but from an inner "rightness" that stands firm in the face of almost anything.

A spiritual life knows joy. Contrary to what we might believe, this is not always consistent with being happy. Most of us can be happy, at least for the moment, simply by getting what we want. On the other hand, as an inside job, joy has far more substance than happiness. Joy doesn't arise from something fleeting and magical in the moment; instead, joy honors the marvelous magic of everyday existence.

A Spiritual Connection is our greatest resource. It is our answer to chronic worry, fatigue, frustration, loneliness, and, especially, our inner restlessness and discontent. The most wonderful thing about spiritual connection is that it is available to each and every one of us, regardless of what we have or don't have, where we've been or haven't been, where we're coming from, or where we think we want to go.

Why would we want to grow spiritually? *Because to do anything less is to settle for less.*

Roadblocks to Spiritual Consciousness

Despite all these marvelous benefits of spiritual awareness and growth, many of us have developed obstacles that prevent us from entering into a relationship with our spirituality. Some of these things that stand in our way include:

Misunderstanding our cosmic unrest

Although every woman has first-hand experience with the inner sense that "there must be more to life than this," we have habitually taken our discontent as a sign that something in our external world needs attending to. Instead of acknowledging our restless nature as a symptom of spiritual unrest, we do everything within our power to subdue, placate, or fix it by putting our focus elsewhere -- into drama and distraction, addictive behaviors, co-dependent relationships, denial, geographical relocations, greater achievements, and doing,

doing, doing in any and all forms. Although some of these efforts may sooth or cover up our inner restlessness for a short period of time, eventually we get thrown right back again into our discontented and unsatisfied soul.

In reality, cosmic unrest doesn't concern itself with what we have or don't have materially. It also doesn't require fixing, acquiring, achieving, or doing. Its purpose is much more meaningful than causing us to initiate changes in our external circumstances. Rather, cosmic unrest is God's way of calling us into relationship with the Real.

Misconceptions about spirituality

The fact that many women are confused about the nature of spirituality and how it relates or doesn't relate to religion can cause a problem. There are some who think that you can't possibly separate the two, while others see no correlation between spirituality and religion at all. A woman can certainly consider herself spiritual and religious at the same time, yet one does not necessarily depend upon the other. Some spiritual women never "get religion" and some religious women, although expert at reciting scripture and verse, are totally disconnected from their own inner wisdom/spirit/truth, as well as from the God of their understanding.

Like most things, our view of spirituality was learned and developed through the people, circumstances, institutions, experiences, and relationships we have each encountered on our own particular path. Just as we are who we are for reasons, there are also reasons behind our religious convictions or lack of them. Some of these are so strong or negative that many of us may have to clean the slate from old messages and beliefs before we can even think about embarking upon a new and meaningful spiritual journey.

Mary refers to herself as a "recovering Catholic." Coming from a long line of faithful church-goers, she had a mother who bordered on being a religious fanatic. Whenever Mary did something that upset her mother, the response was, "God is going to punish you for that!" Mary grew up to equate anything spiritual with this punishing God of her childhood.

Beth also grew up in a religious home with a father who was an Episcopal priest. At church or in the public eye, the man was warm, engaging, and seemingly compassionate. Yet, at home, he was a tyrant – cold, strict, and a harsh disciplinarian. This was very confusing to Beth. As she became older, she unconsciously assigned the same characteristics to God that she saw modeled on an everyday basis by her father. Rather than feel connected to any higher source of comfort and support, she grew up thinking of God as hypocritical and a bit phony.

In Jean's home, materialism was the God of choice. Focused entirely on the attainment of worldly success and security, her parents didn't have a strong opinion one way or another concerning spirituality or religion. Quite simply, it was a subject that was never brought up. So why, as Jean grew, would she be anything but indifferent to the idea of "spirituality?"

Some of our misconceptions about spirituality or religion may initially appear to be authentic ones. Take Suzanne, for instance. She would be the first to tell you of her deep and abiding faith in God. However, if we were to examine her faith more closely, we would see that it is contingent on things going "according to Suzanne." The moment life throws in unexpected or undesired circumstances, she quickly puts God in the background while she scurries about scheming, plotting, and conniving to make things happen according to *her* will and desires.

Sarah is another woman who will vehemently argue that, "Of course, there is a God!" But when asked what God actually does, she has no specific answer. Her God is far removed from anything remotely resembling real life -- a great idea, yes, but not very useful when it comes to the pots and pans, boardrooms, or everyday decision-making.

Some of us will confess that while we once believed in Something Greater than ourselves, a life circumstance changed everything. Perhaps we were abused, neglected, or taken advantage of. Maybe we are heartbroken due to the loss of a loved one and have blamed God for our difficulties. This may have even been reinforced by well-meaning people who have said, "It must be God's will." How could we be expected to trust a Higher Power who could *will* such tragic and horrible things? And if we are presently experiencing the dark night of the soul because of a tragic or devastating life event, we may feel totally incapable of believing that God ever existed in the first place.

Resistance to the concept of a Higher Power

While many of us are simply indifferent to the idea of God, some of us are just plain resistant for reasons we may not even understand. Either way, coming to believe is not as huge a stretch as we might think. After all, if we did some honest soul searching, we would have to admit that, over the years, we have inadvertently assigned the Higher Power status to a number of false gods. Just look at our areas of dependency. For the woman alcoholic, is not alcohol a Higher Power? If we depend on a pill to change our mood or give us courage, are we not giving it the power to do for us what we think we cannot do for ourselves? When we put people on pedestals, or allow their actions and opinions to dictate our feelings and the level of our self-worth, are we not making them "gods" of sorts? What about those of us who put our faith in financial security or money, depending on it to give us stability, happiness, and prestige? It is clear that we can identify with the concept of a Higher Power; it is just that we've been putting our faith in the wrong things.

Confusion about how to begin

Perhaps one of the reasons for our maintained indifference to things of a Higher Order is that we don't know how to get from here to there. Maybe we have had moments of wishing we were more spiritually inclined. Perhaps we know women who are connected with their spiritual selves, women who seem to be so much more content and less afraid that we are. As much as we would like to be that way as well, we feel certain it could never happen to us. After all, how can we begin to believe when, clearly, we don't? Or, for those of us who say we do, how can we develop a relationship with our spirit and the Great Spirit that is meaningful and real?

It won't be that difficult. For openers, regardless of what our past spiritual or religious orientation has or has not been, now is as good a time as ever to ask ourselves the most important question of, "How well has it worked?" How well has our faith -- or our spiritual indifference -- translated into everyday life? What impact has either of these had on our ability to let go, heal, change behaviors, be at peace, and/or take positive action? How well has our faith or our spiritual indifference influenced our opinions about who we think we are, or affected our relationships with others in a positive way?

If the answer is "not very well," then maybe it is high time to start anew – to clean the slate and become willing to leave our resistance, our indifference, and our mental gymnastics of trying to figure it all out behind us. The good news is that we don't have to do this alone or in the dark. Directions for growing spiritually are outlined in the rest of the chapter. As simplistic as these directions may initially appear, the only way we'll know that they work is by taking a leap of faith and following their lead. After all, what have we got to lose?

Getting Started

In the event that our mind is open, and we have decided that we want and are worthy of something *more*, where do we begin? How do we get started? What do we do first? It can be confusing to know that we want to make an about-face, yet not know how. The following suggestions should help. It is good to remember that the simpler we keep this whole process, the more profound our experience is likely to be.

Slow Down

No matter where we are emotionally or physically during this transitional period, if we really want to pursue the spiritual path, we must begin by *slowing down*. Let's be honest. When it comes to doing, we all do too much. We operate on automatic pilot, we react without thinking, we push our way through, we "make it happen" at any expense. We've been acting this way for so long, we don't even realize how fear-motivated most of our busyness is. We also have no concept of the extent to which this fear-based activity keeps us asleep to our own true nature while preventing any real relationship with the comfort and guidance of a Greater Reality.

We pay a high price for being chronically busy. Primarily, being overly-busy keeps us unconscious. And when we go through life half asleep, we continue to try and recreate what doesn't work in the first place. Without even being aware of it, we repeat the same mistakes over and over again, and yet we keep expecting different results. It is as if we jump out of bed each morning and plant our feet firmly into the same old ruts of doing business "our way." These well-worn ruts not only keep us stuck in many dysfunctional behaviors, but far remove us from our spiritual truth.

Slowing down is how we begin to wake up. This often involves going against our human and cultural tendencies, so the only way we can do it is by making a conscious decision to stop filling our lives with busyness, and then to take deliberate steps to slow our frantic pace down. A good place to begin taking these steps is at the beginning of each day, before we jump headfirst into that first daily rut. Instead of rushing off, helter-skelter, on automatic pilot, we can choose to sit with ourselves for a few extra moments, maybe even practicing some of the breathing exercises listed in the previous chapter. Throughout the day, we can consciously make the effort to slow things down a bit, to take the time to touch everything a little lighter, to encounter our tasks a little more gently, and to pause in the midst of our doing to give a moment's reflection on our "being."

Consider a Retreat

Another great way to get started on a spiritual journey is to take ourselves "apart from" our normal everyday routines by going on a spiritual retreat. Nothing is better for the body, mind, and spirit. Whether they are a day, a week-end, or a week-long, retreats offer an affordable and gentle way for us to connect with our innermost spirit, with the God of our understanding, and with other individuals who are seeking a spiritual path.

Most retreats have a theme; some may even be specific to the particular crisis or change we are presently in. There are spiritual retreats for separated or divorced women, for those who need healing, for women in 12-step recovery programs, and for individuals who simply want to discover more about themselves, or deepen their relationship with God. We can find what's available in our vicinity by inquiring at our local church, checking the internet under spiritual retreats, searching the yellow pages, asking friends, or looking on this book's website.

Spending time at a spa is another means of retreating from our everyday normal routines in order to get in touch with our spirit. Being on the receiving end of a massage, facial, or body wrap helps to momentarily slow our mental and physical busyness, and gives us the opportunity to move into our heart-space, the place our spirit lives. We can also access this inner spirit by making retreats into nature. Camping, hiking, beach-walking, even visiting a planetarium, can awaken us to the fact that life is full of wonders and mystery. When we can connect with the larger reality of life, we are then able to put our own problems – indeed, our lives – into better perspective.

That was certainly Maria's experience. Devastated with a diagnosis of uterine cancer, she worked hard to come to an acceptance of the fact that her life would never be the same again. Yet, at the same time, this life threatening disease catapulted her into a deeper spiritual awareness than she had ever thought possible. So much so, that after completing her chemotherapy and radiation, she wanted to do something meaningful to ritualize the end of her treatment and the beginning of new life. While meditating on how to best do this, she had the vision of herself white-water rafting the Colorado River. As luck would have it, there was one available spot during the last week in August of that year. She took it and, leaving her family in Boston to fend for themselves for a week, she flew to Arizona where she spent eight days on what she refers to as a spiritually transforming journey through the Grand Canyon. At the end of the trip, she knew beyond a doubt that she was utterly magnificent, yet as insignificant as a grain of sand on the desert. This is one of the many benefits of taking time apart from the normal in order to connect with the Real.

Listen to Spiritual Music

Another easy and gentle place to begin getting in touch with one's spirit is through the medium of music. It is little wonder music is called the universal language of the heart. No matter who we are, there are few other things that can so thoroughly permeate our defenses and open us to our spiritual origins. If we are really looking to embrace a spiritual way of life, we might consider adding more intentional music to our lives in place of all the meaningless chatter. This means turning off the television and finding a classical station on the radio instead. Or going to a spiritual bookstore where musical tapes and CDs are sold, and picking up some music to sooth the soul. Even though we all vary in our musical likes and dislikes, there is certain music that touches and inspires us all. If we explain to the shop owner what we are looking for, they will know what to recommend. We not only need to ask the question and buy the music, but we also need to take the time to slow down, even sit down, listen to it, and allow it to work its magic.

Read and Write

Shifting our consciousness from the material plane to the spiritual world requires us to incorporate new behaviors in our everyday lives. Reading something of an inspirational or spiritual nature is a great way to tap into our own spirit as well as begin to awaken to a Higher Consciousness. We can read something light and easy in the beginning, such as one of the *Chicken Soup for the Soul* series. There are many wonderful daily meditations written as well, for instance, *Streams in the Desert* by Elizabeth Cowman, or *The Language of Letting Go* by Melody Beattie. Some women get inspiration and spiritual strength from reading scripture or poetry. It doesn't matter where we begin in our spiritual reading, only that we do.

We are then encouraged to take this morning reading one step further by asking ourselves how it pertains to our personal life. Is there a connection between what we read and our own situation? It helps to take pen in hand and journal about this. In other words, to not only do our spiritual reading, but also to take a few extra minutes afterwards to connect with the reading on a deeper and more personal level. The more often we read and write about things of a spiritual nature, the more likely we are to have our thinking aligned to a higher level of consciousness. This will definitely have a positive impact on the ways we feel and respond during this transitional time.

Redefine Our Concept of God

In order to grow along spiritual lines, many of us will have to come up with a new concept of God/Higher Power. Maybe we've been rejecting the idea of God completely because we grew up believing that God was judgmental, punishing, and scary. After all, *we are who we are for reasons.* But this is a new day and new circumstances and, regardless of how we feel, we have the power to start all over where spiritual matters are concerned. In other words, we can redefine our concept of God and come up with one that meets our spiritual needs. We can make a conscious decision to believe that God is accepting, loving, and gentle; that God always has our best interests at heart; that God even has a sense of humor! By exchanging our old views with some new and more positive ones, God can become for us what we have always needed; a supporting and ever-present source of comfort, guidance, and love.

Keep an Open Mind

The only way to embrace spirituality is to keep an open mind. Even if we are known for being a Doubting Thomas, we don't need to let negative skepticism or the misconceptions of a lifetime sabotage our desires for spiritual awareness and connection. Instead, we can give our inner debating society a much needed vacation, and we can stay open to *all* spiritual possibilities. We can use what works for us, and leave the rest. Once again, what do we have to lose?

Enlisting the Power of Prayer

Nothing has more potential to transform a woman's spiritual life than prayer. Prayer is one of the most powerful practices there is to effect change; not just in the circumstances of our lives, but also in our behaviors, personalities, and attitudes. Prayer is the means by which we tap into our own spiritual potential, while developing and maintaining an ongoing relationship with something Greater Than Ourselves – a Higher Consciousness, Great Spirit or God. This spiritual communion is available to each and every one of us during each and every moment.

Still, despite the powerful and positive effects of prayer, many of us are reluctant to avail ourselves of it. Perhaps this is because we have preconceived ideas regarding prayer. We might be under the impression that one needs to be religious in order to pray, or to belong to a specific church or synagogue. Perhaps we think that prayers are meant to be memorized, recited from rote, or poetic. Or maybe we think that prayer requires us to feel a certain way. None of these are true.

Regardless of whether we consider ourselves neophytes, staunch non-believers, or well-versed veterans of prayer, we can all start at the same place; by enlisting the help of a Higher Power. It only takes a moment to invite the God of our understanding (or non-understanding) into our daily lives; into our ups and downs, ins and outs, highs and lows. This prayer of invitation is the most pivotal and powerful prayer we will ever make, for it opens the door to a relationship that has the power to transform us. We don't have to be fancy when speaking to this God of ours; in fact, if we pray to God in the same way we speak to our closest friends and loved ones, this relationship is bound to be a successful one. The more often we communicate with God through prayer, the more we will see God's work and feel God's presence in our lives. The results will be undeniable.

Depending upon present circumstances, some of us may think we are already working long and hard on our relationship with God. We pray fervently and frequently, imploring God for *specific* outcomes, especially in matters concerning others. We pray that the significant people in our lives become healed, come to their senses, change self-destructive behaviors, or be granted their hearts' desires. Yet, when nothing seems to happen, we fall back into our God-doubt and spiritual apathy.

Instead of taking this as a sign of God's indifference, we might want to investigate a little further. Is it really that God has not responded to our prayers, or that God has not responded the way *we* wanted God to respond? Perhaps our bigger problem is that of thinking we know what would be best. Maybe it is time we stopped trying to figure life out and left it in God's hands instead. After all, God and life are both mysteries. Chances are, if we were honest, we would see many past instances where life didn't happen the way we thought it should but, from our vantage point of time and distance, we now see how God's long-range wisdom had better results than our short-sighted desires might have had.

However, there are some times when life circumstances are just downright unjust and unfair. We lose the people and things we hold most dear. Even though we pray long and hard, we feel that God doesn't hear us, or that God isn't there. We have tried to be spiritual and do all the right things, yet the results are heartbreaking. How are we supposed to pray now?

Usually, during these trying times, we pray with great difficulty. If this is our case, it is important to understand that it is not so much *how* we pray, just that we do. Even if our prayers are full of resentment, doubt, or anger, that's okay; God can take it. After all, the important thing is that we are keeping our channels of spiritual communication open.

Linda will attest to the importance of this. After twenty-three years of marriage, one beautiful summer afternoon her husband had a fatal heart attack while mowing the lawn. Her attempts at CPR were not successful, leaving her feeling guilty as well as heartbroken. As the weeks went by, and the initial shock and numbness wore off, Linda became filled with rage. How could God have let this happen?! Night after night, day after day, she would rail at God, blaming God for letting her soul-mate die.

However, even in the midst of her bitterness and rage, Linda managed to maintain a relationship with her Higher Power. Right from the beginning, her prayers became the foundation upon which she was able to heal her enormous wound. As she healed, her spirituality grew, and her inner wound became her greatest strength. From it, she derived increased love and compassion for the pain of others.

Sometimes our pain and anguish are so great that we simply cannot pray under any circumstances. If this is our case, we would do well to share this with those who are on the spiritual beam so that they can pray for us until we are able to do so for ourselves. This is vastly important because, although it cannot be proven how or why, *prayer works.* It changes things, it affects outcomes, it heals, it helps us clarify our values and priorities, it empowers us to do the work of adjusting to the crises and changes that life constantly presents, and it places us firmly and squarely on the path that leads to wholeness, fulfillment, connection, and serenity. Prayer works; it really does.

Today, we have a choice. No matter what is going on in our lives, and regardless of what we might have previously thought about prayer, we can make a decision to ask God for help. Prayer is a gift we give ourselves. So if we want to increase our chances of feeling connected and supported by a Power Greater than ourselves, we must be willing to try something different, to be consistent in our efforts, and to be willing to be surprised by the results. Perseverance is the key. We don't want to give up before the miracles happen – and as we keep on praying, the miracles most assuredly will happen.

Our Need – God's Opportunity

Chances are that most of us have more than a casual acquaintance with the feelings of helplessness and powerlessness. In the past, we may have had few resources for dealing with situations that rendered us totally vulnerable. In fact, our past experiences of feeling powerless may have contributed to some of the less-than-lovely behaviors or attitudes we live with today, ones we may have picked up in order to survive or to cope. We'll be looking at these more specifically in some of the following chapters.

For right now, however, we're going to shift our focus from the material and behavioral plane to the spiritual one. In doing so, we are also going to make a major shift regarding our feelings of vulnerability and neediness. Instead of considering them as huge liabilities, something we want to get out of, and rid of, as quickly as possible, we are going to claim our vulnerability as our greatest gift. We do this by making a conscious decision to *allow our need to become God's opportunity.* In other words, we can use our vulnerability as the motivator to turn it over and turn to God during times of distress or fear. When we can surrender our need to God's care, nothing is ever lost, suffered through, or agonized over in vain – absolutely nothing.

Granted, this is a very profound concept. Let's look at how well it works. There is probably no better wide-spread example of using our need for God's opportunity than that displayed in the fellowship of Alcoholics Anonymous. Throughout the world, millions of men and women have found a spiritual path that began with their desperate cries for help. By admitting that they couldn't give up drinking on their own unaided will, and by being willing to accept the concept of a Higher Power, their lives were transformed. Many will attest to the fact that they began their spiritual journey with great reservations.

Carolyn was one of these. Growing up in an affluent Chicago suburb with two social-climbing parents, the gods of her childhood included membership at a fancy country club, invitations to all the right places, and attendance at a prestigious Methodist church, where it seemed that all God wanted was money.

As a teenager, Carolyn rebelled, turning her back on the establishment, her family, and, of course, any concept of a Higher Power. Being extremely self-sufficient, Carolyn put herself through college, secured a great job, rented a charming apartment in the middle of Chicago, and found herself a boyfriend. She thought she was taking good care of getting her needs met.

However, as the years passed, she became more and more consumed with the inner restlessness, longing, and discontent of her cosmic unrest. She knew there had to be more to life than what she was experiencing, but because she had no way of knowing what she needed or how to get it, she ended up trying to fix and fill the void in ways that didn't work. She drank heavily, smoked, had a habit of looking for love and settling for sex, and tried to find fulfillment in creative and/or intellectual pursuits. Nothing satisfied for long.

It was through a series of coincidences that involved meeting the right people at the right time, that Carolyn was introduced to the fellowship of Alcoholics Anonymous. From the very first moment, she knew this was where she belonged. She loved the meetings, the people, the literature, and she realized that drinking had been a huge problem for her for several years. Still, she had one reservation. The program professed to be of a spiritual nature. It spoke of a God, one that does for the members what they cannot do for themselves.

This posed a huge problem for a self-sufficient person who had come to rely solely on herself. Besides, the only God she had ever known offered little and asked for lots. No, she certainly wasn't about to give her power away to such a God as that!

Despite her misgivings, she knew that the people in her recovery groups had something she did not. She could see it in their relaxed attitude, their ability to laugh at themselves, and the stability and serenity they seemed to maintain in their daily lives. So, one day, after reading in the A.A. literature that "the only scoffers at prayer are those who have never tried long enough," she asked a God of whom she had little or no concept for help. From that moment on, her life began to change in ways she never could have imagined. Ever so gradually, her inner discomfort and unrest were replaced with feelings of safety, certainty, and security. She began to feel wanted, needed, and loved.

Carolyn's decision to let her need become God's opportunity resulted in a profound and transforming spiritual awakening. Over time, with God and A.A., she has come to experience herself as a spiritual being having a human experience. She understands at the very depth of her being that she will never be alone again. As she says: "If anyone had ever told me that this would be the result of that first simple prayer, I would never in a million years have believed it."

Living by spiritual principles also provides an antidote to our deep-rooted, ever-present fear. In fact, it is often said that "faith is the opposite of fear." While certainly this is nice in the telling, it can make the novice at prayer, especially those of us still loaded with fear, feel guilty. We think that we should have enough trust in a Higher Power to get beyond our fear, when in reality, we're not there yet! Perhaps it would help for us to change the way we think about this. Rather than assume that faith is the opposite of fear, to try imagining that "faith is fear that says its prayers, and then goes on to do the next right thing in spite of the fear."

This is faith in action, and it begins by asking God for help in whatever form we need it. Whether we need courage and strength to show up at the home of a friend who has lost a loved one, to meet with a lawyer, go on an interview, drive in heavy traffic, make a presentation, come to terms with a diagnosis, or ask somebody for help, rather than relying on something artificial like alcohol or tranquilizers to get us through, we ask God to give us the strength to do what needs to be done. Then we act as if our prayers are already answered, by suiting up and showing up even in the face of our fear. We take a leap of faith, trusting that the net will appear in time. This is how we allow our need to become God's opportunity.

The great thing about faith in action is that it constantly reinforces itself. The more we try it, the greater our chances at succeeding. And the more we succeed, the more we grow into the comfort and confidence that *God does, indeed, do for us what we have not been able to do for ourselves.*

This has certainly been June's experience, in circumstances both big and small. "I suffer from phobias," she confided. "Probably the biggest one I have is of public speaking. I would go to the ends of the earth to get out of having to stand in front of a group of people and talk about anything! So when my boss asked me to teach the new bylaws to a group of employees, I immediately broke into a cold sweat. 'There's no way I can do this,' I thought. My fear was overwhelming! I briefly considered calling in sick on the day of the presentation, or just plain quitting my job. I shared this with my best friend, Sarah, who always seems so confident. After teaching me some breathing techniques to help me relax, she suggested I ask God for help. This was certainly a novel idea for me, but I was desperate and willing to consider anything.

"The morning of the presentation, I felt sick to my stomach with fear. I did the breathing exercises as she had taught me, and said my prayers, but I still felt terrified. My palms were sweaty; my heart racing. I asked myself, 'What's the worst thing that could happen?', and then decided not to even go there! So, summoning up courage that wasn't my own, I walked into the room, and a miracle happened! I did my job, and I did it well! I admit, in the very beginning, I felt a little shaky. But after just a couple of seconds, I could feel the strength coming into my voice. I couldn't believe how relaxed and self-confident I began to feel. I'm thirty-six years old, and I know it sounds childish, but I really believe that God answered my prayers. One thing is for sure: I won't have nearly as much fear next time."

If we ask God for help, it can be guaranteed that help will come. But God works in subtle and mysterious ways, and our spiritual growth, while certainly taking place, is seldom realized at the speed we want. So in order to know that, yes, we are growing spiritually, yes, our prayers are being answered, yes, we are coming to rely on a Higher Power, we must find ways to stay alert to God's presence.

Taking an inventory of our day before we go to sleep each night is a good way to start paying attention. We might ask ourselves such questions as:

- Did my day go smoother because I started it with prayer?
- Did I find clarity regarding a situation that used to confuse me?
- Did I have a prayer answered, even if the answer was different than what I anticipated?
- Did I worry less today because I asked God for help?
- Was I able to do something that normally intimidates or frightens me?
- Where else did I notice God's presence, even in small ways?

The more habitual we become with this inventory-taking, the greater our chances of seeing God's handiwork in ways we might otherwise miss. By paying attention and keeping our spiritual eyes open, we will come to appreciate that both small and large miracles are an everyday occurrence. And the more spiritually attuned we become, the more we will recognize that the many "coincidences" in our lives are really part of God's plan for us.

Mary loves to tell the story of walking down a crowded city street on a drizzly February day in New England. She had on a long, gray woolen coat that was pilled and frayed in places. Her dingy brown boots had also seen better days. She felt like her hair was too long, her body too fat, and that she didn't have on enough makeup. "I really felt old and worn out," she reported, "Like everyone was okay, and I was just a frump."

At precisely the moment that she was mentally telling herself how awful she looked, a stranger who was passing by, stopped and touched her on the sleeve. "You look like a million bucks!," she said.

As Mary reports, "I felt like God personally stepped in to tell me that I was okay, just as I was. I think about that incident every time I'm ready to mentally beat myself up, and it makes me smile all over again."

Linda finds that her God has a great sense of humor. She loves to share the story of going on an eight-day silent retreat at a Jesuit retreat house on the coast of Massachusetts. Prior to this retreat, she had spent several months working hard to meet a deadline, and was feeling emotionally and physically exhausted. As the time for the retreat approached, she began to get cold feet. The idea of spending eight days in silence, reflection, and meditation began to feel more like work than a vacation. Aside from that, she had been moving through life so rapidly, the fear of slowing down began making itself known.

In the midst of her anxious indecision, she called a good friend. "Look," she told her friend, half kidding, and half serious. "I really don't want to go on this silent retreat. I've already taken the time off, however, so why don't we go to the Bahamas instead?"

Her friend agreed to investigate whether there were any affordable packages to the Bahamas during that particular week. There were not.

"Oh, well then," Linda sighed. "I guess God intends for me to be on the retreat."

When she arrived, she found the facility beautiful, with the ocean and huge rocks on one side of a big stone mansion, and a pond on the other. The dining room boasted a wall of windows that let in both the view and the sun. Coffee, tea, and snacks were always available, self-serve. Beside the coffee machine was a big plastic container of assorted cups and mugs, obviously left from those who had come on previous retreats. Some of the mugs were plain white, others covered with various inscriptions: "I'd rather be playing tennis; Moms are the greatest; A friend is a gift you give yourself."

On her first morning there, Linda grabbed a mug, filled it with coffee, and took it outside to watch the waves come in and out. It was only after a few moments of sitting there sipping that she happened to notice the inscription on the mug in her hand. "The Bahamas," it read.

These may be small examples of God's presence, but God intervenes in large ways as well. There is a story told of a recovering alcoholic who, after many years of a sober life, was at a sales convention in Chicago when he was struck with the overwhelming desire to drink. Leaving in the middle of a conference, he headed for the nearest bar. He walked down a side alley, took a short flight of steps into a basement bar, and ordered a scotch. The bartender mixed the drink, set it before him, leaned forward and gently said, "You can have that drink if you really want it, but I was in New York last month and heard you speaking at an AA meeting."

The man never took that drink nor had a desire to take one since. It is more than coincidental that of all the bars in Chicago and of all the bartenders who work there, this one was put in his path at precisely the moment he needed it most.

Entering the Calm

Although saying our prayers and paying attention to the ways in which they are answered is a great beginning on a spiritual life, if we want to continue evolving along spiritual lines, we must do more. Primarily, we must find ways to become quiet, to become still. There is no getting around this. Embracing a spiritual way of life demands that we enter the silence. For it is within the silence that we learn to listen and listen to learn. This is where we hear our small inner voice, and this is where the God of our understanding speaks to us.

Yet entering into the quiet is usually a woman's biggest challenge when it comes to spiritual growth and awareness. We have become so accustomed to the noisiness of our lives that even the *idea* of getting still is enough to make some of us squirm. Our first thoughts are that it is just too difficult, beyond our reach, or that we don't have the time for it. Besides, we don't know how to enter the silence! "I just can't do this!" we insist to ourselves. "I don't even know where to begin."

We needn't be alarmed; the following pages will help us. By using the tools described here, we can find ways to begin quieting our minds and emotions long enough to get beyond their habitual chatter and chaos. All this requires, once again, is our initial willingness to try, and a discipline to persevere. It is important to note that any woman on a spiritual journey extols the benefits of meditation.

What is meditation?

Meditation is the practice of moving beyond our mental distractions and emotional chaos into a state of serenity and stillness of being. Meditation enables us to "get over our false sense of selves," by moving us through and beyond our many thoughts and memories, hurts and pain, sense of urgency, and need to be in charge. By temporarily removing us from our fear-based distractions, meditation enables us to get clarity about whom and what we really are. At the same time, meditation provides us with much needed emotional and physical relief, especially beneficial during a time of crisis, change, or transitional angst.

By allowing us to enter into the space where our authentic self/spirit lives, the practice of meditation helps us to discover rooms in our interior house that we never knew existed. It is also our primary means of connecting with Something far greater than ourselves, and of consciously deepening our relationship with this God of our understanding. Therefore, meditation is our gateway into wholeness.

How do we meditate?

There are many ways to meditate, several of which are highlighted following each chapter in this book. Some meditation techniques focus explicitly on the breath; others use the repetition of a single word, phrase, or sound such as "om;" still others consist of guided imagery. There are also several books written on the subject of meditation, as well as audio and video tapes. It might be beneficial for us to start using one of these tapes, or to join a class such as Tai Chi, Yoga, or Qigong, all of which place emphasis on becoming centered and still. Regardless of which meditation practice we might choose, they all require time and repeated efforts to reap the full benefits. However, even the smallest beginnings will result in improved emotional health and spiritual serenity.

Meditation guides us through a process of letting go, letting go, letting go. It gives us the means by which to relax and relinquish our grip on worry, control, struggle, and that underlying sense of urgency. At the same time, we can let go of the thoughts, feelings, and emotions that typically keep us so distracted. One of the biggest problems of being human is that we have come to identify ourselves by these very things. In fact, on some level, we believe that we *are* our thoughts, feelings, and emotions. No wonder we find it difficult to leave these things behind as we journey into a foreign land of stillness and silence! To further complicate matters, it can be guaranteed that the moment we try to quiet our thoughts, all matter of inner distractions will begin competing for our attention. Our minds, instead of becoming quieter and calmer, will become hyperactive, uprooting old pain, fear, and unresolved issues, and hauling them to the surface of our consciousness. Getting beyond these can be challenging at best, especially during our early attempts at meditating.

Because of this, many women quit before reaping any of the benefits. The discomfort is more than we think we can take, especially when we are convinced that we must *do something* with the feelings, memories, or thoughts that our meditation raises. But we don't have to do a thing with them. There is no need to resolve or to debate anything that comes up during the process of getting still. In fact, we can take the power away from our thoughts and feelings by simply *observing* them; to take note of them, yes -- but then to gently float them away, as we journey beyond them into the stillness and the relief that lie at the center of our being.

If all this meditation stuff sounds like too much of a stretch for us, especially at this particular time, we could begin by "reflecting" rather than meditating. Reflection is different than meditation; instead of encouraging us to get beyond our thoughts and feelings, reflection invites us to sit and think quietly and calmly. Many women find it helpful to reflect upon certain readings or meditations. For instance, we can read a daily meditation book or a passage from scripture, and then reflect upon what we've read. This can be done in several ways: by taking a few moments in silence to think about the reading and how it applies to our life; or, as we mentioned earlier, by writing down our feelings or responses to the meditation. It is also helpful to share what we've read with a friend. R&R – reading and reflecting – is how we begin to make the written word a living reality rather than just a good thought.

Despite what we might have previously thought or heard, it doesn't require a huge block of time to incorporate meditation or reflection into our lives. Although many practices suggest an hour a day, that amount of time is usually out of the question for most of us. However, tremendous benefit can be derived from simply sitting still for twenty minutes a day. Or even ten. In the beginning, five minutes of being quiet may seem like a lot. That is okay. We just need to do it -- to sit in the discomfort when it arises, and put in our time. If we persist with this practice, eventually we will want to meditate more than not.

When and where do we meditate?

Finding a meditation practice that suits us is often a whole lot easier than finding the time and space in which to accommodate it. In a culture where couples find it necessary to schedule a dinner date, extra time and space do not simply present themselves. We improve our chances for success immensely when we plan exactly when and where we are to meditate. In other words, we don't just say, "I'm going to meditate twenty minutes every day." We know exactly when and where this is going to take place.

There is no right or wrong time for prayer or meditation, but because many of us don't have extra time within our regular daily schedule, it might work better to book-end our days with our newly-found spiritual practices. It is a simple matter to create extra time by getting up a few minutes earlier and going to bed a few minutes later. Doing this will undoubtedly require us to change some of our old habits. We must resist turning the radio or television on first thing in the morning, or staying up late watching something we've already seen or in which we aren't even that interested.

Deciding *where* to pray and meditate is another concern. The space should be comfortable, quiet, and free from all distractions. Although these accommodations aren't always easy to find, we must take special measures to ensure we won't be disturbed. This is why we may want the privacy afforded in the time before our children or significant others get up, and/or after they go to bed. At such times, we most certainly will need to take the phone off the hook and turn off our cell phone or beeper.

Some women find it helpful to create special altars, windowsills, or corners in a room for their prayer and meditation practice. If we belong to a particular religion, we might want to put out some artifact that brings us more into tune with our religious conviction; for instance, a statue of Mary, Jesus, or Buddha; candles, pictures, or incense. It is important to make our prayer space special in every sense of the word, because it *is* special. It is our time to be with ourselves and to communicate with our God.

Embracing spirituality is not just another thing to do -- God knows we have enough of that. Instead, it is a way "to be." Few uses of our time will ever be as well spent as this. Meditating is like putting money in the bank, in this case, our spiritual bank. The more we put in, the better prepared we become for anything that might come down the pike. Life changes in-between heartbeats; it is helpful if we are in spiritual readiness.

For years, Simone believed that her relationship with God was a strong one. She prayed daily and even dabbled in meditation when time allowed. Although her life was chronically full of loose ends, she felt reasonably happy and fulfilled. That is, until the morning her husband Ray told her he didn't love her anymore and walked out the door.

"I always thought I believed in a Higher Power, and that this God had a plan for my life. I was certain that Ray was part of that plan, a BIG part. After all, before him, I had been alone for a long time. Not just alone, but in retrospect, I see that my life had been one of self-imposed isolation. It was miraculous that he and I ever met, let alone got married. When he left that way, so suddenly without warning, I fell apart. We hadn't even discussed it! I was shocked! It felt as if I was undergoing an amputation without anesthesia. To say that I fell into despair is putting it mildly. I felt sickened, betrayed, and abandoned. Everything I had previously believed was up for grabs – love, commitment, even God.

"It seems strange, but I guess my survival instincts must have kicked in. During those first months when I could hardly keep my emotional head above water, I did two things that I credit today with saving my life; the first was exercise and the second was meditation. Not only did these practices help me survive, they have ultimately transformed me.

"The exercise didn't come nearly as hard in the beginning as becoming quiet did. I was used to getting out and walking; it was a great outlet for my anxiety and my feelings of despair. However, sitting in the silence was a whole different story. In the beginning, it seemed to make me feel worse rather than better. Meditating brought up all kinds of inner feelings of pain and loneliness. Still, I made a conscious choice to stick it out. I needed the relief that I felt certain it would eventually provide. I also desperately wanted to connect to *Something* that I couldn't even put into words.

"It is funny, as much as I thought I had a real relationship with God before this, I realize that, honestly, it was very shallow. I treated God like the friendly neighbor. I'd give a wave now and then, provided I had the time and things were going my way. Then I would get caught up in my own self-centered fear, doubt, and control, and forget it! Instead of relying on my Higher Power, I relied solely on my own ability to figure it out, fix it, or "make it happen." I see so clearly now how fear-based I've always been! And do you know the biggest fear I had? The fear of abandonment.

"It's been a year now since Ray left, and a strange thing has happened. Even though it has been the absolute most painful period of my entire forty-eight years, I wouldn't change a moment of it. My daily practice of prayer and meditation has allowed me to finally come face to face with my biggest fears. It has brought me to a level of self-acceptance that I never thought possible. I'm not nearly as isolated and fragmented as I used to be. In fact, in many ways, I've never been healthier or happier. Today, I finally know myself to be lovable and worthy, just as I am. I went to the bottom of the pit, that's for sure. But when I did, I not only found myself, but I found God."

Thomas Merton once wrote that, "When we find God, we find our own true selves; and when we find our own true selves, we find God." Similar to Simone, any one of us is capable of doing this. All we have to do is say our prayers, and then pay attention to how God responds. The more spiritually conscious we become, the more we will come to rely on our instinctual truth/spirit to make wise decisions and to take right action. The more we embrace spirituality as a way of life, the greater our chances of living in full knowledge that our Higher Power is with us and supports us, in both the large and the small.

There is a story told about the parents of a newborn baby girl. Upon arriving home from the hospital, their four-year old son met them at the door, asking if he could talk to this newest member of the family by himself. The parents, unsure of how he might respond to his new sibling, left the intercom on during their son's first unsupervised visit. This is what they heard him ask his new little sister. "Tell me again what God looks like. I'm beginning to forget."

At the moment of our birth, two things happen simultaneously. We begin to forget and we long to remember. Spirituality is our answer for both. It is our greatest resource.

Suggestions for Growing Spiritually

1. Slow down by taking moments throughout the day to enter into the calm. Turn off the television, computer, and radio. Read something inspirational. Be still and listen to the quiet.

2. Can you relate to the inner longing and restlessness of cosmic unrest? If so, in the past, have you attempted to fill, placate, or fix it with outside solutions? Write in your journal about your own experiences with cosmic unrest. Is it possible for you to consider cosmic unrest as God's way of calling you into relationship?

3. Are you resistant to the concept of a spiritual being? Trace the origins of your current belief systems. Examine how well they work. Make a decision to stay open to spiritual growth and awareness.

4. Take deliberate action to connect with your innermost spirit and with God. Meditate, go on a retreat, take a camping trip, spend time in nature, walk along a beach, or sit quietly with yourself.

5. For the next 90 days, make a commitment to invite the God of your understanding (or non-understanding) into your daily affairs. Take note of how God responds by doing the nightly inventory outlined on page 76. Remind yourself that the greatest skeptics of prayer are those who have never tried it.

6. During this same period, create time and space for daily reflection or meditation. Begin by using the meditation that follows, or buy a tape or book on the subject. Consider joining a meditation group, yoga class, or drumming circle. Persevere in your efforts.

7. Write in your journal: *A Spiritual Connection is my greatest resource.*

Meditation on Moving into the Calm

Prepare to enter the silence by finding a time and space in which you'll not be disturbed. Make yourself as comfortable as possible. Close your eyes and concentrate on the rhythm of your breath. Inhale through the nose and exhale fully through the mouth. Take your time doing this. There is no hurry. There is no place else you need to be. There is nothing you need to be doing. This is your time and your space.

Spend a few moments simply breathing. Feel your abdomen rise and fall with your every breath. Relax. You are safe. As you begin to enter the calm, thoughts may come flooding into your mind, attempting to distract or upset you. Unresolved problems may surface in search of a solution. You may think that you're supposed to figure something out or find answers to a current situation. Now is not the time to do so. You do not need to engage with these thoughts, nor struggle in trying to find answers. When these thoughts present themselves, as they are wont to do, all you need to do is simply observe them. Notice what they are saying. Then imagine yourself falling into the space beyond these thoughts. Watch your thoughts get left behind as you drift right through them.

Continue to fall gently into the silence, into a place free of all stress and distractions. As you do so, you may notice emotions come rising to the surface of your consciousness. You may feel sad or anxious. Once again, you do not need to fix or resolve anything. Just as with your thoughts, simply observe your feelings as they come up. Then fall right into them and beyond them. Watch your emotions as they are left behind while you continue your gentle descent into the quiet, into the calm, into your own center of being-ness. All is well. Breathe.

The Fourth Solution: *Learn to Let Go*

Underlying Principle: To embrace the new, we must let go of the old.

In one form or another, all transitional periods require letting go. Yet our ability to do so is often hindered by our fear-based and deeply-ingrained need to hold on. This does not simply refer to those people, places and things in our lives that we are so quick to identify as the "problem." It also pertains to the bigger handicaps of self-limiting attitudes, misconceptions, negative emotions, excessive worry, self-pity, and other inner "baggage" that depresses, exhausts, and immobilizes us. The Fourth Solution counters our tendency to hold on by giving us tools to examine these inner constraints and then to take the action to do some necessary emotional house-cleaning. By teaching us that letting go is a decision whose benefits include freedom and peace of mind, this chapter opens us up in preparation and expectation of something infinitely better.

Our first three Solutions have provided a foundation for our journey through this critical or transitional period. By helping us to practice self-acceptance, giving us the tools to maintain balance, and arming us with the strength of a Higher Source, they have prepared us for the work we must further undertake in our quest for fulfillment and connection.

We now venture into the middle trilogy of Solutions that reveal some of the deeper issues a woman must address to successfully navigate through this crisis or change and come out stronger and more complete in the process. These issues include our need to let go, our need to identify and heal our inner wounds, and our need to confront and change the ways in which we typically self-sabotage and sell ourselves short.

The intent of these next three Solutions is that of remembering, recovering, and redirecting: remembering who we are really are, recovering our sense of connection, and redirecting our energy so that it works for us, not against us. Although much of this work will be painstaking, following the lead of these next chapters will help us "get over ourselves to find ourselves." In other words, we will get over our false sense of who we think we are and reconnect with our true selves. Our inner core of fear, self-doubt, and pain, will be replaced by a healthy sense of self-worth. We need to do this, because *when there's no healthy self at the center, we tend to be self-centered,* even when we're the last person to know it.

Although there is no significant order to these middle steps, we'll begin by addressing our need to let go. Based upon the underlying principle that *to embrace the new, we must let go of the old,* letting go poses a problem for many of us. In fact, most women know how to hold on much better than we know how to let go. It could be no other way. From early infancy, we have been taught the importance of keeping a firm grip on things: "Hold on to my arm so that you don't fall; hold on to that dress, you might wear it someday; hold on to your children, they will be gone soon enough; hold on to your husband (boyfriend or lover), you'll never find another; hold on to that job, it is a competitive world out there; hold on to your looks, it's the best thing you've got going for yourself." Some of us grew up having to hold on just to survive.

Over the years, these underlying messages of "hold on" have become insidiously absorbed into the unconscious fabric of our psyche. Convinced that our youth is our beauty, our home reflects our worth, our husband/job/savings account is our security, our career is who we are, our children are an extension of ourselves, is it any wonder that the idea of letting go of any of these poses such a major threat to our self-esteem and feelings of security?

Because of this threat to the perceived status quo, we tend to hold on to people, places, and things in our lives long after our feminine intuition and good common sense tells us it is time to let them go. In fact, some of us are so resistant to the very idea of letting go, that our previous attempts may have resembled the less-than-glamorous behavior of a dog with a bone. We let it go, only to go back and pick it up again, chew on it some more, put it down, walk away, go back and pick it up again, each time leaving more of our teeth and claw marks on it.

Why is this? In a word, fear – fear that if we let something go, we'll end up with nothing, or at the very least, not enough. This irrational fear keeps us from letting go even when we know it is the right thing to do. We are like the woman struggling to stay afloat in the middle of a raging sea while clinging to a huge boulder. Upon hearing her cries for help, God looks down and advises loudly,

"Let go of the rock."

"But it's *my* rock!" she defiantly shouts back.

We, too, are defiant in our justification for holding on to the things in our lives that we think we need. There may be reasons for our holding on so tightly, but rather than provide us with purpose, fulfillment, or security, holding on threatens to drown us instead. At the very least, it keeps us highly distracted. When we are perpetually treading water while clinging tightly to our rocks, we're not swimming to any distant, meaningful shore.

If we were to take a closer look at the individual things to which we so tenaciously cling, we might notice that they can be easily divided into two distinct groups – the "rocks" we are aware of and can call by name, and those that exist just beneath the surface of our consciousness; out of sight, yet causing our spirits and energy to slowly sink to the bottom. Both types of rocks require our attention, so we will address them one at a time.

The "Rocks" We Know

Most of us can quickly point the finger to what we think causes our psychological and emotional energy to get depleted. We can identify those "rocks" in our lives that, in our opinion, not only prevent us from moving forward, but also keep us stuck. These may include a marriage or relationship into which we put all our attention and energy even though it is not salvageable; a job that has no future or is toxic; friendships that make us feel used or abused instead of affirmed and loved; a role or status in life that we struggle to maintain even though it no longer suits us.

At some level of our being, we know that holding on to these things keeps us stagnant and unfulfilled. Despite this, we continually try to maintain the status quo. Our fear-based justifications for this are several. To begin with, even under the best of conditions, letting go is not an easy undertaking. What we typically need to let go of is familiar and, unfortunately, the familiar feels right even when it is wrong; it feels safe, even when it is not; comfortable even when it isn't; and a sure thing, even when it is anything but sure.

Sometimes, we don't let go because we've become used to the tension involved with holding on. In certain cases, we're actually *addicted* to the chaos and turmoil holding on creates. After all, it keeps us distracted from our greater fear of the inner void, from our anxiety of wondering what we will do once we've let go, who or what will fill the empty space, and even who we will be.

Because these fears can be overwhelming, it might help us to understand that letting go is seldom intended as a two-step process. In other words, we don't decide in one breath that we need to let go of something, and then magically have the wherewithal to do it in the next. Some of us may think that this is how it is supposed to work. We may even try to convince ourselves that this is the way we have let go of things in the past, quickly and effortlessly. If this is our pattern, chances are that we have deceived ourselves. Letting go in a healthy manner involves a *process,* one that takes time and one that has a beginning, a middle, and an end, just like the *process* of all change.

The *process* of letting go begins with awareness. In other words, it begins by recognizing exactly what we need to let go of and why – identifying it – calling it by name – actually saying the words out loud. Believe it or not, this is often the most difficult part of letting go for a woman. We're afraid that if we verbalize it, we might have to do something about it. We're terrified that by actually admitting to being unhappy with the status quo, we'll be forced to make a change. Once again, our fear steps in to worry, "What will that mean? How will I do this? What will replace it?"

Despite this fear, once we've admitted our need to let go, we've taken the first big step by bringing our need into conscious awareness. However, there is good news and bad news about this. The good news is, awareness precedes all change. The not-so-good news is, it doesn't guarantee it. Changes seldom happen automatically or immediately. In fact, the very nature of letting go is that once we identify our need for change, we move into the most difficult place of all places: the divine discomfort that lies between knowing we need to let go of something, and actually having the resources, the courage, or the willingness to do so. This divine discomfort could last weeks, months, or in some cases, even years before we are really ready and able to take the necessary action to move on. In the meantime, it might feel as if we're suspended between two worlds; like a woman on a flying trapeze who knows she needs to let go of one bar before she can grab hold of another, but is terrified to actually do so. The thought of falling is overwhelming. Yet, the only way to move out of the divine discomfort is by being willing to take the risk to let go.

Another seldom acknowledged point to be made about the process of letting go is that it does not necessitate a struggle. What a contradictory statement for those of us who so often cry, "I'm struggling to let go of this relationship! I'm struggling to get out of this job! I'm struggling to let go of my children!"

Let's take a moment to really think about what letting go implies. In no way do those two words - "let go" - suggest resistance. On the contrary, they indicate a willingness to open up, to surrender what we cling to, and to release it into the universe. In fact, if we compare the meaning of "letting go" to "holding on," we will notice immediately that "holding on" is what takes energy and effort. If we think we're struggling to let go, chances are that we're really struggling to hold on. And the more we struggle, the more we reinforce our attachment to the very thing we're trying to let go of.

To resist is to persist. It is like being caught in quicksand. The more energy we put into the struggle, the deeper we sink.

In light of all this, how can we let go without the resistance and the battle? How can we manage to open both our hands to release whatever we're clinging to so that we can be ready to embrace something new that may be more in alignment with our authentic needs?

This was an issue Mary struggled with for years. In her case, she was consumed with a relationship that she knew was not working out. Her boyfriend had some deep-rooted intimacy problems, most of which concerned his feelings of unworthiness. Unfortunately, when people feel unworthy, they tend to act that way as well. His symptoms included chronic tardiness, a fondness for other women, an unwillingness to talk about it, and a basic inability to act like a worthy partner.

Despite all of this, he was a kind man and Mary loved him deeply. For several months, torn with conflicting emotions, she struggled with the decision of whether or not to give up the relationship. She would be determined to do so one moment, only to reconsider the next. This emotional push-pull consumed her as she felt constantly yanked in opposite directions, in and out, back and forth.

One day, in the midst of her struggle, something short of miraculous happened. Mary had a moment of truth, of pure insight. In her words: "For far too long, I struggled between trying to get out of this relationship and trying to make something work that obviously wasn't, for either one of us, really. Finally, one morning while writing in my journal, I began to think. What if, instead of struggling so hard to get free from this man, I shifted my focus instead? In other words, rather than obsess and strain to let go of Michael, *what if I put my efforts and attention on where I want to go instead?* What if I stopped wasting my energy in the distraction of the struggle and focused this same energy on walking purposefully down my own path?"

These thoughts inspired Mary to begin asking herself some long-overdue questions: Was she using this relationship as a *distraction*, a means of *not looking* at work she might need to do on herself? What else was important to her, anyway? Was she happy with her career? Was her creative self being fulfilled anywhere? Who else was she in relationship with? Was it time to develop more women friends?

She next made a list of what she needed to do and wanted the most. Getting a therapist was right on the top. After all, if she was using this relationship as some sort of a distraction, she wanted to find out why. This decision was followed by others, such as taking an oil painting class and applying for a new position within her company. The more she directed her energy and effort towards her own personal goals, the more her life unfolded in surprising and fulfilling ways. Eventually, the relationship with Michael came to an end. But it wasn't a struggle in the least; it was just a byproduct of her willingness to take action on her own behalf and to be open to the many other possibilities in her life.

As simplistic as it may sound at first, this is the basic formula for letting go of every outer circumstance or person we have previously struggled to leave behind. Whether a relationship, job, or problem, all we need to do is to take our attention and energy off of what we're trying to let go of, and put it on where we want to go instead. Rather than struggle, we only need to shift our focus by locating our individual light and moving in that direction. And what if we haven't a clue what our own light consists of? Not to worry. We don't have to figure it out right now. It, too, will be a byproduct of our willingness to follow the path outlined in this book and to continue taking right action on our own behalf.

Beneath the Surface "Rocks"

Now let us address the second category of rocks to which we insidiously cling. These unconscious, beneath-the-surface rocks consist of all the negative emotions and attitudes we've picked up over the years that we continue to haul into and through every situation and relationship in our lives. For the most part, we are oblivious to the huge impact they have on what we say, do, think, or feel. Rather than contribute anything positive, they waste our precious energy by keeping us busily distracted in trying to stay afloat. Probably the biggest one of these is the rock called "Illusion."

Oh, the energy we use trying to make our lives conform to our illusions of what they should be! Some of these more common illusions of ours include:

Life is fair.
True love lasts forever.
Families are always loving.
I'll never grow old/get sick/die.
Everything will stay the same.
Husbands will never leave.
Someday my prince will come.
If I pray long enough and hard enough, I'll get what I want.
If I do everything right, I will have the perfect marriage, the perfect children, the perfect job.
If I try harder, I can make it work.
If I love him more, he'll change.
By the time I'm a certain age, I'll have my life together.

Our subscribing to these faulty misconceptions creates a multitude of problems. It causes us to place unreal expectations on what we *should* do and what our lives *should* look like. When things don't measure up to these illogical expectations and illusions, we feel disappointed, disillusioned and not good enough; in short, like failures.

If we really gave it some thought, we could probably recall numerous times when our illusions have been exposed for what they really are. Even those of us who are only half-awake will have to admit that life isn't fair; true love doesn't always last forever; things change all the time; many families are anything but close; perfectionism can never be maintained; the days of knights on white horses have long passed; and we all grow old if we're lucky enough! And while God does answer our prayers, it is often not the way we might have expected or wanted. That's the real Truth. Still, we insist on maintaining our false beliefs in spite of overwhelming evidence that these illusions are flawed. How often do our inner convictions need to be challenged for us to begin to realize that maybe, just maybe, they really are illusions?

A great benefit of transitional periods is that they give us an opportunity to re-evaluate what is real, and what is not. Now is the perfect time to confront, re-think, and discard those illusions that keep us in a perpetual state of discontent and unhappiness. After all, they really don't serve any good purpose. And just think how peaceful our life might be if we stopped struggling to conform it to some preconceived illusionary notion of what is correct and right! Imagine the serenity we would experience by living with expectations that are reasonable as well as attainable. For openers, our tendency to feel chronically disappointed and disillusioned would begin to disappear. In the process, we would have more energy to put into making changes that are in keeping with what *is* real and who *we* really are.

Illusion and authenticity never co-exist. Therefore, we must be rid of the first in order to embrace the second. The best way to let go of any of our illusions is to shine the light on them; examine them; look them squarely in the face and demand their credentials. At the same time, to ask ourselves, "Is there a direct relationship between my unrealistic expectations and my sense of disillusionment? Is it possible that by letting go of some illusionary concept, I might open the door to a greater reality for my life? If I stopped trying to make my life conform to a preconceived notion of what it should look like, might I be able to lighten up, loosen up, and enjoy life more?"

Challenging the authority of our illusions is how we begin to let them go. And anytime our fear causes us to falter, we need only remind ourselves that fear is nothing but *F*alse *E*vidence *A*ppearing *R*eal. In other words, it is another illusion.

Letting Go of the "Worry Rock"

Worry is right up there on the scale of major negative energy drainers. Women worry. We worry about the real and the imagined. We fret about the weather, our children, our partners, our health, our finances, our jobs, our age. We worry about what is going to happen next, and how it might affect us and those we care about. We ruminate on what we said or did yesterday. We picture all kinds of worrisome scenarios for tomorrow. Some of us have been worriers for so long that we actually believe our worrying serves a purpose, that it somehow helps the person, situation, or circumstance that we worry about. We might even think that if we're not worrying, we're not doing anything constructive!

Because it is so important to separate fact from fiction in all areas of our lives, we have to honestly admit that *worry has never improved a situation or changed an outcome*. Most of our worries don't even have anything to do with the present moment; they concern themselves with something from the past, something that has yet to occur (and possibly won't), or some figment of our imagination that has little to do with reality. Our propensity to worry carries far more consequences than we could possibly imagine. When we allow worry to take over our conscious and/or subconscious mind, it becomes a living entity, a force that grows in strength. In so doing, it keeps us preoccupied and exhausted as it drains the energy out of our day.

When we're in the worry mode, crazy as it might seem, we typically find ways to enlarge and expand our worry, to actually nurture and feed it. For instance, if we're worried about our finances, we become obsessed with watching any bad financial reports on television, or reading them in the newspapers. If worried about a relationship, we call up every friend we know who will add fuel to the fire. When worried about decisions we should have, could have, would have made differently, we dredge up every other wrong decision we think we ever made. As if our worries weren't large enough on their own, we take active measures to make them bigger and more powerful. And the more energy we give to the "what ifs," the less we have to cope with the "what is."

Despite what we might think, we are not victims to our obsession with worrying. Since it serves no good purpose whatsoever, we must find ways to let go of our *habit* of worrying, as well as what we're actually worried about. Once again, the way we begin is by identification. What is it that worries us? What keeps us from sleeping through the night? What interferes with our peace and serenity? Are we worried about our financial security? Our partner, or lack of one? A relationship? Our health? Our future? Our travel plans? Our children? Regardless of what it is, we cannot begin to let go of it without first calling it by name.

My son was not quite three when I was diagnosed with breast cancer. As anyone can imagine, this was certainly a cause for great worry on my part. A year later, I became even more worried when a routine x-ray revealed something suspicious on one of my bones. The doctors didn't *think* it was consistent with cancer, but then again, they couldn't guarantee it.

Obsessed with the possibilities (all negative, of course), I lost sleep. I couldn't eat. And I spent many moments poking and feeling the suspicious area trying to detect any possible malignancies. One day, I even went so far as to drag out my old college Anatomy and Physiology books! There I was, sitting at the dining room table anxiously looking for information, when my son called to me from the next room where he was watching a National Geographic special.

"Mommy, Mommy," he cried excitedly. "Come quick!"

"In a minute, Robert," I replied. "I'm busy right now."

"Hurry!" he encouraged.

At this point, I was so consumed with my worrying that it had taken on a life of its own. After all, I had been feeding it well.

"NOT NOW!" I angrily shouted.

Wounded by my harsh reply, my son began to cry. He walked slowly towards me, tears streaming down his precious face.

"But Mommy, you're missing all the beautiful butterflies."

I could not have had a greater moment of truth if God had personally tapped me on the shoulder. In that one instant, I realized the futility of my worrying. It was serving absolutely no purpose whatsoever except to make me crazy and keep me from being available to anyone else. After all, I had done everything possible regarding my physical condition. I had taken additional x-rays and blood tests, had a bone-scan, and spoken with the doctors. I had no choice but to wait and see. However, what I did have a choice about was how to spend my time. I could choose to spend it worrying about what might or might not happen tomorrow, or I could spend it watching the beautiful butterflies of today with my little boy. I am pleased to say that I have never taken those anatomy books out again, and I have lived to tell the story.

My son helped me learn an important lesson that day – the lesson of letting go of worry. The way it is done is quite simple. When consumed with a worry of any kind, we ask ourselves one question and one question only:

"Is there anything I can do about this today?"

If the answer is "yes," then we empower ourselves by doing anything and everything possible to affect a positive outcome. This might involve getting additional information, calling a lawyer, seeing a doctor, researching a particular matter, sending out resumes, or finding a support system. If there is something we can do, then we do it. But after we have done everything possible, everything within our power, we need to let it go because it consumes us when we don't.

There are other suggestions we can follow to further help us let go of our worry. The first involves our Higher Power. We need not necessarily have faith to follow this suggestion, all we need to do is take an old shoe box or pocketbook and write *God* or *Higher Power* on it. When we begin worrying about something, anything at all, we write our worry down on a piece of paper, and then place it in this "God Box." For some strange reason, the physical act of writing down what we're worried about and transferring it from our head into the box breaks the negative cycle of worrying. We may have to do this several times a day, but if we do, we are guaranteed to feel the benefits. As simplistic as it sounds, it works. (This is a great technique to use with children who worry as well).

Another way to let go of worry is to practice "mind-shifting." This is similar to the thought changing we worked on with our practice of self-acceptance. The way this exercise works is also simple: when consumed with worry, we make a conscious decision to stop thinking about the problem and replace it with a positive thought. Rather than give our energy to the worrisome situation, we simply shift our focus to the positive. Our positive thoughts might include God, love, nature, wisdom, gratitude, or a wonderful experience we once had.

Like any of our other suggestions for letting go, this is also not intended as a struggle, merely a shift. And it does take practice; a whole lifetime of worrying cannot be turned around in an instant. However, with repeated effort, this "mind-shifting" can bring us a lot of relief from our compulsive and chronic tendency to worry.

The more we put these suggestions into action, the less we will worry, and the greater energy we will have for things of a more fulfilling and productive nature. Despite what we might think or how we feel, we *do* have a choice when it comes to worrying. We can adopt it, feed it, and help it grow to such proportions that it totally overwhelms us. Or we can make a conscious decision to let it go, and to focus on the "beautiful butterflies" of today.

To embrace the new, we must let go of the old.

Letting Go of Self-Pity

Without even knowing it, many of us carry the disappointments of a lifetime into each and everyday. Very often, these disappointments are in direct response to many of the illusions we just discussed. But sometimes, life has not lived up to our *reasonable* expectations or desires, leaving us to wonder what went wrong, or where *we* went wrong. It can seem as if everybody else gets what they want in life -- everyone but us. This kind of thinking can cause us to feel oh-so-sorry for ourselves. And practically nothing has more power to consume our energy as much as self-pity.

Take Kathleen, for instance. From the time she was a little girl, she fantasized about a life that included a house full of children and a husband who was attentive, affectionate, and loyal. Rather than exotic trips or fancy clothes, she dreamt of wearing aprons, baking cookies, and reading bedside stories to curious little faces. Her life choices, however, did not turn out to be the best. She married a man who liked his beer and who had a roving eye. Two years after the birth of their son, he left her for another woman. Being a single mom without financial security was not a role Kathleen would have ever chosen as part of her life story.

As much as Kathleen wanted more children, as it happened she never remarried. The older she became, the more she realized that her dreams of being a stay-at-home mom with several youngsters to care for were simply not going to materialize. To say that she was disappointed was a huge understatement. She would often fall into a deep depression carved out by her self-pity and stay there for days on end.

The time eventually came, however, when Kathleen was sick and tired of having her energy consumed with such negativity. Not wishing to grow into a bitter old woman, she made a conscious decision to stop giving so much time and attention to her disappointment about not having any more babies, and to find something else that would satisfy her inner desire to mother. Eventually, a situation presented itself that gave Kathleen the opportunity to become an effective advocate for underprivileged boys in her community. Even though this was a different kind of home for her mothering energy than what she had originally desired, it was one that has benefited numerous children, while fulfilling her in the process.

One way for us to let go of the self-pity that so often accompanies our life disappointments is to take a new perspective on them. Instead of focusing on how bad we feel because we didn't get what we wanted, we need to look at what lies beneath our disappointments. Most of the things that bring on our self-pity represent some underlying desire within us that is not being fulfilled, at least not in the way we want. Instead of continuing to feel bad about this, the question to ask ourselves is the very same one we asked regarding our worries: "Is there anything I can do to change the situation?" If the answer is yes, we take the appropriate action. If the answer is no, we need to accept it. We can do this in the same way Kathleen did: after mourning the loss of her initial desire, she found an alternative way to satisfy the underlying need. We do have other choices.

Jenny was in her thirties when she got married. Even though her husband was a great deal older than she was, she felt that they shared the same values and would make a good couple. Over the next ten years, they had three children. With every new addition to the family, her husband became a little more overwhelmed and a little less emotionally and physically available. He worked constantly, neglecting his family and his own self-care in the process. Periodically, they would go to counseling, but it only put a band-aid on the larger, underlying issues.

Although Jenny considered getting a divorce, she knew in her heart that she would never follow through with it. It not only went against her religious values, but she was also committed to raising her children in a two-parent home. Besides that, she loved her husband and knew that he loved her and the children.

Yet she continued to become more and more disillusioned about their marriage, disappointed that things hadn't turned out the way she expected or wanted. Part of her was in grief over the loss of her "happily ever after" illusion. But what also happened in Jenny's case was that she got caught in the steel trap of self-pity. It became the bitter vise that firmly held her as she chronically complained, "Why is this *my* life? Why couldn't I have a life like Mary's, or Joan's? Why isn't my husband more like Susan's husband? I deserve better!"

As time went by, Jenny became more and more paralyzed by this self-pity. It took complete charge of her thoughts, her emotions, even her conversations. In fact, she became so consumed with feeling sorry for herself that she wasn't able to be available to those three beautiful children she was so fortunate to have.

Yet this self-pity was pointless. Jenny had already asked herself if there was anything she was willing to do about the situation and the answer was, "No." So she needed to find a way to accept the things she could not change, contain her disappointment, and eliminate the toxic feelings of self-pity that only caused more unhappiness in her life.

There is a big difference between feeling our feelings and indulging our feelings. When it comes to our disappointments, the determining factor between feeling and indulging is normally related to the amount of emotional energy we give them. For Jenny, what finally broke the debilitating grip of self-pity she had gotten caught in was her learning how to "indulge within limits." This is a means of setting boundaries around a negative emotion such as self-pity so that it doesn't take over and ruin an entire day.

This is how it is done: when we are consumed with feeling sorry for ourselves, we can designate thirty specific minutes during the day solely for the purpose of self-pity. When the time arrives, we set an alarm to sound in half an hour during which time we do nothing except dwell on our misfortunes and disappointments! We can even put on sad music if this helps – after all, this is *our* self-pity party!

During other times of the day, when our self-pity is clamoring for our attention, we gently but firmly remind it that it will have to wait until the appointed hour. By giving self-pity its own specific time and space, it no longer needs to distract or interfere with the rest of our day. This way, we're available for the many things in our lives that aren't disappointing.

It might also help us to remember that, in some instances, today's disappointments will turn out to be tomorrow's gifts. If we look back over our lives, we can probably see cases in the past when this has been true. We didn't get what we wanted when we wanted it, *thank God*! This might be a good time to recall some of those occasions, especially if we are presently full of self-pity over a recent event or non-occurrence.

Another way to get beyond our self-pity is by reminding ourselves again that *it's not so much what happens to us, as how we respond to it.* We no longer have to take the one black mark in our lives and smudge it all over everything else. If we are feeling disappointed about something, instead of adopting and nurturing our disappointment to the point of chronic self-pity, we might instead make a gratitude list of everything that is going well in our lives. An "attitude of gratitude" is a sure-fire antidote for all kinds of disappointments and self-pity.

Letting Go of "If Only"

It is a lucky lady, indeed, who can identify with the words of Frank Sinatra's famous song, "Regrets, I've had a few, but then again, too few to mention."

Regrets differ from disappointments in that they are far more personal. Often, our disappointments involve other people, places or situations, whereas our regrets have more to do with us -- the opportunities *we* had but didn't take, the decisions *we* made that turned out wrong, *our* personal behavior that, in hindsight, wasn't the best.

If asked, most of us could probably come up with several good regrets at any given moment! Just think of all the possibilities! We regret the things we have done and the things we have failed to do. We regret the decisions we made and those we think we should have. We regret the job we didn't take, the man we didn't marry, the children we never had. We lament over the stock we failed to buy, the house we sold too soon, the time in school we squandered. We regret the money we foolishly spent, the vacations we never took, the chances that won't come again. We regret how quickly the years have passed. Oh, if only........

The fact that we don't usually have denial surrounding our regrets is both a curse and blessing: a blessing because we don't need to spend time digging them up; a curse because regret has a way of making its presence felt right in the pit of our stomach, often pairing up with other disease-producing emotions such as depression, hopelessness, or remorse.

If we really examined the basic nature of regrets, we would realize that most of them have to do with things of the past. Although we know intellectually that it is useless and senseless to "go there," we continue to get caught up in re-living our old mistakes. Even when we try to ignore the "if onlys," we're still aware of their presence. These regrets lurk in the shadows, one step behind us, waiting for a bad day so that they can really attach themselves to our mood. Picking them up and holding onto them only contributes to our negativity and bad feelings, so we must find ways to let them go.

To remove the deeper and more serious of our regrets might require some grief work which is addressed in the next chapter on Healing. However, many of our regrets only need recognition, deliberate attention, and a conscious decision to let them go. With that end in sight, rather than struggle to keep our regrets submerged and therefore manageable (or so we think), we're going to do some necessary emotional housecleaning. In order to do this, we must, once again, journey back on the road of "no longer an option" in order to identify, pick up, and claim the many regrets we may have left scattered about the playing field. Not only are we going to venture back, but we're going to earmark a specific day simply for the acknowledgment and recognition of our "if onlys."

Once we have chosen the day, our primary goal will be to think about, bring into our conscious awareness, and write down every single regret we have ever had, even the itty bitty ones that we think don't count. This exercise does not require us to go into detail, just to make a list, like a shopping list. For instance, "I regret that I never pursued my relationship with Tom. I regret that I didn't try out for that Broadway show. I regret that I never finished my thesis. I regret that I didn't have more children. I regret that I didn't buy a house when they were affordable. I regret that I never put money in a 401K. I regret that I wasn't nicer to my mother when she was alive."

There are many reasons we make this list. For one thing, it will show us in black and white how most of our regrets reflect opportunities gone by. In other words, we are totally powerless to do anything about changing them. No amount or money, intellect, influence, or therapy can affect what has been done or not done. So we must let these regrets go.

Another benefit of writing them down is that it makes our regrets *conscious.* This increased consciousness will help prevent our repeating the same behaviors or making the same mistakes in the future. Writing our regrets down gives us the opportunity to learn from them, not just about what we don't want to do, but about what we do.

After we write our regrets down, we need to go one step further by releasing them physically, emotionally, and symbolically. We can do this by a ritual that involves burning our regrets. This ritual can be done alone, but proves to be more powerful in the community of like-minded women. The ceremony begins by a meditation such as the one at the conclusion of this chapter, followed by a general sharing during which each individual recites her personal regrets list aloud. After the regrets have been shared briefly with one another, the written pages are ceremoniously thrown into a fireplace or other container. As they go up in flames and turn to ash, we make a conscious choice to offer them up or turn them over to the universe, to God, to Whatever or Whomever makes sense to us. At the same time, we make a decision never to take them back again. They are out of our control, out of our hands, and out of our hearts. *We have let go of the old to make room for the new.*

Letting Go of Guilt

Guilt is another toxin that we need to let go of. This can be a lifelong enterprise for some of us. We saw in the chapter regarding self-acceptance just why this might be so. *We are who we are for reasons,* and we have learned to feel guilty for reasons as well. Maybe we are convinced that it is just our cross to bear. After all, everyone else in our family feels guilty for one reason or another, why should we be different? This kind of "internalized" guilt may require professional help for us to get over.

However, the guilt we are addressing at this point in our process is of a different nature altogether; that is, our bona fide guilt. This is guilt we feel as a direct result of behavior that was not what it might have been. Maybe we were unfaithful in a relationship, or revealed a confidence, or betrayed a trust, or told a fabrication. We may have injured another through our deceitfulness, hard-heartedness or indifference. Or maybe the harm we committed was totally without malice; that we acted or reacted on an unconscious level, unaware of the consequences our behavior or attitude had on another. There are times when thoughtlessness can create every bit as much damage as intent.

In the past, we may have justified our conduct, or even denied that our behavior had a negative impact on another person or a situation. But now we are at a new place in our lives, and we are sick and tired of hauling unwanted and unnecessary negativity into each new situation. So we are willing to do what we need to do. When it comes to our guilt, this requires taking a good look at what's "legitimate," and then taking the necessary steps to get rid of it. Even though guilt has an initial good side by making us aware of inappropriate or malicious behavior, it serves no good purpose to continue holding onto anything that makes us feel bad about who we are.

Provided we know what we are feeling guilty about, there is a simple four-step process we can use to clean our internal house of these totally unproductive and corrosive feelings of guilt.

Step One

We write down the specific action, thought, or behavior that we are presently feeling guilty about. Word by agonizing word, we spell out the exact nature of what makes us uncomfortable in our own skins, what bothers our conscience. Did we lie, cheat, steal, gossip, betray? Were we judgmental, malicious, or hurtful? As we write, we ignore the remarks from our inner committee and try not to judge, censure, or beat ourselves up for what we write. We just take pen in hand and, little by little, move the guilt from inside of our head onto the piece of paper. Just doing this much will begin to reduce the negative power our guilt has over our self-esteem and self-confidence.

Step Two

Next, we take ownership of our guilt. The way we do this is by sharing what we have written with another person. Because we tend to be our own worst critics, confiding in another will help give us some much-needed objectivity and may help us realize that we're not quite as unique and terrible as we might have thought. Of course, it is of utmost importance to exercise caution when choosing the person with whom we speak. He/she must be trustworthy and non-judgmental, perhaps a clergy person, a true friend, a therapist, or even a trusted family member.

Step Three

After sharing with a trusted confidant, the next step is to take full responsibility for our behavior by becoming accountable for our actions. Instead of pointing the finger elsewhere in an attempt to blame or justify, we look at the three fingers pointing back at us and take action accordingly. If we have harmed another through thought, word, or behavior, whether intentionally or not, we make our amends as best we can. This might include an apology, financial restitution, admission of wrong-doing, or a decision for changed future behavior. It is important that we use discretion when making these amends. As our objective is not to cause additional harm, we don't bring up past circumstances that might be better off left alone. In fact, we might want to discuss our intentions with somebody else before taking action. "When in doubt, don't." This is not meant as permission to procrastinate because, "when and if we can, we do."

Step Four

Just as we did with our regrets, we might want to make a ritual around burning our guilt-ridden pages. As we watch them go up in flames, we vow never to pick this guilt up again. We have owned it, learned from it, possibly made amends for it, and now we are willing to let it go entirely.

Letting Go of Resentment and Anger

Few women really know how to deal with anger. Instead of expressing it appropriately, we have learned to deny it, stuff it, minimize it, or explode with it. We pay a price for mishandling this emotion. Holding onto anger and resentments makes us sick on many levels. Emotionally, we become consumed with a horrid, toxic emotion. Mentally, being angry at someone gives them free reign over our thoughts; we lie awake tossing and turning at night, while the cause of our resentment probably sleeps soundly. And nothing is more spiritually corrosive than holding on to resentment. Seething with anger is similar to drinking poison and hoping somebody else will die. As Louise Hay asks, "Would you rather be well, or would you rather be right?"

For those of us who recognize that we are angry and why, we are way ahead of the game. Yet knowing is only the first step. We also need to know how to process our anger or, better yet, not to be so quick to pick it up in the first place. Here are a few suggestions:

Don't take offense

Just look at the language we use regarding our personal relationship with anger and resentment. "I'm *holding* a grudge. I'm *carrying* my hurt within me. I *take* offense easily. I *wear* my anger." These action verbs imply a certain amount of willingness on our part to accept and hold on to our anger and resentments. We might be better off to imagine ourselves wearing a bullet proof vest or holding our hands up and saying, "Thanks, but no thanks. I'm not taking any resentment today." If somebody tries to make us angry, we can mentally picture ourselves taking a broom and sweeping the anger off our side of the street and back onto theirs. It is a good way to begin.

Analyze the situation

When looking at what makes us angry, it is important to ask ourselves what part, if any, we might have played in causing or contributing to our anger. We waste time and energy looking elsewhere for answers if we have not first determined whether or not our own side of the street is clean. If we are culpable, we need to address that by taking responsibility for any part we may have played in the situation. Perhaps we owe somebody an apology or amend. If so, we must make it.

Don't personalize it

Because we tend to think everything has to do with us, we often lament, "Why is this person doing this *to me*?" In truth, what somebody else does, or doesn't do, rarely has anything to do with us! Even though it feels so deeply personal, especially when we have been deceived or betrayed, the behavior of others is more about who *they* are than about who *we* are. They do what they do, say what they say, or don't do what they don't do, because they are being themselves! Every person we meet comes with their own inner programming and personal pathology.

If we can learn to depersonalize the behavior of others, we have a much better shot at not picking up the anger to begin with. The way to practice this is by, once again, changing the way we think. Instead of thinking, "Why is he (she, they) doing this to me?," we ask, "Why is he doing this?" Removing those last two words from the equation -- the "to me"-- takes away the supposed intentionality behind the behavior. This is helpful for several reasons. First, we don't take somebody else's behavior personally. Second, if we answer the question of, "Why is he doing this?," we have a chance of getting to know more about the other person. Finally, we come to understand that nothing we might have done or said differently would have changed the situation. Their behavior is simply not about us; it is all about them. If we can consistently depersonalize the behavior of others, our lives will have far less anger and resentment, and much more serenity.

Talk to somebody

When we're in the throes of anger, it helps to find somebody safe to appropriately share this anger with, preferably not another angry woman who might help feed, rather than diffuse, our own. We could speak with a therapist, a family member, a clergy person, or, if in a 12-step program, our sponsor. While sharing our anger can be out of character and difficult at first, just bringing our anger into the light of day is enough to take the negative sting out of it and allow us to eventually let it go.

Go to the source

If we are feeling angry with a specific person over a particular situation, gently confronting the person is an appropriate thing to do. Confrontation only has a bad name because most of us don't know how to say what we mean, mean what we say, and not say it meanly. Instead of going directly to the source and addressing a pertinent issue in a sane, rational, and even loving way, we have become conditioned to talking behind people's backs, exploding in their faces, or treating them with hostile, icy indifference.

Even though the need for it is often fueled by anger, confrontation is only effective when done in a calm, rather than irate, tone of voice and attitude. So before confronting anyone about how their behavior has affected us, we might want to calm ourselves down first by using the breathing exercises we learned in our second chapter on Balance. It is also a good idea to practice the tone and the content of our "talk" with a close friend before we speak to those directly involved.

After becoming calm and rational, we address the source of our anger or resentment by speaking from an "I" perspective. In other words, we don't accuse or point a finger because this is an automatic trigger for the other person to stop listening and defend themselves instead. So rather than attack the other party with a list of their character defects, we keep the focus on how their behavior or the situation affected us; how it made *us* feel. Mary's story illustrates how this works in real life.

Like many women in her parish, Mary felt resentful when, time and time again, the minister would assign her to various committees and groups without asking her first. Although all the other women complained among themselves at his presumptuousness, nobody had ever spoken to him directly about it. Because Mary was not one to talk behind somebody's back, she decided to go directly to the source by calling him up.

After some friendly small-talk, she said in a calm voice, "I was surprised to see my name on a committee we had never discussed. Call me an old fashioned gal if you will, but I like to be asked first."

"Oh", he replied. "Well, if you're not interested in doing it, I can get somebody else."

"That's not what I'm talking about," Mary pleasantly continued. "It has nothing to do with being on the committee or not. It's just that I really like to be asked first. Now tell me some more about this committee and what it would require."

The minister went on to explain the particulars, after which Mary agreed that she would be more than willing to do it. However, a week later when a revised committee list was sent out, Mary's name was no longer on it.

Our sharing is not guaranteed to be received in the manner that we intend; that is not important. We are not responsible for how people may react. Many are just too defensive to hear, and we need to be prepared for this. After all, how they respond is more about who *they* are than who *we* are. And it is far more important to have spoken our truth than to have been heard.

Even though Mary's resentment may seem small compared to our own, the same formula for confrontation holds true in most situations. We calm ourselves down first, and we always speak from the "I" perspective. After we share our feelings, we then need to decide if we want to continue to relate to those who caused us bad feelings. Do we jump back into a relationship with the offenders? This is a personal choice. Sometimes, letting go means moving on from a toxic relationship -- but that's another book altogether!

Write

If we know who we're angry with, we might want to write them a letter. It doesn't matter whether they are still in our lives or even alive; the letter we write is for our own benefit. Once again, it is about taking direct and specific action to let go of our anger or resentment. When we write the letter, we do it the same way we do our confrontation, from the "I" perspective. We put down on paper how we have been personally affected by the situation. "I felt _____ when you _____." If the person is still living, and we wish to send the letter, we might do so. However, it is advisable to share its contents first with a trusted and reasonable friend. If we don't wish to send the letter, we could burn it or put it into our God Box. What we do with the letter is irrelevant. The important thing is that we express our feelings; that we move them out of us so that they can no longer do us harm.

Forgive

As impossible as it may seem right now, in certain circumstances, forgiveness is the key to letting go of anger. It is the vehicle by which we can truly experience the freedom of release from resentments that have previously kept us captive. This spiritual principle of forgiveness begins by making a decision to forgive -- no matter whom, no matter what, no matter how we feel. We are who we are for reasons; they are who they are for reasons, as well. Once we know this, and provided we are trying to grow spiritually, we can go one step further and actually pray for the person(s) responsible for our anger or resentment.

Some of us will immediately be repulsed by this idea, thinking to ourselves, "No way am I going to pray for him/ her/ them! And let them off the hook? After what they did!" This response is the same as taking another drink of that poison meant for them. It still doesn't work, but prayer does.

This is how we do it. Every day for three weeks, regardless of our resistance, skepticism, or downright defiance, we get on our knees and ask God's blessing on the offending person(s). We might even go so far as to pray that good things come their way. (Not a fast train or a speeding bullet, either)! If at the end of three weeks, we still feel angry or resentful, we must continue to pray daily until our hatred, anger and resentments are replaced by serenity and compassion. The amazing thing about doing this is that it actually works. And we are the ones who reap the benefits. Not only are we relieved of the heavy burden of this toxic anger, but we experience even greater spiritual growth and connection.

At this point, we might be thinking that all this is just too much! Granted, we have been given a lot of emotional housecleaning to do in this chapter. Yet, our willingness to let go is vital to our ability to move through, rather than get stuck in, whatever crisis or change we happen to be in. By following the suggestions outlined throughout this chapter, we make a good beginning on getting over the negativity that has previously been a barrier between us and our knowledge of our true selves. We are gradually and steadily replacing our inner core of *fear* with a clear and unobstructed view of who we really are. We understand that when there is no self at the center, we tend to be self-centered, and we no longer wish to be that way. So rather than cling fearfully and desperately to the old, we are willing to be receptive to new and wonderful possibilities with arms that are wide-open and inviting. *To embrace the new, we must let go of the old.*

The drowning woman finally let go of the rock and swam to shore. About a week later, when walking along the side of a cliff, she stumbled and fell over the edge. It was extremely fortuitous that a little branch was sticking out from the side of the cliff and that she was miraculously able to grab hold of it. As she dangled in mid-air, she once again cried out for help. God answered.

"Let go of the branch," God instructed.

"Is there anyone else up there?," she quickly responded.

This so often is our story. Is there anyone else up there? As much as we've been conditioned to want somebody or something else to "save us," we are beginning to understand that faith is the true means by which we let go of anything and everything. And it can be guaranteed that once we stop clinging to the old, and take the leap of faith to let go, one of two things will happen: either a ledge will appear, or we will be given wings to fly.

Suggestions for Letting Go

1. What worried you the most a year ago? Do you remember, or does it now seem insignificant? What are you worried about today? Is there something you can do about the particular person, place or situation? If so, do it now. If not, make a decision to let it go.

2. Put the exercise of "mind-shifting" into action this week. Whenever a worry comes into your mind, replace it quickly with positive thoughts of God, love, serenity, peace.

3. Create your own "God Box" from an old pocketbook or shoe box. Label it with a word or words that work for you -- *God, Higher Power, Allah, Great Spirit.* Write down what you want to let go of -- a disappointment, worry, resentment or anger – and place it in the box. As you do so, imagine yourself mentally and spiritually releasing it as well. Do this as often as necessary.

4. Designate a "Burn Your Regrets Day." Invite your closest friend or friends to participate in it. Do the ritual as outlined on pages 105-106.

5. Find a quiet space and time to ask yourself, "Am I feeling guilty about anything? Do I owe somebody an apology?" If so, make amends whenever possible. If reluctant or confused about doing so, discuss it first with a close friend, mental health professional, or clergy person.

6. In big letters, write in your journal: *Letting go is about freedom, not deprivation. To embrace the new, I must let go of the old.*

Meditation on Letting Go

Bring yourself into a state of calmness by using the meditation on page 87. Continue to focus on your breathing, becoming more and more relaxed with every breath. As you feel your body become heavier and heavier, tell yourself that there is no place else you need to be right now; there is nothing else you need to be doing. This is your time and space. It is sacred. As you continue to breathe deeply, imagine God breathing through you.

After entering into the silence, bring your attention to the very center of your being, into your heart space. Is there something standing between you and your own true self? Does your inner spirit feel weighted down by something old? Are you holding a resentment that it is time to let go of? Is there an ancient source of guilt or shame keeping you in bondage? Do you have a fixation on somebody else that is holding your spirit hostage?

Take a few moments to examine what keeps your heart closed, burdened, hardened, or frozen. Try to identify what saps your inner enthusiasm and energy. When it becomes clear, make a conscious decision to let it go. It does you no good to continue clinging to something you no longer need.

Once you make the decision, picture yourself releasing whatever you need to into the universe. Just as if it were a balloon, let it go, give it to God. In your mind's eye, watch it become smaller and smaller, until eventually you see it no more.

Bring your awareness back to your center. Feel your heart space soften, open, expand. Be at peace. Give thanks. Be hopeful. Know that you're not alone.

The Fifth Solution:
Choose to Heal

Underlying principle: Healing is essential for wholeness.

Many of our crises and changes have the added consequence of placing us among the walking wounded. This is often compounded by the phenomenon that new pain tends to reawaken the old. It is as if we carry a sack inside of us containing the hurts of a lifetime. When we open it up to put in a current loss, any previously unacknowledged or under-healed pain comes flying to the surface, further increasing our feelings of helplessness, despair, and emotional paralysis. The Fifth Solution helps us to counteract these feelings by giving us permission and showing us how to grieve our many losses, the old as well as the new. When we do the work of acknowledging, feeling, and expressing our pain, we begin to heal. As a result, rather than harm us, our wounds become the source of our wisdom, compassion, and inner strength. God often enters a woman's life through the fracture of a broken heart. For this reason alone, wounds that are attended to can be gifts that transform.

In the last chapter, we identified negative emotions and attitudes that have previously consumed our energy in non-fulfilling and non-productive ways. We realize that in order to transition successfully, we need to let go of these things that have habitually distracted and distanced us from the Real.

Yet as important as it is to learn how to let go, there are certain things in life that we simply cannot "get over," nor are we meant to. Primarily, this refers to the pain and heartbreak that we have experienced both in the past as well as in the present circumstances of our lives. Losses that do much more than disappoint or disillusion us -- losses that leave us devastated, shattered, broken, and bereft. In some cases, our wounds are fresh, gaping, and immediate.

But in many cases, the wounds we suffer are old ones that went underground many years ago and have been lying dormant all this while. A transitional period has a way of uprooting these previously unacknowledged or under-healed traumas. In the cases where we are already trying to cope with the pain of the present, the combined stress created by this phenomenon can be more than we can bear.

It is important to understand that, as a society, we have traditionally not been great at healing our losses. Once again, this is not our fault. Our culture, extremely outer-focused, is accustomed to placing the emphasis on how things look. We applaud the woman who holds it all together in the midst of her pain. Just look at our response to Jacqueline Kennedy following the assassination of her husband, the late President John F. Kennedy; we put her on a pedestal for not breaking down in public. The fact is, in this country, public displays of grief and despair often make us uncomfortable. We would much rather deny, minimize, "fix", or remain stoic with our pain than feel it. Assuming that others have the same approach to grief, we get stuck in the I'm-doing–fine-thank-you-very-much mentality that has become our accustomed way of responding to painful situations.

Our culture is also built around immediacy. With this as our model, rather than place value on the *process* of healing or give ourselves permission to take the necessary time and energy to grieve, we concentrate our energies on the external, material things at hand – concerns such as moving on, growing, achieving, filling the empty spaces, and proving that we are okay.

There is nothing wrong with any of these things in and of themselves. However, the problem arises when our motivation is spurred by an unconscious attempt to cover over or outrun our inner distress. When this is the case, which it very often is, our external growth and development become like a tree growing without the benefit and stability of roots. Provided the weather cooperates, the tree appears to do well. But when the winds change and the sands shift -- which they inevitably do -- the tree is totally vulnerable to being blown over at any given moment.

This same principle holds true for us as well. When we charge through our lives without fully healing our pain as we encounter it, we often choose busyness over fulfillment. Still, as busy as we keep ourselves, our unhealed pain lurks closely behind. Whether this pain is associated with a current situation or consists of unhealed grief from the past, the consequences are similar. Our decisions, choices, and behaviors, rather than rooted and grounded in wholeness and stability, are often dictated by the underlying anxiety of grief that has not been given its full due.

Healing is essential to wholeness. In other words, there is no way we can grow and evolve into all that we are meant to be without addressing our need and our right to heal any and every part of us that needs healing – and not from the outside-in as we are so wont to do, but from the inside-out.

The prospect of doing this does not have to frighten us. After all, we are not going to do it alone. The following pages will help us to understand what is to be expected, and how we can best heal -- both our older wounds that have kept us from being at home in our own skins over the years, as well as our current losses that threaten to consume us with their intensity.

Encountering the Shock

Encountering the shock is where any new experience with grief and loss begins. Some of us may be at this stage right now: paralyzed from the trauma of losing a spouse, child, parent, or sibling; full of anguish over the breakup of a major love relationship; in shock over a recent diagnosis; or devastated due to an unwanted and unexpected change of status in our family, marriage, health, or job.

No matter what circumstance has brought us into this first phase of grief, it is an extremely difficult time. Depending on the particular nature of our loss, we might feel as if we have been knocked over by a tidal wave that has rendered us powerless by its intensity and power. Our emotions can be in such a state of flux that, within a span of seconds, we vacillate between feeling depressed, angry, anxious, terrified, or agitated. We may think we're fine one minute, only to break down in hysterics or anxiety the next, or even to laugh inappropriately. Concentration can be difficult; the simplest of tasks requiring a supreme effort. We might feel disconnected from everything and everybody; as if encapsulated in a plastic bubble, separate and alone, able to see and hear, but with senses that are somewhat veiled. Colors are not as bright; food doesn't taste as good. Things that used to seem important now appear trivial and meaningless. It can feel unbelievable that the world still goes on, birds continue to sing, and people have the audacity to laugh.

There are even times, especially when the initial reality of a situation is too painful to bear, that we respond with total denial. As a first line of defense, denial renders us momentarily numb in order to give us a period of grace before the full implications of a devastating situation can be absorbed. Denial can occur immediately upon hearing shocking news and last for several days or even weeks. During this time, the truth may be so unacceptable that we feel certain we'll soon awake to find it nothing more than a horrific nightmare, the workings of an overwrought imagination, or a mistake. By protecting us from the full emotional impact of a sudden loss, denial allows us to survive the first few days or weeks following a traumatic occurrence. It helps us keep our sanity long enough to do what we have to do in the everyday world.

This initial denial can be a good thing. However, if we continue to live in our denial, it can create serious problems over time. For one thing, it prevents us from doing the necessary work of acknowledging, feeling, and expressing our wounds. And when we fail to do this work, our ability to move on from our losses as a whole, integrated person can be compromised. It can be likened to placing a band-aid over untreated physical wounds; even though the wounds are out of sight, they continue to fester beneath the surface, slowly poisoning our entire system.

This tendency to maintain denial at any cost is where we have fallen into difficulty in the past, especially regarding any emotional wounds we may have incurred during childhood or adolescence. Not knowing what to do with our pain at the time, we may have stuffed it way down deep, living our life in denial of it. As a result, our inner unhealed pain has insidiously and unconsciously impacted our choices, our behaviors, and our attitudes; usually not in a healthy way. To make matters even more difficult, every time we encounter a new loss, this unhealed pain from yesterday jumps in to push us deeper into despair.

When Sally's mother died, even though it was an expected death after a long illness, her grief was overwhelming. The pain from losing her mother threw her into memories and feelings that she had thought were long buried, thoughts of a father who had left them many years ago. Sally had been a teenager at the time, the eldest of five children and, of course, very responsible. Because her father left the family for another woman and moved across the country, Sally's mother never spoke of him again nor allowed the children to. Unfortunately, her father had died before she ever had a chance to reconnect with him. Her grief over this loss had never been acknowledged, felt, or expressed. Instead, she had spent a lifetime of busyness, trying to outrun this inner void. The death of her mother threw her right back into these old feelings, making her present grief that much more difficult to handle.

Even when we've grieved our past losses, any new pain has the potential to put us intimately in touch with the old. When Janet's husband died, she acutely felt her previous losses of an unborn baby, a younger brother, and her dearly beloved grandmother. This is what pain does; it taps into the sack labeled "grief" that we all carry within. Dealing with these painful memories is difficult enough when we have done our previous healing work; it can be paralyzing if we have not.

Therefore, whenever we encounter the shock of new loss, we must be willing to enter into the grieving process. If, during this time, old feelings of loss also begin to surface or resurface, we must expose these inner pains to the light and air as well. This is the only way we can begin to heal them. Grieving is not easy, and there are no shortcuts to this process. In fact, there is only one way to grieve any and all of our wounds: not by going around, over, or under our inner pain, but by making a decision to march straight through the heart of it.

The Wounds of Today

After getting through the initial daze and haze of the "shock," and provided we don't get stuck in our denial, we next move into the period characterized as "longing." This is the time when we live in the pain of the open wound. It generally begins two to four weeks following a major loss or death, and under normal conditions should start to subside after several months or a year.

During this time, it is normal to become preoccupied with our longing for life to return to the way it used to be. We continue to ride the emotional roller-coaster of highs and lows, and we needn't ever go looking for our grief because it will always find us, often in the strangest ways, at the most inopportune times. We may have a moment of feeling better, only to walk around a corner and run into a concrete wall of sadness and despair. Certain sights, sounds, or smells can instantly provoke a "grief attack." The changing of seasons, special events, anniversary days, or even a full moon can intensify the anguish of a loss, especially during the first year. There may be times when our emotions will feel so out of control that it frightens us. We may even suspect that we have gone a little crazy.

It is not easy to live in the open wound of grief. This was where Jane found herself two months after losing her husband to pancreatic cancer. He had died in the prime of his life, having taken an early retirement only the year before. Not only was she grieving the loss of her partner and lover, but also the loss of their future dreams for companionship, travel, and of being grandparents together.

Financially, it became necessary for Jane to sell their vacation home in the mountains. While preparing it to be listed with the realtor, she went to the local hardware store to buy a replacement piece of wood-stove piping. As she prepared to leave the store, the owner who had known Jane and her husband for years and who had not yet heard the news, unknowingly asked, "How's hubby doing?"

Caught completely off-guard, Jane blurted out the painful truth that Charlie had died. She then burst into uncontrollable sobbing and fled from the store. Later she was to hear through the grapevine that she "wasn't doing very well."

Jane's outburst in the store was certainly an appropriate response to her immense loss. Yet it made her feel totally out of control. To compound matters, when she heard that she wasn't doing very well, she began to believe it also. So she worked even harder to keep her feelings stuffed deep inside of her, as far out of sight as she could manage. She did this by becoming very busy in her life, jumping immediately into pursing her master's degree. For two years, she worked as hard as she could both in and out of school. To all appearances, she was doing "just fine, thank you." But following graduation, she nearly had a breakdown as she fell headfirst into the black pit of despair she had desperately been trying to outrun. The simple fact is, we cannot grow and evolve in the external world without healing our inner wounds. Not with any degree of long-term success, that is.

Still, it is understandable that we continue to try. When we feel untowardly vulnerable due to our extreme emotional state and don't know what to do about it, it is only natural that our first response would be to repress our feelings as much as humanly possible. In many cases, our family and friends may feel awkward around our pain as well, so we pretend we're okay for their sake, even when we're not. This gets reinforced by people commenting proudly on how brave and strong we're being. The more this happens, and the less external permission and validation we are given for our need to grieve, we more we come to devalue it as well. As time goes by, we mistakenly think that it shouldn't be taking this long, when of course it should, because it does.

During any first year of recovering from a major loss, there are several normal and predictable responses we might fall into. Insomnia is one of them. Night after night, we may lie awake, restless and agitated, not knowing where to go or what to do with our tumultuous feelings and thoughts. If we are surviving the death of a person or of a cherished relationship, we may spend these nocturnal hours doing two things: reliving the joy of the relationship or rehashing the pain of the final separation or goodbye. In the instances where our distress is a direct result of somebody else's decision, we may lie awake struggling to figure things out, to make sense out of the senseless. In the cases where our loved ones were lost to painful deaths, we may be consumed by memories of their suffering, long after they have been set free.

When we are grieving, food often loses its appeal, and our appetite wanes. This normally passes with time. However, if it doesn't, it can eventually lead to the serious condition of anorexia. Excessive weight loss is an insidious and destructive means by which some women attempt to exert control over a life that feels out of control. We are especially vulnerable to falling into a pattern of continuously losing weight when our losses are the result of a perceived rejection, or that tap into our inner feelings of being "less-than." We somehow think being thin is the magical answer. Our next chapter goes into greater detail about anorexia and similar conditions.

During this period of longing, we are also subject to falling into the "should haves, would haves, could haves." Rather than remember what we have done right, we beat ourselves up for what we didn't do perfectly. This also happened to Jane. For over two months, she was at the hospital night and day with her husband. Just getting there involved a long stressful drive on a major interstate highway. One day, shortly after she arrived, Jane's husband expressed a craving for a particular flavor of ice cream that the hospital didn't have. It was cold and rainy out. Friendly's Ice Cream Parlor was five heavily-trafficked miles down the road. She just couldn't do it.

"Although it's a small matter, I've often thought of that missed ice cream," she confessed. "In fact, probably much more often than I've remembered all the things I was able to do for him."

This is so typical of women. Rather than reinforce ourselves for everything we might have done right, we dwell on what we didn't do or what we think we did wrong; what we said and how we said it; when we weren't there; what we wish we had done; or what we wish we hadn't said or done. We compound our grief by feeling guilty.

Getting beyond this guilt can be a challenge. If we are struggling with this, we might want to go back to the previous chapter and use some of the suggestions for letting go of guilt. At the same time, we might remind ourselves that we are not perfect, nor were we ever meant to be. As human beings, we make mistakes. To dwell on them is counterproductive; to learn from them is the goal. Most of us do the best we can under any given circumstances.

Anger is another predictable and normal response that women feel when living in the longing stage of grief. The anger associated with loss usually flares up quickly, seemingly from out of nowhere. Because women seldom know what to do with anger, our first inclination might be to direct it towards the people we feel are responsible for, or who contributed to, our pain. This might be a husband for leaving, a hospital that left our loved one unattended, the doctor who failed to make a correct diagnosis, the nurse who didn't bring the pain medication on time, or even the loved one who died! We mistakenly think that getting angry will bring us relief. While certainly distracting, it is merely another band-aid.

Sometimes we direct our anger inappropriately onto innocent parties. Jennie's husband left and she took it out on the kids. Gretchen's father died, and she became a rageaholic in her office. After Martha lost her seven year old son to a rare kidney disease, she flew into uncontrollable rages at the women who worked for her, women who still had their children. Following the death of her long-time companion, Maria became a wild woman on the highways. Depending on the degree of our anger, there are times when we can be downright dangerous.

We also misdirect our anger by taking it out on ourselves. This self-destructive anger is evidenced every time we refuse to get enough rest, don't eat nutritiously or regularly, isolate ourselves, refuse to let go of our guilt, overuse or misuse drugs or alcohol, or fail to treat ourselves the way we deserve to be treated: with compassion, love, and respect.

As difficult as our anger and guilt can be, the next phase within our process of grieving is even more so. This is the stage of depression and, according to Dr. Elizabeth Kubler-Ross, it is the last stop before eventual acceptance. Kubler-Ross was a pioneer in the field of death and dying who, back in the early 1960's, delineated five stages of grieving: denial, anger, bargaining, depression, and acceptance. Although originally intended for those surviving the death of a loved one, these stages are also relevant to other losses, including the loss of a relationship, or a healthy body, or a beloved pet.

When we enter the depression stage, it is impossible to mistake it for anything else. Depression is unrelenting. It awakens with us in the morning and keeps us company all day long. It makes us dread getting up or dread going back to bed. Depression feels like forever and always. When caught in its paralyzing grip, it is difficult to remember that we have ever been anywhere else, and impossible to imagine that we ever will.

In some instances, our depression itself can take a nosedive, culminating in despair. Despair is a state of abject helplessness and hopelessness, a period of feeling totally disconnected from everyone. Rather than have faith in anything, we feel isolated and abandoned, swallowed up in a black, bottomless pit that completely separates and alienates us from family, friends, and even our God. Despair is as Dante so accurately wrote during the early 14th century, "I did not die, but nothing of life remains."

It is during times like this when it helps to have friends or loved ones who remember better days, those who can help us live in the memory of once believing in something. If we are despairing and lacking hope, we need friends who can gently and lovingly assure us that this, too, shall pass. However, if it doesn't pass, and our despair persists longer than a couple of weeks, this is an indicator that we need professional help to assist us through this final stage of our deep grief. Other symptoms that we might need additional help include:

- having suicidal thoughts
- becoming over-dependent on alcohol or prescription drugs
- the continued inability to sleep, or to get out of bed

- sustained anorexia
- a tendency to chronically isolate ourselves

None of these are normal responses to grief. If we do not have a therapist, bereavement counselor, group, or clergy person to help us, then this is the time to find one. It takes a strong woman to acknowledge her need for help.

Grieving our losses is not easy work, but it is necessary if we want to live lives that are usefully whole instead of fractured, frantic, and/or depressive. That said, the following pages are intended to give us specific directions for working through our grief. By showing us ways to acknowledge, feel, and express our pain, they will help us *gentle* ourselves through this period of longing so that we can eventually enter into the serenity of acceptance and reconciliation.

Acknowledge, Feel, and Express

Give Voice to Feelings

It is not true that time heals all wounds. Time only heals wounds that are acknowledged, felt, and expressed. When it comes to grieving our losses, isolation is our deadliest enemy. It not only keeps others out, but it locks us in. We were not meant to suffer our losses alone. We need and deserve to have support during the dark and difficult hours, and it is up to us to get it.

As tough as it may be, we must resist our impulse to curl up in a physical or psychological ball and, instead, find a safe place to express our feelings; a place where we feel loved, affirmed, and validated.

If coping with the loss of a loved one, we need to be able to talk about them, and about how it now feels to be without them. If grieving the loss of a relationship or a health issue, we need to be encouraged to speak of that as well. If we want to break down and sob, we must feel free to let our tears flow without fear of negative comments, or impatience, or of having our pain minimized. The more opportunities we can find for sharing our feelings, the less potential our grief has for keeping us in bondage.

There is a tragic story told of a woman who lost both her young children in an automobile accident. When asked how she ever survived this excruciatingly painful period of her life, she shared that it was the support of a truly special friend that gave her the strength to get through each day. Every morning her friend would come over and sit beside her bed, quietly inviting her to, "Tell me about the children."

The only feelings that can harm us are those that we keep bottled up inside of us. Therefore, one of the most important aspects of our grieving is to find healthy and appropriate ways to express these feelings. We, too, need to find those who will invite us to, "Tell me about your husband, your brother, your child, your soul-mate. Tell me about your marriage, your operation, your feelings of betrayal."

This is not always an easy thing to do. Not everybody is willing or even able to listen to our pain. In some cases, our family members may be going through the same loss as we are and so are virtually unable to support us. Our friends may be so busy with the demands of everyday life that they are already over-extended. If they have never experienced similar pain or loss, they may lack compassion and patience in their response to ours. They may say inappropriate things, trivialize our loss, or avoid us completely because they don't know what to do or say. Some people are afraid to get too close for fear the same situation could happen to them.

It pays to be discriminating when looking for support. If we have a partner or best friend who is willing and able to be there for us during our time of need, that is ideal. Many women do. But we may want to go one step further by asking specific friends to be part of our support team, friends who are capable of coping with our huge emotional mood swings, or our need to rehash and revisit the incident; those who will give us permission to call them during the toughest times, whether on a Sunday afternoon or in the middle of the night.

This also might be the time to engage in short-term therapy, to find a life coach who specializes in loss and transitions, or to join a bereavement group. As mentioned in the chapter on Balance, there are groups specific to practically any kind of loss we might be encountering. Often, these groups are listed in our community newspapers or church bulletins. In the beginning, it might be helpful to invite a friend to go along with us.

Sometimes, we don't express our feelings because we're afraid that they will consume us if we do. This can be especially true when dealing with life-threatening diseases (ours or somebody else's). We fear that by talking about our feelings, we could make a bad situation even worse; that by actually expressing our deepest fears out loud, we could increase the possibility of them coming true. Nothing could be further from the truth. It is the *repression* of feelings, not the *expression* of them, that drains our energy, compromises our immune system, and puts us in jeopardy for long-term problems. Besides that, the repression of feelings is not a selective process. In other words, if we close our heart, our heart is closed; it cannot differentiate to what it is closed. While we may temporarily shut out the pain and fear, at the same time, we close the door to pleasure or joy. This is one of the side effects of certain medications that doctors are quick to prescribe to "fix" us; they may numb the pain, but they also numb our potential for feeling hope and joy. Even if we need them for awhile, we must be conscious of the fact that they are only intended for short-term use.

There are no shortcuts for getting through the longing period of our grieving process. It takes what it takes, and it takes as long as it takes. We cannot continue going over, under, around, or in-between our feelings. We need to go straight through them, and the only way we can do this is by *hearing ourselves feel.* We may not even know what our feelings are until we open our mouths and let them out. So we talk, and we talk, and we talk some more. We talk even when we're sick and tired of hearing ourselves talk. We give voice to our emotions because we know that this is how we heal – by acknowledging, feeling, and expressing. The more we can do this, the more we will understand that feelings are not right or wrong, good or bad. They are just feelings. When we stop running from them and face them head on, we will discover that they will not paralyze or kill us; we are stronger than we think.

Heal Through Creativity

Remembering that healing requires us to acknowledge, feel, and express our feelings, creative enterprises can also facilitate this process. And we don't have to consider ourselves creative on any level in order to get comfort and relief in some of the following ways.

Writing is a wonderful means of expression that is cathartic as well as potentially creative. Even those of us not familiar with this means of self-expression can buy a notebook and begin. Because we are dealing with the *process* of writing, rather than any finished product, it is not necessary to censure what we write or find fault with our incorrect use of grammar or misspellings. This particular form of writing is only meant to provide *movement* for our fears, loneliness, despair, or sorrow, so that these same emotions don't get stuck inside of us where they can cause great harm.

The way we do this stream-of-consciousness writing is simple. As our feelings come up, we move them out of ourselves by writing them down in a journal of some sort; we just scribble out our feelings in no particular form or order. For some strange reason, when feelings make their way from our head through our heart into our hand and onto the page, something magical happens in the process. To begin with, we get immediate relief by having a hands-on project. At the same time, we get our feelings out in the open rather than keep them bottled up inside of us. The act of writing has provided solace to many a broken heart throughout the centuries. In fact, some of mankind's greatest poetry originated from an inner wound.

There are several other ways that we can physically and creatively promote the healing cycle of "acknowledge, feel, and express." We can attempt to paint, draw, make jewelry, sculpt, or sew. When art is used for the primary purpose of expressing one's innermost feelings, the doing becomes far more important than the actual finished product. After all, we are not trying to create a masterpiece; rather, we are seeking comfort and relief by feeling the clay in our hands, watching the paint as it reacts on the canvas, or experiencing the limitless boundaries of an artist's sketch pad. Several art forms have the additional benefit of providing solace through repetition, such as knitting, weaving, or quilt-making.

Making music, acting, or dancing are additional forms of creative self-expression that can facilitate healing. Drumming, playing the piano, strumming a guitar, even belly dancing can be a means of providing movement for our inner feelings. Any creative enterprise that promotes the cycle of "acknowledge, feel, and express," will not only help us heal, but also may open a new door that would have otherwise remained shut.

Heal through Self-care

Throughout any healing process, it is vital to take care of ourselves. In fact, if we continue to struggle with self-care, we might want to go back and review some of the suggestions outlined in our chapter on Balance. As difficult as it might be to nurture ourselves at a time when we are running on empty, we need to make the effort. It might help to think of ourselves as if we were recovering from a physical assault. This means more than simply resting when tired, drinking plenty of water, and eating well; it also requires that we lower our expectations of what we should be able to accomplish right now.

Exercise can also promote our ability to heal. If we can find a walking buddy with a good listening ear, the benefits will be two-fold. We can walk and talk, and talk and walk, instead of being alone with our pain. Maybe we can make plans to meet a compassionate friend at the local gym or at a yoga class. However we do it, exercise, fresh air, and sunshine are excellent antidotes for any inner hurts we may be experiencing.

At the same time, we must take the action to stay connected with others during this phase of adjusting to our losses. This may require us to move into unfamiliar territory that is not particularly comfortable. Rather than wait for the phone to ring, we might have to force ourselves to pick up that one hundred pound telephone and make the first call. People are generally very willing to be of service when asked, so ask we must. We must especially enlist help for those peak times of grief or longing that cause us the most difficulty. As hard as it can be to put ourselves out there by asking somebody to help us or spend time with us, it is usually a great deal easier than suffering through these lowest periods by ourselves. If we give ourselves the gift of joining a support group, we need to also give ourselves the gift of showing up for the meetings in any and all conditions.

During this entire healing process, it is of vital importance to stay honest about how we feel, not only when speaking with others, but when talking to ourselves. If we're having a bad day, so be it. We don't need to pretend that things are okay when they're not, and we don't need to apologize for not feeling one hundred percent, either. A bad day is not a moral issue; it is just a bad day. The more we can support ourselves during these times, the greater chance we have of moving into an acceptance of life as it presently is. After all, we can't expect others to do for us what we are unwilling to do for ourselves. Now is definitely the time for us to suit up and show up on our own behalf.

Healing Old Wounds

Many of us have been among the walking wounded for longer than we might care to remember. Perhaps we are carrying around wounds that originated a long time ago, in childhood or adolescence. Maybe something happened during our young adulthood for which we had few or no coping or healing skills. Regardless of the particular nature of our earlier wounds, the important question to ask is this: "What have we done with our pain?"

In most cases, we probably did whatever was necessary in order to survive. After all, life didn't come with a handbook of directions on how to cope. Chances are, when faced with trauma, tragedy, or loss, we did what we had to do. This might have included blocking out memories, minimizing the negative impact of certain situations, living in denial long after it outlived its usefulness, or looking for relief in all the wrong places. Unhealed grief is often the birthplace of behaviors, attitudes, and choices that are not the healthiest, nor the most appropriate. The next chapter goes into more detail about the individual nature of these self-limiting and, in some cases, self-destructive responses.

For now, let us just say that as women we have been living with the symptoms of unresolved grief for so long that we think they are normal. Fear, insecurity, lowered self-esteem, and self-defeating thought patterns are but a few of these symptoms. Tell-tale signs of unhealed inner pain manifest themselves in ways that confuse us. We can become teary over the strangest things. We feel anxious or lethargic without knowing exactly why. We are diagnosed with disorders of the immune system, such as chronic fatigue syndrome and fibromyalgia. Most doctors would agree that heart disease, cancer, and depression are all compounded by unhealed grief.

Much as we try to put it behind us, unacknowledged and unhealed grief gets dragged along with us into any new situation. No wonder we feel tired a great deal of the time! If we're presently trying to cope with a new source of heartbreak, any unresolved grief from the past becomes more than just a heavy and unwanted burden. It dictates how well we cope, the decisions we make, and how we feel. This was certainly true in Anne's life.

The daughter of an alcoholic woman, her early childhood was spent being shuffled between relatives. When she was nine, her father divorced her mother to marry another woman, one who was secretly addicted to tranquilizers. Anne's stepmother was ill-equipped to cope with her newly-acquired family of five children, ages five through fifteen. Over time, she became verbally and emotionally abusive, directing most of her anger towards Anne, the middle child, and by far the beauty.

Anne's two older siblings were teenagers. Seldom home, they escaped the bulk of their stepmother's wrath. This left Anne not only to fend for herself, but also to protect her two younger sisters for whom she felt hugely responsible. In many ways, she had been their surrogate mother from the time they were born.

An academic achiever, Anne went through college easily, spending her summers teaching at a camp in Maine, and enjoying a long-term relationship with a man named Mark. A couple of years after her graduation, Anne experienced a series of crises that occurred, as they are sometimes apt to do, all at once. To begin with, after failing repeated efforts to get sober in Alcoholics Anonymous, her birth mother eventually drank herself to death. She was found days after the fact, alone in her Brooklyn apartment. Though Anne's contact with her mother had been minimal, she had long lived with the secret dream that her mother would get well, and that they would be reunited. To make matters worse, Anne knew nothing about the disease of alcoholism and was filled with shame over the circumstances surrounding her mother's death.

Following the loss of her mother, Anne broke up with Mark and began dating someone else. One month later, Mark was killed in an automobile accident when his car was hit by a drunk driver. Not knowing what to do or even how to feel, Anne attempted to take a geographical cure from her pain, and moved to Sweden with her new boyfriend. This move to a foreign country added a huge stress on top of two major losses.

It was in Sweden that she hit her first emotional bottom. Devastated, full of grief and guilt (a common response for someone who feels responsible for everything), Anne entered one of the blackest periods of her life. She didn't know anyone, couldn't speak the language, wasn't getting along with this new boyfriend of hers, and was carrying a whole lot of unhealed, inner pain. She didn't stay long.

Coming back to the United States, she moved to Nantucket Island where one of her younger sisters now lived. It was here that Anne finally got into therapy and began the long, hard work of grieving her many losses, both past and present. She was eventually able to return to college where she obtained a Master's Degree in Social Work and became a therapist in Boston. It is said that we teach what we need the most to learn. Although Anne had made a beginning on healing her inner pain, her new career enabled her to continue doing what she had been doing her entire life -- taking care of the needs of others at the expense of her own.

In 1990, Anne moved in with another man. At the same time, her younger sister Claire was diagnosed with breast cancer. For the next three years, Anne traveled back and forth from Boston to her sister's home in Connecticut. When it became obvious that Claire wasn't going to win her long battle, Anne took a leave of absence to care for her. Claire's death devastated Anne. She felt as if she had lost a child as well as a sibling. She also felt guilty and responsible, even though she had done everything she possibly could.

Jumping quickly back into an extremely busy life, Anne returned to work and, at the same time, became engaged to be married. Internal changes within her agency had resulted in an insurmountable workload; once again, Anne's time and energy were spent meeting the expectations of everyone else while she was slowly dying inside. It wasn't long before life presented her with another cluster of crises and changes. Within a two month period, she discovered her fiancé's unfaithfulness, moved out of the house she had expected to live in as a married woman, and was diagnosed with breast cancer herself. She was forty-five years old. The chemotherapy threw her immediately into menopause and triggered a manic-depressive illness that had been lying dormant for years. Anne's life became pretty much of a nightmare before it began to get better.

Any one of these losses would have been traumatic enough by themselves. However, the fact that they occurred together in such a short span of time was not only overwhelming, but also made infinitely worse by the tremendous amount of unacknowledged and under-healed grief that Ann was already carrying. The combination of past and present losses threw Anne into the darkest despair imaginable. Helpless and hopeless, she was absolutely paralyzed with shock and grief.

Sometimes it takes our darkest hours for miracles to happen. As mentioned earlier, God often enters a woman's life through the fracture of a broken heart. This was true in Anne's case. While in the midst of the Dark Night of the Soul, an organic shift began to take place within her. Her deep despair was so intense that without even knowing it, she finally gave herself permission to heal; not only her immediate losses, but those of a lifetime. Anne's healing didn't happen overnight, but slowly and steadily, empowered by the gift of desperation, she was able to use her deepest depression as a springboard into new life.

Fortunately, as a therapist herself, Anne knew the importance of expressing one's feelings. Though she had been in therapy before, this time she made a commitment to stay with it. She knew she needed to find ways to acknowledge, feel, and express her feelings if she wanted to survive. She also knew the importance of having a support system, and so she actively began to construct one. The Episcopal Church, which was the church of her youth, became a great source of spiritual strength for her. The priest encouraged her to join the choir; although it was difficult in the beginning because of her depression, singing became another means by which Anne regained her voice. Eventually, she even took out the fiddle she had played as a child and joined a small ensemble. Music became literally instrumental in Anne's return to mental and emotional health.

On the advice of her therapist, Anne also joined the fellowship of Al-Anon, a group for family members of alcoholics. Although her mother had been dead for several years, Anne still strongly felt the rejection, abandonment, and guilt she had internalized as a little girl. It was in the halls of Al-Anon that she finally learned the nature of her mother's disease, and she was able to forgive her. This forgiveness was an enormous step in Anne's healing process.

Writing, drawing, sharing, and making music worked together to heal Anne on a spiritual and emotional level. Over time, this healing reached the deepest crevices of her inner wounds. And when this happened, her physical body became healed, as well. Anne has never looked or felt better. She is living proof that out of the darkness comes new life, and that every goodbye has an eventual hello when we trust the process enough to fully grieve our losses and heal our pain.

Using Forgiveness, Ritual, and Faith to Heal

Just as Anne needed to forgive her mother in order to heal, there are times when our healing depends on our ability to forgive somebody or something. This might present a dilemma for many of us. How do we forgive what is unforgivable? How do we forgive the husband who left us financially and emotionally bankrupt or the soul-mate who was unfaithful? How do we forgive the parent who robbed us of our childhood or the alcoholic spouse? How do we forgive somebody whose actions not only wounded us, but left us devastated?

There are no easy answers for this. The previous chapter on Letting Go gave us some suggestions for forgiving. It might also help to remind ourselves that non-forgiveness harms only one person: ourselves. So we forgive, not for their sake, but for our own. And regardless of how impossible this may seem, it is not. In truth, forgiveness is not just a spiritual principle; it is a practical choice.

When Maureen was a little girl, her mother unknowingly married a pedophile who abused Maureen for years. Long after the events, Maureen was filled with rage at her mother for not protecting her. This internalized anger compromised all of Maureen's relationships – both men and women alike. She had hardened her heart in defense. No one was allowed access to her heart, nor was she able to fully give her love away.

Years and much therapy later, Maureen realized that the only way she would ever heal this childhood trauma was by forgiving her mother. Although she had attempted to do so repeatedly, it was never met with long-term success. She would try to forgive, only to take the anger back again and again. Because she knew she was only harming herself by harboring this toxic emotion, she began praying for a solution. Her prayers were answered one day when she was struck with an inspiration. Cutting out two pictures -- one of her mother as a young girl, the second of herself as a baby – she then pasted the infant picture of herself into the arms of her beautiful mother. Carefully and lovingly, she matted and framed the picture, and hung it in a prominent spot in her living room. By the time she had finished, she had taken a huge giant step toward forgiveness. To this day, each time she looks at the picture of mother and child, her forgiving heart softens and opens wider still.

Ritual is another way of promoting our healing process. There are several ceremonial acts that can further facilitate inner acceptance. If grieving the death of a loved one, we could create a special altar and place their picture or other important memorabilia on it, like a special letter, card, or piece of jewelry. We can wear something they have given us or that belonged to them. After Susan's husband died, she had a cross put on the inside of her wedding band and wears it on a chain around her neck. Betty sleeps in her late husband's pajamas even though they are all worn out. When Edie's son was killed in a motorcycle accident, she planted a weeping willow tree in her yard. Marie started a scholarship for her granddaughter who died of meningitis at the age of sixteen. Polly wrote a book of poetry dedicated to her late husband. Marsha named her boat after her father. June has a memorial Mass each year for both of her parents.

The use of ritual can also lessen the impact of our "living" wounds. When Helen took a job on the West coast that she just couldn't turn down, she knew it would mean leaving her soul-mate behind. His children lived on the East Coast, and it was a priority for him to be part of their daily lives. Although the thought of a separation was intensely sad for them both, they both understood and accepted the circumstances.

On the night before she left, they celebrated how full and wonderful their relationship had been. Surrounding themselves with balloons, champagne, and ice cream, they talked and laughed and ate and loved and cried. Before parting, they tied two balloons together before setting them free. As they watched the united balloons float gracefully away, they knew in their hearts that they would always be connected. This last night ritual was their way of honoring what they had shared, and affirming that their relationship was a valuable and life-enhancing experience that would remain within them both forever.

Ritualizing our losses is a way of keeping our love alive even in the midst of our suffering. In the movie *Shadowlands*, a story about C.S. Lewis and his wife who was dying from cancer, there is a very touching scene where they are standing together in a barn, knowing that her time is limited, yet extremely happy in the moment. Looking deeply into his eyes, she tells him to remember the joy he is feeling today, because it will be contained in the sorrow he will experience tomorrow.

The same is true for us: there is joy contained somewhere within all of our grief and sorrow. As Kahlil Gibran so poignantly wrote, "Your joy is your sorrow unmasked. And the selfsame well from which your laughter rises was oftentimes filled with your tears." We cannot experience one without having experienced the other.

While forgiveness and ritual are both fundamental to our healing process, the source of most of our relief and comfort will be through our connection with the God of our understanding. Yet even though spiritual connection is our greatest resource, it was never intended as a short-cut through the grieving process. Even when we feel certain that our loved ones are at peace, or that things happen for a reason, we still have to live through the longing and the deep anguish over our loss. Faith is not, and was never meant to be, the absence of feelings. On the contrary, it is what supports us during our healing process, sustains us in our period of mourning, and gives us hope for a better tomorrow.

Sometimes, however, our losses are so horrific that they deeply challenge our relationship with God. Even the most faith-filled among us can become a doubter in the face of abysmal tragedy. We may feel that God doesn't exist, doesn't care, or has abandoned us completely. After all, how could a loving God allow such a loss to occur?

For this and all the other accusations we tend to hurtle at God when in anguish, there is only one answer:

God cries with us.

Although many religious and spiritual texts have been written about surviving loss, these four words sum it up greater than any number of others:

God cries with us.

When we believe this, we can trust that our God is compassionate, loving, and kind; that our Higher Power isn't responsible for the adversities we face in this life, but gives us the strength, courage, and resources to deal with them.

God cries with us.

By accepting this as truth, we can allow our losses to become God's opportunity. Then and only then, will nothing be suffered in vain.

Moving Into Acceptance

Once we've embarked upon our healing work, it usually takes a year or two, no longer than three years, to make the transition from living in the longing to accepting the things we cannot change. This acceptance will be gradual, coming in subtle yet consistent waves. At this time, our episodes of feeling blue will have decreased. We will be able to recall the wonderful parts of our past without feeling overwhelmed with sadness and grief. Our daily activities will have resumed, and even though our lives have changed, we will find new meaning and hope in them.

Acceptance makes all things possible. This is not only true regarding our monumental losses, but also those losses that aren't as apparent but still affect us deeply. For some, the loss of a pet creates the same amount of pain as losing a beloved relative. For others, losing the ability to see, hear, move, or remember, makes it impossible to do the things we once valued and enjoyed. Following surgery to remove a benign lung tumor, Denise could no longer ride her bike or climb a mountain. Connie's stroke made it impossible for her to continue knitting, one of her favorite activities. Shelley, in menopause, mourned deeply the loss of her child-bearing years.

Comparatively speaking, these losses may not appear major. Yet they are significant to us, and we need to honor and value that fact. We may not get much outside sympathy and validation for these so-called smaller and more personal losses, but that doesn't mean we shouldn't "gentle ourselves" through them the best we can. Acceptance only comes from doing the work of healing: the work of acknowledging, feeling, and expressing our emotions.

Our positive changes also carry the potential for sadness. We move to a better house, but have to leave the old neighborhood; we get a promotion that requires us to say goodbye to long-time colleagues; we happily walk down the aisle, yet give up various aspects of our single life; we have a baby, and our lives are never the same again! As wonderful as some of these changes can be, they each result in the loss of something we once enjoyed. When we can recognize this and give ourselves permission to grieve the losses within our positive choices, chances are we won't be so prone to think we've made a mistake.

Regardless of the nature of our wounds, *healing is essential for wholeness.* By healing our past wounds, we will no longer be compromised by carrying the weight of them. We will feel infinitely lighter in spirit and less likely to fall into the unexplained and sudden "blues." Rather than be habitually susceptible to lethargy, anxiety, depression, or physical illness, our energy and vitality will improve, and we will feel more fully alive.

When we heal, we no longer need to live with our grief nipping at our heels, one step behind. Consequently, we won't be compelled to fill every waking moment with fear-based distractions. Instead, we will slow down, enjoy life more, and make decisions and choices that originate from a feeling of assurance, not anxiety. Healing also makes it easier for us to cope with new challenges and losses as they occur.

Healing is essential for wholeness. There is tremendous value contained in our suffering when we're able to honor our wounds, heal them, and integrate them within us. For the same things that render us helpless and vulnerable today, become the core of our strength, integrity, and vitality tomorrow. Healing brings us into the consciousness that we are not alone, but share in a collective grief to which everyone who has had the privilege to love is vulnerable. Healing promotes genuine empathy for others who suffer similar losses. Rather than fear their pain, the fact that we have "been there and experienced that" gives us compassion and an ability to be of service which could be found nowhere else.

Healing is essential for wholeness. When we fully heal from the inside-out, we no longer feel fragmented and fearful, but know ourselves as women who are marvelously and usefully whole. We experience how our pain can be used as the doorway into authentic and transforming spirituality. A heart broken wide open is far more available and receptive to the healing wisdom and strength of God than it might be otherwise. Every grief has this potential – to open us up, to soften us, to deepen our compassion for others, and to bring us into closer relationship with the God of our understanding.

Suggestions for Healing

1. If you are presently in some kind of pain, take out your journal and write about your feelings to the best of your ability. Go one step further and share what you've written with somebody you trust.

2. Has a recent loss opened up an old wound? Look into your past and examine any old unhealed pain. Use the suggestions in this chapter to help you do this. Get professional help if possible.

3. Develop a support system for your healing process. Get prior permission to call on various people during the more painful or difficult hours or days. This will make it easier for you to do so when the need arises.

4. Consider joining an ongoing support group specific to your loss. Look in the local paper, or call the nearest hospital to see where and when they meet. Ask a good friend to accompany you to the first few meetings.

5. Are you experiencing any of the symptoms listed on pages 126-127? If so, please share this with a trusted friend, religious professional, or therapist. If unsure of where to find help, call the Social Services at your local hospital.

6. If you are currently healing from a loss, try to ritualize your loss by creating a special altar or album, planning a celebration, lighting a candle, taking part in a spiritual ceremony, planting a tree, or making a quilt.

7. Nurture yourself during this time of loss. Eat regularly, rest when tired, get exercise, and surround yourself with nurturing friends. Remind yourself that you only have to go through this pain one day at a time.

Meditation on Healing/Integration (As adapted from a Joan Borysenko workshop)

Begin by settling comfortably into your body. Become aware of your breath, the way it feels when you breathe in, how relaxed you feel when breathing out. Let go and open yourself up to this breath. Become fully relaxed.

Now picture a white light coming down through your body, relaxing every muscle and nerve. Begin by bringing this white light down through the top of your head and feeling it relax your facial muscles. As you continue to breathe, let that light begin to move through you, washing away all your fear and filling you with peace. Bring this light down throughout your entire body, down your neck, your back, your arms, your torso, and right down through your legs and feet. Continue breathing in this light until you feel your entire body encased in its safety and warmth. Let that light fill you with its radiance. As it does, allow it to create a large circle of light around you. You are safe here; safe and warm and loved.

Within this circle of light, look down at your feet and see a cradle with a baby in it. This baby is you. Picture yourself as you might have looked when born -- small, innocent, and pure. A spiritual being come to live a human existence. Pick this baby up and look deeply into her eyes, the eyes of a precious being who has no agenda other than to give love and receive love. Hold this baby in your arms and tell her that she is loved and she is okay, just as she is.

As you place the baby back in the cradle, look out and see a little girl approaching the circle of warmth and safety. She is skipping and running, radiant with curiosity and joy, eager to enter the light. As you look deeply into the eyes of this little girl, realize that this is you when you were three. What was happening in your life at this time? The arrival of new siblings? A death, move, or separation? Continue to look into the eyes of this little girl. If she is wounded in any way, ask her to share that with you. Tell her she is safe now and beautiful just as she is.

As you look up again, see yourself as a child of seven approaching the sacred circle of light. Seven years old -- a magical time. On the threshold between the world of make believe and the world of reality. Look deeply into the eyes of your seven-year-old girl. What was happening at this time in your life? Were you receiving the affirmation, affection and approval that every little girl needs and deserves to have? Or were things in your life unpredictable and uncertain? Take a few minutes to let your seven-year-old share the nature of her wounds. Now hold her in your arms and tell her she is safe and beautiful just as she is.

As you look out again, see another little girl approaching the circle of light. This is you at the age of thirteen. Thirteen – about to leave childhood behind and enter the ways of women. Adolescence. The beginnings of sexual curiosity and exploration. Who were your role models during this time? Did anyone explain the mysteries of being a woman? Who talked to you when you felt confused? Did anything happen that wounded or hurt you? Take a few moments to let your thirteen-year-old share with you. Now take her into your arms and tell her she is safe and beautiful just as she is.

Now into the circle of safety and light, invite yourself as you were at the age of twenty-one. What was happening in your life at this time? Look deeply into the eyes of this girl/woman and acknowledge any wounded or broken parts of her. Reinforce to her that she is safe now, and that she is beautiful just as she is.

This time when you look up, imagine that you see the Angel of God approaching. Look into the Angel's luminous face as she looks calmly and lovingly into yours. Watch her as she, one by one, slowly looks into the eyes of the many parts of yourself – you at twenty-one, thirteen, seven, three, and then you as a baby. As the angel looks at you, feel all of these parts of yourself merging together into the light, bringing you into harmony. As you embrace the whole of yourself, feel your inner wounds and brokenness begin to be healed. Say to yourself,

May I be at peace.
May my heart be opened.
May I know the beauty of my own true nature.
May I be healed.

After staying with this feeling for a couple of minutes, visualize any women in your life who are in need of healing. Bring them into the circle of safety and light. Wish for them.

May you be at peace.
May your heart be opened.
May you know the beauty of your own true nature.
May you be healed.

Now take a moment to visualize our fragile planet earth, a living being of fire and ice, plants and animals and human beings. And in your heart pray,

May there be peace on earth.
May the hearts of all beings be open to one another.
May all lives be whole.

In a moment of silence, express to the light – to God's healing light – whatever is in your heart.

The Sixth Solution: *Stop. Look. Listen. Learn.*

Underlying principle: We all have an inner voice that knows the Truth.

Lacking directions for living, many of us have consequently learned to respond to life situations in ways that have not worked well over time. We have developed roles we insist on maintaining even when they no longer suit us, self-limiting behaviors that damage self-esteem and destroy possibilities, and self-destructive addictions that insidiously take over our lives without our permission or knowledge. Although these responses were originally intended to help us survive, they have ultimately contributed to our falling asleep to our individual liabilities as well as our personal potential. We seldom realize that what we don't know about ourselves can and does harm us. Transitional times have a way of shaking us awake, often exposing these less-than-desirable aspects of how we habitually live, function, and try to cope. Therefore, it is crucial that we not only pay attention to the specific nature of the "ruts" into which we have fallen, but that we also take the necessary action to climb out of them. The Sixth Solution will help us do so. By showing us how to stop, look, and listen, we will be able to connect with, learn from, and come to honor our inner voice that knows the truth. This will empower us to move out of our well-worn ruts and onto the road that leads to wholeness, happiness, and health.

Thus far, we have encountered several solutions to help us through the confusion, uncertainty, and emotional responses of this transitional time. They have included,

- the importance of practicing self-acceptance on a daily basis
- the necessity of staying balanced even when we are tempted to do anything but
- ways to embrace a spirituality that works

- the means of letting go of negative emotions, attitudes, and misconceptions
- how to grieve and heal our many losses, the present as well as those from our past.

This brings us to a critical juncture, a point at which we can either turn around and go back to where we've come from, or continue on our journey. The direction we choose will ultimately determine whether we simply survive this transitional period of ours, or learn to thrive in the face of almost anything. If thriving is what we're looking for, there is only one way in which to proceed -- upward and outward. In other words, we must be willing to climb up and out of the many dysfunctional ruts in which we have been habitually stuck for so many years.

Let's be honest. We all know what it is like to be stuck in a rut. We're aware, at some level, that we make personal choices and behave in ways that are familiar, routine, and perhaps even more than a little tedious. In their most harmless form, these might include such things as always going to the same place for vacations, continuing to wear our hair the way we did in high school, cooking the same old meals, watching the same old shows, getting angry with our spouse over the same old issues. These ruts are not only common, but they seldom create any long-term distress.

However, our tendency to operate on automatic pilot keeps us stuck in other ruts as well, ones that are far less benign. These include our ruts of self-deprecating thought-talk (the same dynamic we spoke of in previous chapters of this book); behaviors that we continue to repeat over and over again despite knowing at some level that they limit our potential rather than encourage it; and addictions that have originated from an initial need to get relief or comfort, but that fail to provide us with either over time. Charging through life the way we do, we also fall into a common rut created by our tendency to *react* rather than *respond* to the situations and people of our lives. When we are half asleep and don't think, we are normally far removed from our own truth on many levels. It is said that the only difference between a rut and a grave is its depth.

Yet, even in the midst of pointing our fingers in an attempt to justify our behavior, or simply trying to ignore the fact that we're stuck in a rut to begin with, most of us know down deep when we are not acting and reacting in our own best interests. We have glimpses that tell us when our personal behaviors are not in keeping with our innermost values and priorities. We even have brief moments of surfacing long enough to hear our inner voice speak its truth. But we generally don't pay attention to these moments. Instead, we quickly fall back into our familiar, complacent-lined, ruts.

It cannot be overemphasized that *what we don't know about ourselves can and does harm us.* If nothing changes, nothing changes. Therefore, if our wish is to grow and evolve and thrive and do all those wonderful things that we are more than capable of doing, then we must first be willing to climb out of our apathetic and comfortable routines. So let's begin this chapter by taking a more exacting look at what constitutes these ruts.

The Nature of "Ruts"

Let us be very clear about one thing: all of our ruts have their beginnings in innocence. For the same reasons that *we are who we are for reasons long past*, so are they. As we identified in chapter one, most of the ways in which we behave, think, and respond were learned years ago, taught or modeled by the families, culture, and institutions of our lives. Other behaviors and attitudes were picked up along the way as a means of survival. Many of these probably served a purpose at one time. However, so very often, the same things that helped us initially cope and survive have resulted in less than optimal habits, ones we have held onto long after any original benefit has expired.

All ruts share common characteristics. They are:

<u>R.</u> Repetitious
<u>U.</u> Unconscious
<u>T.</u> Tenacious
<u>S.</u> Self-limiting/Self-defeating

Ruts can also be separated into three distinct categories -- "thoughts," "roles," and "behaviors." It is important that we look at each one of these groups individually. This will require a willingness on our part to do some self-examination, an idea that may be uncomfortable for some of us. However, if we've been following the suggestions of the previous chapters, we have already made a good beginning on this. We might remind ourselves to remain curious rather than critical during any process of looking at our behaviors. After all, we are not here to beat ourselves up, but to learn as much as we can about the fascinating creature that we are.

We have already discovered that we can't move into the solution of *anything* until we identify the so-called problem, so our first challenge is that of calling our personal ruts by name. In other words, we must identify the areas that keep us hostage. The next several pages are intended to help us do this by providing brief descriptions of some of the more common ruts into which women tend to fall. We don't need to do anything else right now except read on and open our minds long enough to become aware. In every case of authentic change, awareness must come first. That is the primary purpose of these next few pages. Although the solutions will be forthcoming in the latter part of this chapter, right now we are simply focusing on gaining clarity about the exact nature of our personal ruts.

Thoughts

In our first Solution on Self-Acceptance, we discussed the frequency with which we women put ourselves down, and the overall damage it does to our self-esteem as well as to our spirit. This dynamic bears further investigation because it is at the core of our chronic and unconscious self-sabotage.

For many of us, we are stuck, and have been stuck for a long time, due to the way in which we think. Actually, we *think without thinking,* seldom aware of how, why, and how very often we use self-deprecating thought-talk. Every time we give ourselves an inner message of "not good enough," we carve our low self-esteem rut just a little bit deeper. Each time our inner dialogue delivers the messages of, "I can't. I'm not smart enough. I'm not worthy. I'm afraid. I shouldn't be feeling like this!", we get a little more stuck. Our mental preoccupation with "I don't know," "always," "never," and "should" keeps us like the woman perpetually treading water and going nowhere.

Most assuredly, as we previously identified, this tendency to speak so harshly and negatively to ourselves has been internalized over the years from messages we received early-on in life. If, over the years, our feelings were denied, ignored, discounted, or even punished, we have probably learned to do the same. Now, as adults, we no longer need to be told by somebody else that our feelings aren't real or justified; we tell it to ourselves. In some cases, we have even become indifferent to our own intuition and authentic inner voice.

Some of us even go so far as to mentally beat ourselves up when life doesn't go the way we think it should or that we want it to. Circumstances disappoint or people betray, and we somehow think it is our fault. Even when we are the so-called victims, we take responsibility and mentally punish ourselves for the outcome of situations. For instance, somebody ends a relationship with us, and we beat ourselves up even more by thinking, "I never should have picked this person for a friend or lover. What's the matter with me for trusting a liar? How could I have done this to myself again?" Instead of affirming ourselves for being brave enough to take a chance, to dare to love, or to choose to trust, we contribute to our pain with our harsh self-accusations.

Over time, by continuing to barrage ourselves with self-defeating thoughts, we actually come to believe these negative inner messages, and to doubt our own capabilities. By constantly self-reinforcing that, "I'm not good enough," or "I'm too nervous," or "I can't do it," we become immobilized. Instead of taking a chance to stretch into something new and different --something that will expand as well as empower us --we unconsciously talk ourselves into staying in whatever dysfunctional or unhappy "rut" we happen to be in. In other words, we fulfill our own prophesy.

Left unchallenged, our thoughts have the ability to harm us in ways we can't begin to imagine; sometimes, they even make us sick. Now is definitely the time to start questioning their validity. But we can't do any of that until we first become aware of how frequently we sabotage ourselves by the way we think.

Roles

Other repetitious, unconscious, tenacious and self-limiting ruts are created when we insist on maintaining various roles in our lives that no longer work for us (and perhaps never did). Maintaining a role is similar to wearing a mask. Once again, we come by our roles innocently enough. They may have been directly or indirectly assigned to us years ago, learned from parents or others who were influential during our early care. Some of our masks were undoubtedly picked up as a means of shielding us against vulnerability or used as an armor to cope with painful situations. Others may have been put on in an attempt to give us an identity. Even though some of these roles/masks may have originally served a purpose, at this point in our lives, they are simply keeping us stuck in the same old rut. Descriptions of some of the more common "role ruts" to which we women fall prey follow.

The Victim. A woman caught in this rut is full of the "poor me's." She feels that life is basically against her; if something can go wrong it will; and that everything bad happens to her. Rather than take active steps to help herself, she blames others, feels powerless, and spins her wheels in "awfulizing." It is one thing to be a victim; it's quite another to remain one.

The Rescuer. This woman gets her sense of identity and self worth by trying to fix and rescue others. There is an unconscious superiority/inferiority attached to this role. The Rescuer wears her mask as a smokescreen to avoid looking at something deep within herself that needs addressing, healing, or changing.

The Peacemaker. Every family has a woman who attempts to keep peace at any price. The Peacemaker is she who placates, tries to smooth things over, and attempts to make peace out of chaos. She avoids conflict like the plague, and consequently never addresses the underlying issues within the family, her place of business, or herself.

The Intellectual. It is said that the longest eighteen inches in the world lie between our head and our heart. The woman caught in the rut of intellectualizing epitomizes this. She uses her brain and her wit as a protective shell to keep everyone at a distance. It is her first line of defense against true intimacy and a genuine heart-connection.

The Shrew. Women who are stuck in this rut relate to others with anger, nastiness, and intimidation in order to get their way. Usually this "bitchiness" is a cover-up for inner feelings of fear, inadequacy, vulnerability and/or shame.

The Martyr. The martyr takes the victim role to new levels. Long-suffering and a master at self-deprivation, this woman sets up situations in which she sacrifices everything for others while making sure that they understand she's doing so. Underlying guilt is often her prime motivator, and she has no qualms about trying to make others feel guilty as well.

The Judge. Although this role has an outward attitude of "I'm better than you are," the woman who wears this mask is usually a secret, harsh self-critic. Any woman caught up in judging others usually has a very low opinion of herself. In fact, very often a woman's tendency is to assign her *own* less-than-desirable characteristics onto others.

The Beauty. When a woman derives her identity primarily from how she looks, her mask becomes continually more difficult to maintain. The Beauty finds it traumatic to age and can get hooked on such things as compulsive dieting, chronic exercising, or cosmetic surgery. Her over-involvement with physical appearance keeps her extremely self-centered and unable to authentically connect with others, or even with herself.

The Dependent. A woman caught in this role continually looks for someone else to take care of her, to bail her out, to do for her what she really could and should do for herself. The Dependent gets mileage out of being helpless and acting childish. She doesn't trust her own capabilities enough to take responsibility for her own well-being.

The Drama Queen. For this woman, everything is a crisis. She spends her time and energy putting out one chaotic fire, only to ignite another. The Drama Queen seldom sees her own complicity in starting and maintaining the chaos and confusion in her life. High drama is used as a fear-based distraction, keeping her from looking at something that goes far deeper.

The Passive-Aggressive. A woman wearing this mask will often use manipulative and indirect measures to get her needs met or her point across. She will say what she thinks somebody wants to hear, yet do something entirely different. She asserts herself either passively and underhandedly, or with inappropriate aggression. Both are attempts to cover up underlying feelings of unworthiness and powerlessness.

These are just a few of the role ruts we have fallen into over the years. There are many others including the Entitled, the Hypochondriac, the Loner, the Loser, the Pollyanna, the Perfectionist, the People-Pleaser, the Independent, and the Self-Saboteur, to name a few. The biggest problem with being stuck in any of them is that they keep us a stranger to ourselves. At the same time, wearing a mask and playing a role keep us apart *from*, rather than a part *of,* the significant others in our lives.

This was the case for Camille. For years, her identity was derived from being the clown. She felt certain that the only reason people invited her to parties or to a function was because she was entertaining. As the years passed, her role as "she who makes you laugh" began to feel more like a responsibility than a gift. Rather than bringing out the best of who she really was, it did just the opposite. Her humor, often self-deprecating, became the armor that kept her isolated and hidden, separate from those she so cleverly entertained.

Sarah's role was to keep peace in the family. With an hysterical mother and a father who drank too much, this was not an easy undertaking. In fact, it was impossible. Still, Sarah would go to any length to try and avoid conflict so that things would *appear* peaceful, even though her own inner world was filled with turmoil. Not only did she exhaust herself in the effort, but she felt like a failure every time she couldn't bring about a miracle.

Marie was a people-pleaser who came from a long line of the same. Like her mother before her, she would turn herself inside out to get the affection and approval of others by trying to do what she thought would make them happy. All of her energies were consumed in trying to please all the people all the time. Naturally, in the real world, this is just not possible. So when the inevitable would happen, Marie would be left wondering where she went wrong.

Even though it is largely unconscious, there are reasons we continue wearing our masks and staying stuck in our roles:

- because they are familiar
- so that people will like us
- to get what we want
- because we think we *are* our roles
- because we don't know how to change, even if we wanted to
- because we worry about what we might look like without our mask

The underlying factor for each of these is the same --- fear. Fear that tells us not to look too closely because we may have to make changes that challenge or frighten us; changes that might cause us to feel unlovable or vulnerable for a time; changes that we may not know how to make. And, especially, the fear of not knowing what lies beneath our familiar role or mask.

Behavioral Ruts

Our next category of ruts consists of the many behavioral responses that we have become stuck in over the years. Some of the more common behavioral ruts a woman tends to frequent are described briefly below.

Constant Busyness. There is a reason that this is not the first time we have looked at our chronic busyness. Without a doubt, this is the deepest and most justified behavioral rut in which a woman of today gets stuck. Being busy is not only encouraged but praised. Some will argue that it is not a rut at all, but a necessity, or even a virtue! Let's face it, it gets results. There are things that must be done, and we are the ones to do them! Besides, empty spaces fill us with anxiety or guilt. What we fail to realize is that chronic and constant busyness doesn't allow time for examining our motives, our values, or our priorities. It prevents us from taking stock of where we are, where we've been, and where we might want to go. Moreover, it is impossible to get to know ourselves, others, or even God with an agenda that is crammed full of activity.

Needing To Be in Control. This rut is created from the illusion that once we get everything and everyone lined up and doing what they are supposed to be doing, we'll be fine. A woman who needs to be in control takes on an inordinate amount of responsibility for things that are really beyond her control. She has a chronic need to micro-manage, directing and exercising undue (and often unsolicited) control over people, places, and things. When we live in this rut, we usually have an additional need to be "right." Even though the potential to make mistakes is a human one, we cannot allow ourselves the prerogative of being wrong, so who's right becomes more important than what's right. Ironically, attempting to always be in control is the primary reason a woman so often feels that her life is unmanageable.

Blaming Others. Constantly blaming others is our attempt to make someone else responsible for our own feelings, actions, and results. When we are stuck in this rut, we don't usually get far beyond it. Blaming others becomes the way we either justify our own actions and deeds, or avoid looking at ourselves completely. Rather than make essential changes in our own behavior or attitude, we stay stuck by putting our attention in the wrong place. In fact, if we really examined this tendency to shift the blame, we would probably uncover the well-hidden fact that we often blame others for what we suspect of ourselves.

Procrastination. This rut is carved out of fear-based inaction and reinforced by our negative thought-talk as it convinces us that we can't do it, we're over our heads, we're lazy, or we just don't care. Rather than risk failure *or* success, we do nothing. We become stuck, discouraged and angry with ourselves for not finishing something we have started, or for not doing what someone else has asked us to. We stay stuck because we're afraid we might not get the results we wanted, or live up to the expectations of others. Procrastination is a dream's worse nightmare; it is a rut that turns our deepest desires from possibilities to "not an option."

Gossiping. The practice of spreading usually untrue or exaggerated details about others is a rut that attempts to make us look good or feel better by comparison. This commonly backfires. For one thing, when we're stuck in this rut, there is a part of us that believes we are only liked because of the information we share regarding others. We also live with the ongoing suspicion that others do the same regarding us. Although it may not seem so on the surface, most chronic gossipers have deep feelings of remorse and inferiority that block authentic growth.

Being Habitually Overwhelmed. This is another behavioral rut that, like procrastination, capitalizes on inaction and, therefore, does nothing to promote wholeness and growth. Like all the ruts before us, being overwhelmed feeds on itself and ends up taking on a life of its own. For example, something happens that initially causes us to feel overwhelmed: perhaps a change in the status quo; an unrealistic expectation we have placed on ourselves or that somebody else has placed on us; an unexpected onslaught of extra work or duties; or the staggering weight of an emotional excess created as a result of a crisis or change. Regardless of the cause, we respond by feeling overwhelmed which, in turn, results in inaction. This inaction causes us to accomplish little or nothing, which then leads to lowered self-esteem. Lowered self-esteem causes us to feel even more overwhelmed, which leads to greater inaction, and so on. All of our ruts share this same underlying dynamic of feeding on themselves, creating an ongoing cycle that basically goes nowhere faster and faster. This is how the cycle looks:

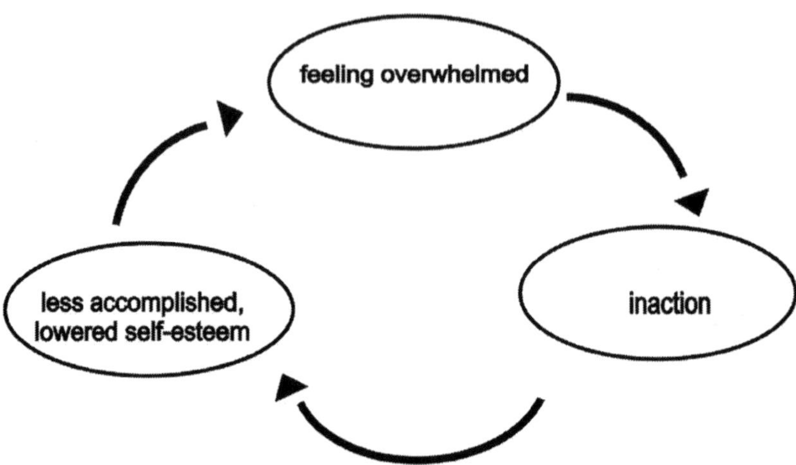

The Rut of Being Overwhelmed

Regardless of the particular rut in which we may presently be caught, the only way we can begin to make any *real* progress is by breaking out of the dead-end cycles that they each create.

We'll examine ways to do this shortly.

When "Ruts" Become "Pits"

Sometimes, our behaviors feed on themselves to such an extent that they go beyond being ruts, and turn into self-destructive pits. In a word, this refers to our addictions, one of the most misunderstood ways in which women get stuck. Whether we are acquainted with addiction personally, by association, or not at all, the more we can move beyond the myths and misconceptions surrounding it, the better our chances of identifying it, if and when we need to.

Although there is much written on the subject of addiction, the following pages are an attempt to give some short and simple answers to a complex and deadly serious subject. If there is any section of *The Joy is in the Journey* that should be read carefully, it is definitely this one. And if ever we need to remain curious and not critical, it is as this section is read, because it could save our life or someone else's.

What is Addiction?

Addiction is the chronic and habitual use of a substance, behavior, or relationship which, over time, becomes excessive and compulsive. The addictive process is characterized by a mental preoccupation with a particular substance or behavior (thinking about it all the time), a physical craving for more, (if one is good, two is better), and ultimately, a compromised spirit or loss of spiritual values. Addictions are camouflaged by denial, and typically create an emotional roller-coaster that fluctuates between euphoria and depression. They manifest themselves in numerous ways. Some of the more common ones include excessive and compulsive drinking, smoking, the overuse or misuse of prescription or illegal drugs, gambling, over-or-under eating, spending, working, sexual promiscuity, or total preoccupation with what somebody else is doing or not doing.

Addictive behaviors not only prevent us from realizing our potential for personal fulfillment, balance, and service to others, but they also negatively impact every level of our being. Left untreated, addictions can and will destroy us physically, mentally, emotionally, and spiritually. They will also stifle any current relationships we may have, as well as the possibility for future ones.

The contrast between the characteristics of our "ruts" and the "pits" of addiction into which we fall can be seen in the following comparison:

R. - Repetitious	P. - Progressive
U. - Unconscious	I. - Insidious
T. - Tenacious	T. - Toxic
S. - Self-limiting/defeating	S. - Self-destructive

Addictive behaviors are progressive. Left unacknowledged and untreated, they will *always* increase in extent or severity. They are insidious, sneaking up on us gradually, often without our knowledge or permission. Addictions are toxic – they poison us, and cause our behavior to be unstable and unpredictable. They are self-destructive, so much so that they ultimately result in death, if not of the physical body, then of the soul. Whereas ruts will keep us churning round and round in the same cycle, there is no accounting for how far we can fall when caught in a deep, dark, bottomless pit.

How Do Addictions Begin?

There is not a woman alive who grows up wanting to become an alcoholic, a drug addict, morbidly obese, a compulsive shopper, a chronic gambler, totally enmeshed in the life of another, or a sex and love addict. Just like our behavioral ruts, our addictions begin innocently.

Sometimes our tendency for an addictive behavior comes with the territory. Research indicates that women who grew up in homes with active alcoholism or food addiction have a far greater chance of becoming addicted to *something* during their lifetime. In addition, there is a genetic component to addiction. In other words, we can inherit both a physical and an emotional predisposition to becoming dependent on a substance, person, or behavior.

Some addictions begin as a response to over-sensitivity. There are those of us who are born seemingly devoid of any emotional protection to buffer us from the impact of common life occurrences. Even on a good day, we live with an underlying feeling of intense vulnerability and over-sensitivity. Being thin skinned makes us susceptible to needing *something* to help us cope with life's hurts, tragedies, and anxieties. Unfortunately, we often get hooked on that very something.

For many, an early childhood, adolescent, or even an adult traumatic experience may trigger an eventual addiction. As we saw in the previous chapter on Healing, when *any* trauma or tragedy isn't acknowledged, addressed, or dealt with in healthy and healing ways, the pain from it does not dissipate on its own; it merely goes underground where it creates an inner distress and lowered self-esteem from which we want and need relief. When we don't know appropriate ways to get comfort, courage, or good feelings, we can end up looking for it in all the wrong places.

Addictive behaviors are also influenced and supported by our society. Just look at the blatant messages we receive regarding how to cope with difficulty or distress. We needn't look far to be encouraged to pop a pill, take a drink, smoke a joint, have an affair, or shop till we drop. We have been taught to equate food with comfort, alcohol with courage, and pills with changing our mood in an instant.

Encountering a critical time puts any of us at a higher risk for developing an addictive behavior that may lie dormant within us. When we are living in the discomfort, confusion, or vulnerability of a transitional period, it is only natural to want something to make the pain and fear go away, even temporarily.

When Mary was 55, her long-time husband decided he no longer wanted to be married. For years, they had enjoyed a nightly cocktail before dinner and an occasional glass of wine with the meal. Now alone, Mary continues to make herself a cocktail. Because she has nobody at home to cook for, she sometimes will have another drink or two, rather than dinner.

When Barbara's company merged with another, she lost her job in a highly competitive field. Her work had become her identity, so she felt totally lost without it. Not knowing how to fill the empty spaces or how to cope with her newfound circumstances, Barbara began taking comfort in food. In the beginning it was no big deal, but before long she was eating even when she wasn't hungry. Junk food became her drug of choice, and as the weeks went by, she became more and more dependent on it to alter her mood, give her comfort, and momentarily numb her.

When Bernice's husband died suddenly, the pain was excruciating. The doctor gave her a prescription for a mild tranquilizer to help her through the initial shock. She took it as prescribed, at least in the beginning. As the months went on, one pill didn't seem to work as well, so she began taking two. Over time, she found additional doctors to write prescriptions for her increasing dependency on tranquilizers.

Unfortunately, in so many cases, what begins as a temporary solution turns into a permanent problem by setting an addictive cycle in motion. Let's look at the dynamics of this more closely.

The Addictive Cycle

Addiction begins the same for everyone, with an initial need for relief (from pain, discomfort, anxiety or stress), or with a desire to enhance our feelings of joy and well-being. Either way, we look for something to alter our mind or elevate our mood. As we have mentioned in previous chapters, there are certainly healthy ways to do both of these (meditation, moderate exercise, breathing correctly, support groups, or therapy). However, most of us tend to want more immediate gratification and relief, causing us to gravitate towards behaviors that don't require quite so much time and concerted effort. Reinforced by a society notorious for treating the symptoms while ignoring the underlying needs, we seek fast-acting solutions for getting out of or altering our feelings. Often, these "quick fixes" include a pill, a joint, a drink, food, extreme busyness, shopping, gambling, sexual activity, or smoking. In the cases where we use these substances or behaviors for short periods of time and in moderation, they may have the intended effect. They help us relax by momentarily taking the edge off our feelings; they increase our ability to cope; they enable us to enjoy life more fully; and/or they help us get through the first few days of a major crisis or change.

Unfortunately, we are not all masters at moderation, and we can easily and unknowingly end up using these same behaviors or substances excessively, compulsively, longer than intended, or with increased quantity and frequency. When this happens, rather than help us cope and thrive, our compulsive behavior backfires by developing into a cycle of addiction. The very thing we become addicted to, rather than decrease our pain and anxiety as intended, actually increases it because the addiction leads to poor life choices and lowered self-esteem. Just like the cycle of our ruts, the self-destructive cycle of addictive behaviors also feeds on itself to such an extent that the solution eventually becomes the problem. This is how it works:

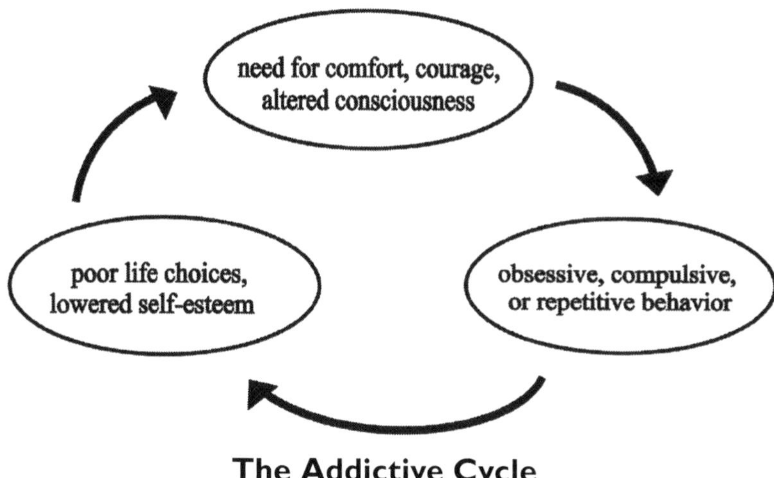

The Addictive Cycle

As we have seen, any number of triggers can set this cycle in motion, especially during a critical or transitional period. When we are trying to cope with a multitude of emotional responses, we need relief; how and where we find it is a huge factor in determining whether or not we will get stuck, fall into a pit, or move *through* our critical period into the many possibilities for our lives.

Recognizing Addiction

One of the fallacies we have come to believe regarding addictions is that the problem doesn't exist until it is blatantly obvious. Nothing could be further from the truth. Just because a woman doesn't show for the first several months of pregnancy, doesn't mean she's not pregnant. The same is true for addictive behaviors. The majority of men and women who suffer from an addictive behavior are not only functional, but usually well-accepted members of their communities. In fact, for many, keeping up appearances is of paramount importance, whether in the work environment or in the home.

In a world full of denial, it is no wonder that so few of us recognize our own addictive behaviors for what they really are. We unconsciously deny the extent to which we are dependent on drinking, smoking, or mind-altering prescriptions. We convince ourselves that our over-eating, workaholism, gambling, or promiscuity doesn't harm anyone, except maybe ourselves. We ignore the fact that our obsessions with significant others have taken over our sanity and are blocking our serenity.

Denial is one of the biggest characteristics of someone who has become dependent on an addictive behavior. Rather than contribute to a solution, denial is generally our largest handicap. Denial is, quite simply, our inability or refusal to acknowledge the truth. When our behavior is too painful, shameful, or frightening to look at, or when we feel incapable of doing anything about our dependency, we deny that it is a problem. This denial is evidenced each time we minimize, justify, or out and out lie to ourselves, as well as to others, regarding the extent of our behaviors.

It is a wonder we ever get beyond denial. Indeed, how do we recognize and even admit that we have a tendency to overuse or abuse a substance or behavior? How do we know when and if we have become stuck in the self-destructive pit of addiction?

The short answer to this question is a simple one**:** *If we suspect something is a problem, then it likely <u>is</u> a problem.* In other words, if we find ourselves wondering from time to time, "Do I drink too much? Is my compulsion for work interfering with my family or other relationships? Am I obsessed with my love life at the expense of everything else? Is the way I'm eating contributing to my health problems?" If we worry that something might be a problem, chances are good that it is.

Another way to determine whether or not we are caught in an addictive behavior is to ask ourselves: *"Does this behavior create a problem with my health, safety, or personal relationships?"* Remember, the behavior could be *anything* done excessively or compulsively. "Does my behavior create a problem with my health, safety, or personal relationships?" If the answer is yes, the answer *is* yes. If overspending is creating a problem, than overspending *is* a problem. If love addiction is creating a problem, than love addiction *is* a problem. If drinking is creating a problem, than drinking *is* the problem. If smoking is creating a problem, than smoking *is* the problem. If obesity is creating a problem, than over-eating *is* the problem.

Another relevant question to ask is, "Where does the behavior lead?" In other words, does my use of a substance or behavior end up making me feel bad about myself? Does it eventually lead to guilt, shame, remorse, or regret? Does it cause me to make poor life choices? Does it hurt other people? If the answer to any of these is yes, then we really need to look at the behavior. Any behavior that ultimately makes us feel bad about who we are and what we do, ends up creating an even greater need for relief.

Even though our denial tries to convince us that our behaviors really aren't that bad, if we are caught in any addiction, it is progressive and self-destructive if left untreated. Rather than help us get through a crisis or change, addictive behaviors compromise our ability to make healthy choices. Instead of allowing us to be who we really are, they keep us a stranger to ourselves, and prevent us from opening to new experiences, possibilities, and authentic relationships.

One of the main characteristics of an addictive behavior is that it will always cause our world to become smaller instead of larger, to shrink rather than grow. Addictions take our spirits hostage and interfere with our ability to live lives of integrity and honesty. They also get worse as time goes on, eventually bringing us to the brink of the despair mentioned in the previous chapter. In Dante's words again, "I did not die, but nothing of life remains."

We don't have to wait until we get to this point before we do something about our destructive pits and self-limiting ruts. We have gained some insight regarding their specific nature, so now it is time to learn how to climb out of them. The way we begin is by paying attention to our glimpses.

Paying Attention to our Glimpses

Despite the denial surrounding our areas of dependency, most of us are aware at some level when we engage in behaviors that are harmful to our physical, emotional, and spiritual health. We have all had moments when our blinders were briefly removed, and we saw ourselves more clearly than we perhaps would have liked. We have heard our inner voice whisper its dissatisfaction, concern, or discomfort over some of our choices. We have momentarily recognized the negative impact of our self-limiting behaviors and compulsive natures. We have all, at some time, experienced a glimpse of truth about ourselves and our situations.

The glimpse is the primary way that our inner voice tries to get our attention. It is an intuitive moment in which our denial and self-justification are briefly distracted, and we have the insight to see our behavior for what it really is. Glimpses happen when we least expect them, usually when, for some reason, our defenses seem to have taken a break. In their pleasurable form, glimpses serve as windows into the more beautiful aspects of our soul, putting us in touch with the fact that we are whole and complete just as we are. An awareness of this nature might occur during any moment in which we have lost our mind and come to our senses - tucking in a sleeping child, watching the sun hit a wet blade of grass, marveling at the sparkle of a million diamonds on the sea, or catching the special look in a loved one's eyes. Random and unanticipated, these glimpses provide us with the unquestionable knowledge that we are much more than we ever thought possible. Of all the gifts that God bestows upon us, the glimpse is undoubtedly one of God's greatest.

But glimpses aren't designed simply to highlight our magnificence. Other important types of glimpses are not so pleasant to receive. These glimpses come as a wake-up call, to illuminate truths about some of the less than desirable ways we have learned to behave or cope, ways that are not in our own best interest, nor in the best interest of others. These moments of painfully acute and honest insight happen to everyone. Often, we just pretend not to notice them, afraid that if we do, we might have to give up something or change a behavior.

Mary is a recovering alcoholic. Like many, she recalls a lifetime full of glimpses, ones she had become expert at side-stepping and ignoring. Long before entering a program of recovery for her drinking, she had several intuitive moments of knowing that her use of alcohol was problematic. One such glimpse occurred when she was twenty-five years old, years before she actually stopped drinking.

"I remember it as if it was yesterday. I had already been divorced, dropped out of college, lost a good job, and was pretty much at an all-time low in terms of self-esteem. The only way I knew how to cope was by drinking. Of course, at the time, I just thought I was having fun.

"One night at a party, I went to the bathroom and got a glimpse of myself in the mirror. For just a split second, the fog cleared and I saw myself as I truly was -- drunk, bloated, blotchy, and unkempt. Locking eyes with my reflection in that mirror revealed a thousand unspoken words of truth. For one brief second, I knew in my innermost being that alcohol was a problem. But I was young. I even owned my own home. How bad could it be? So, armed with denial and self-justification, I quickly moved away from that moment of truth and went on to have another drink. But I never forgot it.

"Over the next six years, these glimpses of my drinking problem periodically made themselves known. However, my denial was one step behind. 'What was the big problem, anyway?', I would think. Sure, there were those who mentioned how much I drank, but I ignored or dismissed them. And even though I had problems directly related to over-drinking -- car accidents, blackouts, an arrest or two - I could always blame them on something else; I had failed to eat, my boyfriend hurt my feelings, or the streets were icy. I looked for people who drank more than I did, and compared my drinking to theirs to make myself feel better. Despite all evidence to the contrary, I actually believed that booze was the magical elixir that held me together and made all things possible. In hindsight, I see that I could not have been more mistaken!"

Unbeknownst to Mary at the time, she had fallen into a pit of ongoing, self-destructive drinking behavior over which she was powerless. Rather than Mary controlling when and how much she drank, drinking controlled her. It made her decisions, chose her friends, and determined where she would go or not, what she would do or not do. And through it all, she had no knowledge that it was getting worse over time.

Like Mary, many of us are stuck in our denial regarding our addictive behaviors. And although we get glimpses of ourselves -- taking more pills than prescribed; finishing up the half gallon of ice cream after everyone has gone to bed; downing another drink in the solitude of our kitchen or in the shower; smoking a joint in the morning just to get out the front door; spending money we don't have; jumping in bed with somebody we hardly know -- we ignore them.

Our glimpses also highlight some of the behavioral ruts we previously identified. We catch a snapshot of ourselves in the midst of trying to micro manage everything and everyone. We see ourselves yelling at a child, or insisting that we're right, when we know we're really wrong. We watch ourselves allow indecision to keep us paralyzed, because we're afraid of making the wrong choice. We become briefly aware of our inner discomfort while telling a tale out of school. We catch a glimpse of ourselves racing helter-skelter from one frantic activity to another, knowing for a painful, fleeting moment that something is wrong with this picture.

We're not the only ones who have glimpses concerning our behaviors. Even when *our* denial remains intact, our family and friends recognize both the ruts and the pits we've fallen into, no matter how hard we try to disguise or minimize them. Very often, these people live with the hurtful consequences of our behaviors. Our spouse suffers first-hand the rejection created from our workaholism. Our family lives with the financial insecurity caused by our overspending or gambling. Our children endure the embarrassment and chaos created by our unpredictable behavior when drinking or taking drugs. Our friends get the back lash from our inability to tell the truth. In the past, our significant others may have even tried to communicate their concerns or pain to us, only to be pushed away by our defensive, angry denial.

If this is our truth, and we've had a glimpse into some behavior that makes us feel "less than" rather than "more of" ourselves, we cannot take it lightly. We must *stop, look, listen* and *learn* now, because the opportunity may never arise again. Glimpses only last a fleeting moment, but they have the ability to open the door to a freedom for which we have always searched -- the freedom to be the women we were meant to be.

Into the Solution

Paying attention to our glimpses is only the first step in interrupting the self-perpetuating and damaging cycles of roles, behaviors and addictions that keep us on a treadmill going nowhere. It is one thing to know the truth; it is quite another to act on that insight. So we must remain curious not critical; stop operating on automatic pilot; stay alert to catching ourselves in the middle of – or perhaps before we engage in – negative actions, thoughts, and behaviors that don't really work well for us; and take specific suggestions to keep from sticking our head back into the sand or guillotine!

Combat Negative Thought-Talk

When it comes to our unconscious and self-limiting thought-talk, our biggest challenge is to learn how to distinguish between the many voices within. Although some of us may require professional help in this area, most of us can make a beginning by listening to the ways our inner committee negatively dictates what we feel and do (or don't do, which is more likely).

By learning to pay attention, we can begin to catch ourselves in the middle of one of these mental assaults on our own character, and immediately STOP. LOOK. LISTEN. LEARN. The following questions will help us do this:

- From where are these negative thoughts coming?
- Are they from an old place?
- Whose voice is doing the talking?
- What good purpose do these thoughts serve?

By taking an objective and curious stand outside of ourselves, we can not only watch our negative thought-talk in action, but also we can learn from it. We can even begin to question its origin, its validity, and its authority. Then, we can go one step further and counteract it with dialogue that is more positive and helpful. This is the same technique of "thought-changing" that we learned in the First Solution on Self-Acceptance. Without a doubt, it is one of the biggest and most critical shifts a woman can make.

For instance, when our mind negatively questions, "What else could possible go wrong?," we can immediately tell ourselves that, "I'm sure the next thing will go right." If we catch ourselves thinking, "I can't do this," we can become as the Little Engine and begin reciting over and over in our mind, "I think I can, I think I can, I think I can." Even habitual self-responses like labeling ourselves as stupid or clumsy when we make a mistake are destructive. Therefore, in *every* case where we begin to give ourselves negative messages of doom, gloom, and failure, we need to stop ourselves immediately, and begin retraining our minds to give inner messages of hope, encouragement, validation, and affirmation instead. Thinking a positive thought is the first step in breaking any destructive cycle of negative thought. The more we can Stop. Look. Listen and Learn how to speak kindly to ourselves, the more we'll be able to access and increase the volume of our little voice within that knows the truth.

Move Beyond Self-Defeating Roles/Behavior

When attempting to step out and beyond our behavioral ruts and/or the roles we have learned to play, our first step is to call them each by name. At this point, we might want to go back and review the several roles and behavioral ruts listed in this chapter. If we either identified with them, or were resistant to what we read, we might want to investigate further. In both cases, we can ask ourselves the following questions:

- What is the payoff for maintaining this role or behavior?
- Do I think that it's the reason people like me?
- Do I really believe that this is who I am?
- What are the consequences for staying stuck in this role/behavior?
- What closed cycle has this behavior created?
- How might my life be different if I chose to take off my mask?
- What would *I* look like without it?

Now would be a good time to take out our journal and answer some of these questions to the best of our ability. Sometimes, discussing the results of our writing with a close friend and asking for input can be very enlightening. As uncomfortable as it may be to grow in self-awareness, it is the only way we can stop accepting our "ruts" carte blanche, and challenge their authenticity instead.

Once we identify the exact nature of our "ruts," we need to take the appropriate action to break their cycle and step out of them. This often creates a dilemma. How do we break the cycle? How do we change the behaviors of a lifetime? How do we let go of the very things we think give us an identity? In other words, how do we get from here to there?

The answer is so simple, many of us miss it. In fact, it is the same solution we used for letting go of troublesome situations and personalities in the Fourth Solution. Simply put, *we head in the opposite direction of where we are stuck.* For example, if we are stuck in the rut of people-pleasing, the way to get "unstuck" is by beginning to please ourselves. So we head in that direction by asking ourselves what would please *us*. Then we act accordingly.

If we're stuck in the rut of procrastination, the way to get out of it is to move towards its opposite, in this case, deliberate action. If we're stuck in the rut of constant busyness, we head in the direction of inaction and stillness. If we're stuck in the rut of blaming others, we head in the direction of examining our own behavior. Once again, we do this without criticism or struggle, but with curiosity and persistence.

The following diagram illustrates the concept of breaking the cycle of a "rut" by awareness, and then managing to stay out of the same rut by heading in the other direction. *We never struggle to get out of our ruts; instead, we simply put our energy into walking towards their opposite.*

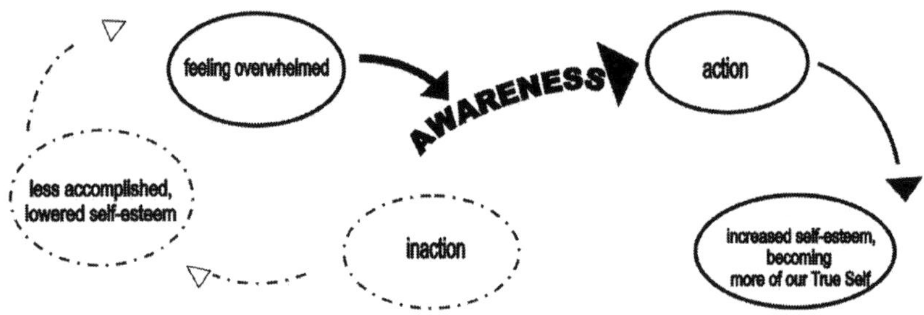

Awareness breaks the cycle, making it possible for us to move into right action.

When we take the necessary and right action to keep from falling back into our rut of choice, this action sets up a *positive* cycle that, in turn, feeds on itself. This is definitely easier said than done, but it does work. Chances are we may have to start with baby steps and talk ourselves through each little one. Yet over time, provided we continue to honor our needs for balance and spiritual connection, our new behaviors will become easier and easier to maintain.

It is important to note that when making any pivotal change or climbing out of any rut, the pendulum may initially swing too far in the opposite direction. In our fear that we're not going to make it out, rather than simply stretch ourselves, we tend to over-reach. We should not let this alarm us. The beginnings of instituting new behaviors are seldom smooth.

Maureen is a good example of that. For years, she lived in the rut of passivity. She would "go along to get along," never actually telling you how she really felt about anything. In her attempts to climb out of this behavioral rut, she joined a woman's group whose focus was on self-assertion. As time passed, she learned her new lessons well, almost too well. Instead of becoming gently assertive, she initially became rather aggressive in her responses.

In fact, one day, her significant other wanted to discuss an ongoing problem and said to her very nicely, "We really need to talk about this."

"No," she rudely replied. "*You* need to talk about this."

On another occasion, he asked her a legitimate question about how she felt regarding something he had done.

"Don't ask me any questions if you're not prepared for the answer," she smartly retorted.

If we're aware ahead of time that we might at first go too far in the opposite direction when making changes in any of our behaviors, we will, perhaps, not judge ourselves too harshly when and if we do. After all, anytime we're learning a new song, we're bound to hit a few sour notes before we get it right.

At the same time, however, we must realize that not everyone is going to be happy with us climbing out of our ruts and changing. In fact, it may create several negative reactions among family and friends who have adjusted to, and perhaps even like our particular dysfunction. Maybe our ruts have been compatible with theirs and they fear losing a rut-mate! We cannot let their opinions dissuade us in our efforts, because when our choices and decisions are founded upon a true sense of self rather than motivated from a fear-based rut, everyone benefits in the long run.

Combat Addictive Behaviors

There is one important rule of thumb when it comes to recovering from addictions: *Addictions are never meant to be faced and conquered alone –never, never, never.* They are much stronger than any human will-power, and can only be successfully combated in the face of two or more with a common purpose. Even if we manage to stop the addictive *behavior* (which is really only a symptom) by white-knuckling it, we still need to address the deeper issues that led up to the addiction in the first place. To do this work, we need the support and help of others. We need people who will show us how to get well; those who will stand beside us and support our efforts at recovery; friends who will give us a kick in the butt every now and then, just to let us know they're behind us all the way.

The group process has long been proven as the most effective means of recovering from addictive behaviors. With that in mind, if you suspect that you or your loved one is addicted to *anything,* please make a phone call to your local mental health services or Alcoholic Anonymous Central Service where somebody will direct you to the appropriate twelve-step program. If you are addicted, this phone call will -- hands-down --be the most important gift you could ever give yourself.

We all have an inner voice that knows the truth. We have heard this inner voice encourage us to speak kinder to ourselves, and to step up and out of our habitual ruts. We have heard it implore us to get the help we need to recover from our addictive behaviors. We have experienced our glimpses as well, in their moments of pulling back the curtain to reveal things about ourselves that we have really known all along. Now is the time for us to wake up and pay attention to both our glimpses and our inner voice, so that they may become the catalysts for our breaking out of our old habits, thoughts, behaviors and addictions. Although it will require committed and steadfast action to get out and stay out of these familiar places, we can do it. If our deepest desire is to move on in authentic and fulfilling directions, with worthy goals and suitable companions, we must stop, look, listen, and learn so that we can make the changes that will ultimately bring us to where the riches truly await.

A woman was dreaming that she was wandering through a dark, deep forest. Dazed and confused, she had no idea how long she had been lost, perhaps a lifetime. She was hungry, lonely, frightened, and weary. No matter how far she walked, she always seemed to wind up where she began. Discouraged and disheartened, she was ready to give up all hope, when one day, she stumbled upon a path. It was narrow and ill-defined, hardly discernable. And yet, she followed it, hoping and praying that it would bring her out of the woods.

The path eventually stopped at a huge, high gate that was shut tight and locked. On the other side of this gate was a beautiful castle, with people milling about in the courtyard, laughing, playing, and talking with one another. The woman could hear music and smell the delicious aroma of fresh meat cooking on an open fire. Oh, how she yearned to be part of all this!

How long she stood there, she did not know. Finally, the gate opened, and a maidservant came out. She left a few scraps of bread for the woman to eat, and some water for her to drink. It was barely enough to sustain life but the woman consumed them quickly. She then proceeded to wait for more. She waited and waited.

The next day at exactly the same hour, the gate swung open and the maidservant appeared with bread and water. Once again, the woman consumed them quickly. And so it began. Each day, the woman would be waiting at the gate, willing to accept the crumbs that were offered. Although they kept her alive, they did not nourish her at any level of her being.

As time went on, the woman began to be aware of a still small voice within, one that would gently encourage her to, "Move on. Move on." But the woman was paralyzed with fear, afraid that by venturing forth she would miss out on the scraps and end up hungry, thirsty, frightened and lost once again. She didn't realize that the crumbs she settled for were merely a small sample of what could be. So rather than move on, she stayed in her rut outside the gate instead. Because of this, she was never to discover that just around the corner, barely out of sight, was a banquet that could have been hers for the taking – if only she had listened to her small voice within and honored the wisdom it imparted.

Suggestions for Listening and Learning

tead of continuing to charge through life on automatic t, make a conscious decision to STOP. LOOK. LISTEN. LEARN.

2. Remembering to remain "curious not critical" during periods of self-examination, assign a day to pay attention to how you think. Try to catch your negative thought-talk in action. From where do these inner messages originate? Can you begin to question their authority and validity? At the same time, give yourself some positive feedback instead. Spend a day pretending to be the Little Engine That Could: "I think I can, I think I can, I think I can."

3. Did you identify with any of the role ruts listed on pages 152-154? What does your mask consist of? Where did it come from? Why do you continue to wear it? What would happen if you were brave enough to take it off? Answer the questions on page 171 to the best of your ability.

4. Go back and review the section on behavioral ruts, pages 156-158. Are you stuck in any of these? Is there some other "rut" you can identify in your own life? If so, what would constitute the opposite of this behavior? Step out of your rut by heading in this opposite direction. Use the graphic on page 172 to help you with this dynamic.

5. Do you suspect that you are caught in the grips of an addictive behavior? If so, make a decision *right now* to get help for yourself. Make the call that will save your spirit and possibly your life.

6. Pay attention to the "glimpses" in your life by using the meditation that follows. Begin listening for your own inner voice. Learn to honor its wisdom.

Reflection on the Glimpse

Make a concerted effort to bring all activity to a halt. Carve out a little corner of the universe where you will be comfortable and undisturbed. If you wish, play some background music. Be sure that it is instrumental only as the voice you need to listen to right now is your own. In this quiet place, take a few deep breaths to relax yourself and to clear away the mental clutter that constantly engages and distracts you. Consider your mind as a deep pond, one that is covered over with fallen leaves and other debris. As you breathe deeply, imagine yourself taking a mental brush and gently sweeping all of these things to the side, leaving the surface clear, allowing you to take a good look at what lies beneath.

Understanding that glimpses of truth are one of God's greatest gifts to us, try to recall an instance in your own life when you knew beyond a doubt that you were far greater than you normally realize. Think of a glimpse experience that unquestioningly put you in touch with your higher self, a time of inner "knowing." We have all had these moments, so think hard. Perhaps it occurred when you were feeling peaceful and in the moment, maybe on a vacation, while listening to an inspirational talk, during a hike, bike, or kayak experience, or in the midst of doing something for somebody else. In your present state of clarity, bring this momentary glimpse you had of your higher self to the surface of your consciousness. This is who you really are.

Now, confident in the knowledge that you are truly far more than you may think, take another deep breath and reflect upon the other type of glimpses that God bestows upon us, those that reveal in stark honesty the very things that prevent us from connecting with and accessing this higher self. In the safety of this moment, bring to mind a time when you heard your inner voice caution you about a behavior that was not in your highest good, or when you had a glimpse of your lower self in action. Did this action involve over-doing something? Perhaps it was related to your tendency to over-drink, over-spend, over-eat, over-compensate, over-look, take over, or obsess over?

Maintaining a curious not critical attitude, reflect upon the circumstances that surrounded any such glimpses that might come to your awareness. What were the messages given to you from your small inner voice during these times? Bring these messages into full consciousness so that these glimpses of undesirable behavior can become a catalyst for promoting positive changes. Make a decision to not only trust your truth but to also begin living it.

The Seventh Solution: *Take Right Action*

Underlying Principle: Right action promotes positive change.

There comes a point during any transitional period when we must chirp or get off the twig. This involves doing the next right thing: taking action that is in alignment with our deepest values and fondest wishes. While doing so can be challenging, it only stands to reason that the more self-accepting, balanced, spiritually inclined, unencumbered by emotional baggage, healed, and free from self-defeating behaviors and attitudes we are, the more likely we will be to take right action into positive change. This often requires us to step out of our comfort zones and be willing to be stretched and remade, even to risk the possibility of failure. The Seventh Solution helps us suit up and show up for the changes we want and need to make. It highlights the importance of discernment prior to action, teaches us the wisdom of the "wait," and outlines specific steps for keeping our "attention on the intention" in order to make our dreams and goals materialize. By taking right action on our own behalf, we will not only bring new life to ourselves, but we will also acquire the ability to carry that same positive energy and potential into the larger world.

At the very beginning of this book, we learned that all change includes a necessary and critical period of adjustment. During this time, there are certain things we can do to better ensure the best direction for our lives and how whole we will be in the process. The chapters we have read thus far have addressed these concerns. They have not only enabled us to cope with our present circumstances, but also have helped us to get over our false sense of self in order to discover the wonderful and spirit-filled self at the center of our being.

If we have followed the suggestions and progressed on our journey, we should now be ready to move on. In fact, we may be chomping at the bit to do so. However, when contemplating any action, rather than do so prematurely, it is wise to first take time for discernment. After all, we don't want to confuse motion with action. We've been there and done that, perhaps for most of our lives. We are now at a point where we want the Real Deal; that is, we want to take action that is more in keeping with our innermost desires and values. The problem is, we don't always know for certain what these dreams and values are. This not-knowing causes us great insecurity, often rendering us stuck in indecision. This can be especially true when we are vacillating between the option of moving on from a particular person, place, or situation, or staying put.

Sometimes decisions are made for us. Situations occur that leave us in the tumultuous wake of an event or somebody else's actions. Other circumstances arise that are beyond *anyone's* control. Both can initiate changes that we would not likely have chosen for ourselves, as well as generate emotional upheaval, financial insecurity, and mental anguish. As we are now well aware, we must grieve the loss of the life we once knew and enjoyed in order to come into an eventual acceptance. Like all of our processes, this is not an easy undertaking; yet it must be done. When we fail to accept the things we cannot change, we become like the woman who stands in front of a closed door and bangs her head on it. Even though numerous other doors are wide open and inviting, our lack of acceptance keeps us stuck in a place that is no longer an option. And while this head-banging may be our immediate reaction to the crises and changes in our lives, it no longer needs to be our long-term response.

There are times for acceptance, and there are times for action. But in matters where we get to cast the deciding vote, how can we be sure what to do? How can we know whether it is high time to call something quits or, instead, to bloom where we're planted? Should we move on from our present circumstances/relationships, or should we stay put? Should our energies be expended trying to change something within an existing structure, or should we be looking elsewhere? Distinguishing between what to accept and when to initiate change is a question of discernment. It is what Reinhold Neibur spoke of in his famous Serenity Prayer when he wrote:

God, grant me the serenity to accept the things I cannot change,
The courage to change the things I can,
And the wisdom to distinguish the one from the other.

Many of us have a passing acquaintance with this prayer. However, if we are standing at the threshold of wanting to take right action to promote positive change, we must understand the message within this prayer at a visceral, rather than superficial level. In other words, we must learn how to instinctively and intuitively discern between actions that promote our intrinsic values and priorities, and those that do not; between choices that will move us closer to fulfillment and connection, and choices that will continue to keep us stuck in the same old, same old. There is only one action that promotes positive change -- and that is the right action that comes out of deliberate discernment.

The Wisdom of Discernment

Taking time to determine our next move before jumping right into it is the wise and prudent thing to do. Yet we women are accustomed to moving ahead quickly (and sometimes irrationally), and we don't always value or give a lot of attention to the discernment process. Now is the time we must do so. If we are presently ready to take action on our own behalf, we must first determine to the best of our ability whether or not the proposed action will promote fulfillment and connection, or simply lead into more of what has previously left us empty and depleted.

A good way to enter into our discernment process is by borrowing our Time Energy Awareness chart from the Second Solution on Balance. As we will recall, this is a very helpful tool for determining where our energy goes, and where it gets refilled. Caroline Myss, a medical intuitive, motivational speaker, and author, has been a ground breaker in this field of energy awareness. Based on years of research, she believes that our lives are comprised of energy transfers. In other words, every encounter we have involves some transfer of energy between the parties. These energy exchanges occur in relationships, working environments, places we live, and people with whom we reside. Myss explains it as being similar to plugging ourselves into an electrical socket. What we need to determine is this: are we plugging into a circuit that replenishes our energy, or simply drains it?

We would all agree that relationships and situations consume energy. However, there is a big difference between healthy and non-healthy uses of our energy. The healthy situations and relationships in our lives replace energy as well as consume it, by maintaining a somewhat equal distribution of give and take. This is great when it happens, but let's face it -- that is not always the case. As women, we have all experienced encounters that leave us totally fatigued. We intuitively know which people, places and situations exhaust us. If we were to be even minimally honest, we could probably list several individuals who sap our energy and enthusiasm rather than promote either. Still, we keep plugging into these people and situations, waiting for something or someone to change, thinking that this time it will be different. It is similar to trying to get a drink from a dry well, or going to a dead battery to get recharged. No wonder our zest for living has escaped us. It has been slowly discharging.

To guard against this phenomenon, prior to taking any kind of action, and in order to help us discern if action is, indeed, called for, it is important that we gather some information about our present energy transfers. Whether regarding a job, situation, or relationship, we can ask ourselves the following questions:

- Is there a healthy energy exchange of give and take in this relationship, job situation, life circumstance?
- Does this situation (person, job, place) emotionally exhaust me?
- Or do I get energized from it instead?

If we determine that, yes indeed, we are somehow being drained of our energy reserve, we need to investigate this dynamic a little more closely. Are we being drained because we have unrealistic expectations of how things should be? Are we giving our energy away when we don't really need to? Are we saying "yes" when we could be saying "no?" Could we remain in the relationship, job, or situation simply by making changes within our own behavior? These are important questions to consider.

In some cases, our motivation to move on may really be a very cleverly disguised excuse to run away. We might think it would be easier to make an outward change than to take responsibility for addressing our inner "stuff." Maybe the situation we're in or the people we're currently with challenge some unacknowledged pathology within us that requires looking at. Perhaps we just don't want to be held accountable. In order to get some clues about this, we might want to review our past history before taking action. Are we in the habit of moving on the moment the going gets tough? Are we running away from facing something within ourselves? It is always good to remember that the woman who gets on a bus in Boston is the same woman that gets off the bus in San Francisco. If we think we need to revisit some of our previous Solutions prior to taking action, we probably do.

On the other hand, if we feel certain this is the time to make some kind of move, and we have an idea what that would entail, our next step is to follow the good idea through. In other words, to really think about the total implications of what would be involved; sometimes the idea of something proves to be far more appealing that the actual reality. So we are wise to visualize *all aspects* of our potential changes, rather than fantasize certain parts of them; to really give consideration to what the challenges, concerns, and consequences of the actions might be. Granted, our next move may be one that stretches us, but we don't want to run the risk of over-reaching to such a point that we set ourselves up for certain failure, disappointment, or worse – the same old, same old cleverly disguised.

The more thorough we can be during this phase of our discernment, the better our chances of taking right action to promote positive change. We could even go one step further by taking pen in hand and listing some of the more negative possibilities of our projected next move, as well as the romanticized ones. For instance, if we are considering quitting our job to become a stay-at-home mom, we can list the benefits of spending more time with our children, while on the other side of the coin, give voice to the reality that staying home full-time with children can have its lonely and isolated moments. Or, if we are thinking about leaving our job to get rid of the wicked witch of a boss we have, we must also consider the possibility that we could get the same type of boss in a different setting -- unless, of course, we work for ourselves, and even that does not guarantee success.

All changes have some aspects that are stressful, challenging, or simply boring. If we follow the idea completely through *prior to making change*, we won't be taken so much by surprise. An additional benefit of following the idea through is that it gives us the opportunity to question whether or not our actions will ultimately compromise or even violate our deepest values and highest priorities. In fact, before making any decisions, we might want to answer the following questions:

- Is this action in alignment with my basic values?
- Will this action or change bring me closer to my personal dreams and desires?
- Will it help me become more of who I am?
- Will it contribute to my ability to maintain physical, emotional, or spiritual balance?
- Is this action a fear-based distraction, intended to cover up something about myself that I'm not willing to face?
- Might there be a reason that God has put me in this situation? Is there something I'm supposed to learn?
- Am I having trouble moving on because I'm waiting for something or somebody else to change?
- What would I be leaving behind if I chose to move on?
- What would I be taking with me?
- What price would I pay?
- What would I be giving up if I chose to stay put?

It might also be wise during this period of discernment to consider what impact, if any, our decisions and actions will have on those closest to us. If we are truly in touch with our intuitive and spiritual nature, we must remain sensitive to the concerns of others, taking their feelings into account before making changes that will affect them. It is not suggested that we sell our soul for anyone, or that we accept unacceptable behavior under any circumstances, but, whenever possible, we do need to look beyond our immediate gratification to determine if our decision is in the long-term best interest of all involved.

Another way to cultivate our discernment process is through our prayer and meditation practice. There is hardly anything else that will produce such prodigious results as this. All we need to do is to continue saying our prayers, asking for guidance, and then paying attention for the answers. In other words, we need to take periodic breaks from our daily and often frantic routines; to stop, look, listen, and learn from our newly resurrected *inner voice that knows the truth.*

The Wisdom of the Wait

Sometimes, the best action we can take is that of no action at all. In other words, we can wait. Even though waiting is not a concept with which we're particularly comfortable or familiar, there is a wisdom in the "wait" that can be found nowhere else. If what we are interested in is taking the next right action, it may be necessary for us to first take two giant steps backwards and hibernate for awhile before jumping into something new.

Perhaps we are at a point in our lives where it feels as if all the doors are shut tight, and we have no clear path on which to embark. This can create such anxiety and discomfort that we may want to take action just to move out of the spot we are in. *Anywhere* can seem preferable to the cold, dark hallway. Perhaps in the past we have left the hallway prematurely and paid the consequences for our folly. In fact, we may have even become so compulsive in our behavior that, once the snowball started rolling downhill, we tried to change everything else at the same time –our job, our marriage, our hairstyle, where we live. If we feel tempted to do this, we most certainly need to progress as slowly and thoughtfully as possible.

This might require changing our basic attitude about waiting. Instead of considering waiting as an unproductive waste of time, to think about it as giving us the time in which to ready and re-energize the vessel so that we will be more than prepared to go forward when action is called for. We might also want to change the way we go about waiting. We no longer need to hold our breath, clench our teeth, or whine, worry, and wonder while we wait. Neither do we have to stay passively glued to mindless television, sleep fifteen hours a day, or medicate ourselves with alcohol, eating, shopping, or some other drug! We have Solutions today!

If we are currently in a period of the discerning wait, there are certain steps we can take to empower ourselves while we're here. Even though we may not have a clue what to do next or with whom to do it, we can use this time productively by taking care of routine business. For example, we could go back to our Second Solution and work more diligently at putting the suggestions for Balance into action. We definitely need to remember that *every situation is improved by self-care.* It is a practical matter to treat ourselves gently, patiently, and lovingly as we wait. This means getting enough rest, eating healthfully, staying current with our exercise program, remaining connected with our friends, and, of course, saying our prayers.

The period of waiting is also a great time to take care of the more mundane aspects of living. We can get that yearly physical we've been putting off, have our mammogram, get our teeth cleaned, sort through our clothes, organize our file cabinets, or begin a new exercise program. If we want to de-clutter our mind, we can begin by de-cluttering our house, getting rid of the many belongings that threaten to suffocate us. After all, we don't want a bunch of stuff interfering with our next right action!

Most importantly, we can choose to assign *value* to the process of waiting. Any woman who is growing along spiritual lines knows that waiting is an integral part of any authentic growth process.

Waiting gives us the benefit of time so that we can make decisions in deliberate and adult ways, rather than in an adolescent, knee-jerk fashion. Wise women take comfort in the truisms: *Everything takes as long as it takes; Good things come to those who wait; Anything worth having is worth waiting for.* Let us not minimize the fact that waiting helps prepare us for the next chapter of our lives by giving us a grace period in which to determine our next right action.

When Julie moved to a new city with her husband and two sons, she left everything familiar behind, including her family of origin, her community, good friends, and her job. Yet she was excited about the move. The career change was a great one for her husband, and her children would be attending an excellent school.

Upon arriving, everyone in the family had a place where they naturally fit; everyone except her. After she finished the major job of reorganizing a new house, hanging the curtains and pictures, and unpacking the many belongings, she wasn't sure what to do next. Where did she belong? Sure, she was Darren's wife, Ben and Paul's mother. But who was *she,* and what fulfilled *her*?

In order to move quickly out of her discomfort and insecurity, Julie was tempted to apply for a job in the same field she had been in before. There were several such jobs advertised locally, and her references made her an excellent candidate for many of them. Still, her deeper truth knew that even though this would temporary fill the void, this work no longer gratified or fulfilled her. Actually, it hadn't done either for a long time.

During the first few months following her arrival in this new community, Julie was approached frequently to join various clubs and groups such as the garden club, the woman's club, and the library. Although membership in these community organizations would certainly keep her busily distracted from the void she felt inside, Julie was a wise woman, one who had been working hard at developing personal insight and deepening her spirituality. Because of this, even though she felt anxious with the not-knowing, she was aware of the danger of taking on something new just to get out of the discomfort. She had no desire to consume her time with busyness, but wanted to fill it with work and play that suited her soul and gave meaning to her life.

Her answers did not come immediately. In fact, they required several months of living in the "divine discomfort." In retrospect, Julie claims that this was some of the most valuable time she has ever spent. Living in the wait allowed her the opportunity to really develop a vision for what she truly wanted to do. In this case, it involved designing and crafting hand-made jewelry, something she had always dreamed of. Julie's decision to stay in the hallway for as long as was necessary is the reason she is currently doing the work for which she was born. Her pieces are displayed and sold all over the country.

Although waiting may initially feel like a big waste of time, we must be patient with it and with ourselves during this period. After all, we are working to grow spiritually, and a woman who is in touch with her spiritual nature is also in tune with the rhythms, cycles, and seasons of life. She recognizes that the wait is an integral and vital part of the whole of creation. Even the human breath has a period of wait. We breathe in; we breathe out. And for just a moment in-between, we pause. We wait.

The oceans do the same. World round, the tide comes in, the tide goes out, but in-between, for just a second, the sea remains quiet while it waits. And every woman knows that during the seemingly unproductive winter months, a tree's roots are storing up energy in order to bloom at a later date. The good news is, this dormant phase is only temporary. If we can enter into it with a spirit of willingness, and allow it to take as long as it takes, it will be the some of the most productive time we have ever spent.

When life calls upon us to wait, we wait. Not with dreaded apprehension, but with hopeful expectation. Our willingness to do this will be the key that will eventually unlock the right door for us, the door into *right action for positive change.*

Eight Steps for Right Action

The following eight steps can be applied to any right action we might need to take in order to promote positive change. Whether targeting a troublesome behavior, making a radical shift, modifying an existing situation, moving on from something that no longer fulfills us (and perhaps never did), or embarking upon a lifelong dream, these steps will work for us if we work them.

Step 1. Visualize our Dreams/Goals/Ideas

The first step in taking right action is to have a vision of what we hope to accomplish. Whether it involves making a career change, leaving a marriage, going to college, moving to the country, getting sober, becoming an artist, finding a new mate, adopting a child, buying a house, fixing one up, giving up smoking, obtaining a master's degree, learning to play the violin, losing twenty pounds, or writing a screenplay, the only way to begin is by having a clear vision of our goal. In other words, to mentally picture the changes we would like our actions to bring about.

Many of us, however, have never really developed the art of envisioning ourselves doing something outside our normal realm of possibility. Suffering from vision-deprivation, we may have difficulty imagining ourselves doing anything that seems out of character or involves stretching. In fact, when Martha's therapist asked her what she wanted to do in her life, she responded with, "I don't know."

"Well, who should I ask?" he countered.

If this is our case, we might want to explore ways to pay more attention to what our inner spirit/voice has to suggest. After all, the answers for fulfillment and contentment are inside all of us if we would listen to them. We have been given tools to do this throughout the previous chapters: prayer, meditation, reflection, and contemplation are all guaranteed to bring our unconscious desires to the surface. Even when we're tempted to think of these as a waste of our time, we do them anyway. Because the more disciplined we become in matters of the spirit, the greater our chances of having visions for future goals that are in keeping with our basic values and priorities.

If in doubt about what the next right thing to do might be, we can put the question out to God before we go to sleep at night; to ask God to show us what kind of positive action we need to take at this point in our lives. At the same time, we need to be willing to listen for God's answers. These answers come from many places – from the people put in our path, through opportunities that "coincidently" present themselves, and even through the doors that close tightly behind us.

Answers to our dilemma of what to do next can also be accessed through the medium of dreams. Carl Jung was famous for his work regarding the collective unconscious and the psychology of dreams. Any Jungian therapist would agree that when our psyche/soul realizes that we are paying attention to its wisdom, we tend to dream more frequently and vividly. Once our spirit knows that we are listening at all, it will find ways in which to communicate. Even those of us who don't think we dream, or can't remember their content, can develop the habit of early morning reflection and writing. All we need is a journal and a willingness to be open to the experience; a willingness to get up a little earlier, sit with blank pages in front of us, or to just write anything in order to get in the daily habit of showing up to the page. If we do this consistently, it will amaze us how much truth will surface among the scribbling. It is kind of like sifting for gold; every now and then we will find a nugget of pure wisdom in the midst of all the sand. This early morning writing has more potential to reveal things about ourselves and our dreams and desires than almost anything else we could undertake.

However, if we are really at a crossroads of indecision and confusion and haven't a clue what to do next in our lives, we might want to enlist the help of a professional. Jungian therapists are great resources for helping us get in touch with our unconscious self. Hiring a personal life coach is also a great idea during times of indecision. Coaches are skilled in helping us identify our values, consider various options, and find ways to stimulate our envisioning process. In some cases, identifying what we *don't* want is the first step to eventually discovering what we do.

Step 2. Set an Objective

Once we have an idea of the positive action we want to take – and remember, this can be the action to leave something just as much as to take on something new-- our next step is to set an objective. In other words, we need to be precise and clear regarding what we wish to accomplish. One way to help facilitate this is by writing a "statement of intention." This is a sentence that specifically addresses the "what" and "why" of our goal/idea. For instance: I want to give up smoking because it makes me feel bad about who I am; I want to get my master's degree because it will give me the credentials I need for moving into a higher position within my company; I want to get out of this job (relationship, committee, position) because it is draining the life-blood out of me. Even when we don't necessarily know where we're going next, we can still take the positive action of leaving or changing the status quo.

This was true for Paula. For fourteen years, she had tolerated the long trek from her Chicago suburb into the city. During this period, she had two children. As time went by, she felt more and more that she was missing out on the most important thing of all: being home with her son and daughter, ages eight and ten respectively. She was also tremendously dissatisfied with her current job. Although the benefits and salary were excellent, every day she felt like she was selling her soul just a little bit more.

It was definitely the time to make a change, so in January of that year, after talking it over with her husband, she set an objective of leaving her job before summer. She immediately felt better just by making that decision to leave! At the same time, however, she was filled with doubt and confusion. What would it involve to actually say goodbye to everybody? How would her boss take it? What would be the impact on the family's finances? Even though her husband made a good salary, they had become accustomed to a rather high standard of living. Was she willing to compromise this? Another consideration was the fact that she normally spent one night a week in the city with friends. Was she prepared to give that up? Would she be better off to find a part-time position within the firm, something that piqued her interest? That way, she would still have an income yet be able to spend more time at home. The more Paula thought about it, the more she realized that she needed to do some homework before she could begin to set an objective.

Step 3. Do the Homework and Outline a Game Plan

Basically, when considering any change, it behooves us to become students, fact-finders, and data collectors, the nature of which will depend entirely upon what our particular change/shift/move involves. We might need to seek advice from those who have traveled down the same path, research the internet, speak to a realtor, become clear regarding the financial implications, check licensing/credential requirements, find out when and where meetings are held, go to the Small Business Administration, join a group, or speak with the Human Resources Department at our organization. The more informed we become at this stage of the game, the more empowered we will be to make our desired change.

Not having a clear objective in mind, and in an attempt to get some clarity about her next move, Paula began by devising the following game plan:

- talk with husband around question of finances
- write a list of personal interests
- write down goals/accomplishments
- speak with the company's Human Resources Department
- find out about the policy and availability of part-time positions
- buy a notebook for networking contact information
- begin telling key people about desire to make a change
- network within company; maintain visibility at functions, workshops, or meetings of anything that is of interest
- follow up all leads, no matter how out of character they may seem

She also found it helpful to put this list in order of importance: what needs to be done first, second, third, and so forth. At the same time, knowing her propensity for procrastination, she determined a reasonable date for each task to be completed and wrote it alongside the goal. Staying true to this time line became very important for her in achieving these objectives. It was a form of self-accountability that also provided the opportunity for regular completions, a vital component for staying true to any plan of action.

Doing our homework and coming up with a game plan are crucial undertakings for bringing our dreams and goals into the light of day. When developing our game plan, we might want to consider the following questions:

- What will the change/idea/move involve?
- How much time?
- How much money?
- Do I need additional education?
- Does it require a new computer or other tools/equipment?
- Does it involve networking or researching?
- Should I join a support or professional group?

Making a game plan that encompasses these questions will help us counteract the old familiar bogeymen of fear, procrastination, and feeling overwhelmed. Provided we make the tasks within our game plan manageable and right-sized, we set ourselves up for success, rather than failure.

We also need to create the time and space for our goals and dreams to come true. As mentioned in our Second Solution, if our days are packed solid, there is no extra room for new possibilities. Once we determine how much time and energy it might require to put our goals/dreams/changes into action, we must make the corresponding adjustments in our schedules. In other words, we must be willing to let go of something old in order to make room for something new and different.

Step 4. Develop a Support System

It is a spiritual principle that *"we" can do what "I" cannot.* The degree to which we become empowered to carry our ideas into actual change will depend a lot on who is supporting us. Whether our goals are big or small, behavior-modifying or radically life-changing, we need and deserve to have our own cheerleaders. We also need to be intentional and deliberate in our asking for their help. This often means stretching – once again – to overcome our reluctance and actually ask somebody to be part of our support team. Just as we learned during our chapter on Healing, we need to let them know right up front what we need.

This is the way in which Meagan approached some of her closest friends when she needed support to bring a dream to fruition: "After years of saying I was going to, I've finally decided to put my best poetry and photographs together in a book. But I know myself. I procrastinate, I get overwhelmed, I discount the quality of my work, and I never follow through on my good intentions. Yet this is something I really want to do so I'm trying to find ways to stay true to my dream and not give up the moment it gets tough. I know this is a big thing to ask of you, but can you be there for me, even at the times I find it difficult to be there for myself? It's perfectly okay if you say no, but if you say yes, then I'm going to be counting on you. This might mean that I need to call you up, sometimes maybe every day. I might ask you to look the book over at certain times and give me your honest opinion. But mostly, I need you to remind me that this is something I have always wanted to do, and that I'm capable of doing it. "

Once we've enlisted the help, it is up to us to use it. That is, provided we really want to do what we say we want to do -- take right action to promote positive change. It might help us to remember, once again, that most women love to be of service. We are doing a friend a favor by asking her to show up for us on occasion. And if by chance we don't have the people we need in our lives right now, all we have to do is ask God for them. After all, it is said that "if you pray for elephants, you'd better have a big backyard."

Step 5. Put in Today's Effort

It is also said that, "If you pray for potatoes, you'd better pick up the hoe!" Fortunately, the great news about taking any right action is that we only have to put effort into it *today*. A house is built one brick at a time, a book is written one page at a time, a relationship is dissolved or deepened one moment at a time. Think about it. If we had to pick up a board that was 365 feet long, we'd give up before we started. But if we cut the same board into one foot sections, it is an easy matter to pick up the pieces one at a time.

Keeping our effort in the day is what makes all positive change possible. Yet, even though it is only one day at a time, we still have to do the work of today. This means suiting up and showing up regardless of how we feel or whether or not we even want to. *Taking right action to create positive change doesn't always feel right!* This is especially true when the action we are taking is new and unfamiliar. The fact is, it may even feel wrong, like we must not be doing it right. *Taking right action to create positive change doesn't always feel easy!* Sometimes, it just feels downright difficult. There are days when we want to do anything else but show up for our lives; days when our dreams and desires seem to be little more than that; times when our best-laid plans seems ridiculous or impossibly hard. These are the times we must keep trudging regardless of our fears, doubts, or resistance; to act "as if" we can reach our goals even when we are convinced that we can't. It really helps during these times of "action angst" to go back and revisit our initial visualization; to remind ourselves exactly what we hoped to accomplish and why we're doing this in the first place. It is very easy to lose sight of the larger picture when we get bogged down in the daily details of making change or achieving specific goals, so we take active steps to counteract this. At the same time, we remind ourselves that we are only responsible for the effort; the outcome will take care of itself.

Step 6. Maintain Accountability

There is a big difference between *talking* about right action and *taking* it. This is where accountability comes into play. Accountability is like personal insurance to protect ourselves against procrastination, indifference, losing sight of our vision, and taking our eye off the ball. The accountability factor is often what determines whether a woman will achieve her goals and dreams, or leave them behind in the stockpile of other never-to-be-realized good ideas and great intentions. When we fail to make ourselves accountable, the very best of plans fall by the wayside. To paraphrase John Greenleaf Whittier, "The saddest words of tongue and pen are these four words, *what might have been*."

Knowing that accountability is the key to making positive change is only the beginning. We must also take the appropriate action to set ourselves up for success. One way is by hiring a personal life coach to help us stay true and accountable to our own ideas. In fact, the accountability factor of the coaching relationship is one reason it is so effective in promoting positive change. A personal coach helps an individual develop an action plan in keeping with her dreams/goals/ideas, commit to doing x, y, and z, and then holds her responsible on a weekly basis for having completed the agreed upon tasks. A personal coach listens, supports, encourages, makes suggestions, and always maintains curiosity about the client and her process.

Personal coaches are not the only professionals we might consider hiring at this time. If our desired action is related to career issues, we might want to employ the services of a career management counselor, or someone with a marketing background to help us in setting reasonable goals.

In some cases, we might enlist the help of one or more of our closest friends, explaining what our goals are and asking for permission to "check in" periodically regarding our progress. Perhaps a group membership could help. One of the primary reasons for the success rate of 12-step recovery programs is the accountability factor through sponsorship and regular attendance at meetings. The reason Weight Watchers is so effective is because members are responsible for weighing in each week.

There are other ways we can stay accountable to ourselves, especially regarding some of our smaller changes such as those needed to support our balance and spiritual growth (which, of course, in turn support our ability to make the bigger changes). We can learn to write things down, make notations on a calendar, or use gold stars to mark our successes. Jane puts a big red X on her calendar every time that she meditates. Maureen writes down every morsel of food that goes into her month. Ginny marks the days she exercises in her monthly planner with a purple heart. All of these things not only serve to maintain our good intentions, but reinforce our commitment to our larger goals.

Step 7. Stay Vigilant for Self-Sabotage

For some strange reason, when we are the closest to realizing our dreams and goals, we are also the most likely to sabotage ourselves and our progress. We must guard against this.

The more common ways that we self-sabotage is by allowing ourselves to get completely out of balance, and by failing to keep our spiritual consciousness as a priority. Letting either one of these slip by the wayside deeply compromises our ability to move forward successfully. We must never forget that balance and spiritual consciousness provide the strong foundation on which positive changes are more likely to be made.

Another common pitfall to be aware of, especially when on the cusp of making a pivotal move, is a resurgence of self-defeating thought-talk. All it takes is a whiff of success to cause many of our inner committee members (remember them?) to increase their efforts to detain, deter, or discourage us. This is our fear speaking, *again.* Terrified of any change, even positive ones, our inner dialogue attempts to maintain the status quo by overwhelming us with its self-limiting message of, "I can't."

"I can't do this. I don't have enough experience, education, guts, talent. I'm not smart enough, disciplined enough, strong enough. I'm too confused, indecisive, unsure, over-sensitive, overwhelmed. I've always been this way. What makes me think I can change now? This is more than I can handle. I'm not ready. I'll do it later. It's too big a risk. I don't know the right people. What the heck was I thinking, anyway?"

This is the voice of self-sabotage, and even though we've been working on this throughout these chapters, our negative inner voice tends to become louder and more noticeable when we are on the verge of making a pivotal, positive, or radical change. Rather than encourage our efforts, this inner voice fills us with nagging doubts, causing us to procrastinate, or to not even take the first step to begin with. In cases where we are already in a positive process, this is the voice that entices us to give up before the miracle happens, the project is finished, or the way is clear.

Regardless of these convincing undertones of self-defeat, we still don't need to give this inner dialogue the power to dictate what we do or don't do. Instead, we can face it head on by recognizing it for what it truly is: self sabotage in the form of *fear* -- fear of change, fear of inadequacy, fear of the unknown, fear of failure, and even fear of success! As we have discussed before, the only way to overcome or manage our fears is to get them out of the shadows, hold them up to the light, look them squarely in the face, and then do what we need to do in spite of them. In other words, we tell our inner fear, doubt, and insecurity, *"I hear you loud and clear, but I'm a woman in transition and you're no longer calling the shots."*

Another form of self-sabotage that raises its ugly head when we're in the midst of making positive change is our extreme susceptibility to falling back again into the same-old, same-olds. These same olds don't simply apply to our same old fears and doubts, but they also include the same-old boyfriends, old habits, and old behaviors. Insidious and subtle, these same-olds in their many forms seem to come out of nowhere to curtail our progress. Regardless of their nature, they share one thing in common: they attempt to lure us back into fear-based distractions, dysfunctions, or turmoil, usually at a time when we are just beginning to make some significant changes in our lives or lifestyles.

Whether our self-sabotage comes in the form of a person, situation, or nagging doubt, the only way to counteract it is to cut it off at the pass. In other words, our best defense is a good offense. This means we must stay vigilant for the re-emergence of these same-olds *in all their many forms* and refuse to give them power.

How do we do this? The answer is the same one we've been using throughout this text. We don't have to figure anything out, and we don't have to struggle to get freed from these same old- same olds. What we do instead is to simply shift our focus. We take our attention off of what threatens to distract us, and put it instead on where we are or where we wish to go. Instead of giving our attention to the fear, the negative behavior, or the old boyfriend, we put our attention on our original intention and stay vigilant to keeping it there. No struggle, no wrestling match – just a shift in focus.

Step 8. Keep our "Attention" on the "Intention"

One of our biggest setbacks to making significant changes in our lives is the fact that we go back to sleep so easily. Our great ideas and good intentions all too often get put to the side, displaced by the distractions of everyday life. Keeping our "attention on the intention" is one way to stay awake so that we don't get sidetracked from achieving the desires of our heart. There are several ways we can do this:

- By making a daily renewal of our commitment to whatever plan of action we are working to carry out.
- By writing our intentions down each morning and posting them in a visible place so that we can remain *conscious* of what we are striving to do and why. For instance, we could write our statement of purpose and post it on our refrigerator door or on the top of our computer.
- By putting our intentions on a piece of paper and carrying them in our pocket, taking them out and looking them over periodically to remind ourselves to stay on task.
- To make a daily list of things to do that will help bring our goals/dreams one step closer to actualization.
- At the close of every day, to take an inventory on how well we have stayed faithful to our commitment/intention.

Whenever life threatens to deter or distract us from what we have determined to be the right course of action for us, we simply bring our focus back to what we need to do *today* in order to accomplish our long-term goal or objective. Provided we keep our eye on the road ahead, on our own light, on our own intention, and calmly and steadily walk towards it, our right action will continue to promote positive change. It can be no other way.

How it Works

After three years of living with Ken, and *two* cancelled wedding days, Wendy knew it was time she chirped or got off the twig. Despite her supreme efforts to "make it happen," it was obvious that this relationship was not going to culminate in the marriage she had hoped for. Ken was simply incapable of making the commitment. So, after several months of living in the push-pull of emotional turmoil, Wendy knew the status quo had to change; she had been too miserable for far too long. Fortunately, her pain was so great that she began asking herself some very honest questions. Why was she willing to put up with this? After all, she was thirty-eight years old. She wanted to be married. She wanted to have children. And she didn't have another three years to give to a relationship that obviously wasn't going anywhere. So she began to *visualize* what she would ideally like to see happen in her life. This vision included a loving and available partner as well as babies.

It was obvious that she had to make a decision and, although the thought of leaving Ken seemed next to impossible, there eventually came a day when the pain of staying far outweighed the thought of going. It was following another hurtful incident in which Wendy once again felt abandoned and unloved, that she had her moment of truth: this was not what she wanted.

Her decision to leave the relationship presented several difficulties. For one, Wendy presently lived with Ken in a house that he owned. She had also recently quit her job to become a freelancer in her consulting business which was still in the early stages of development. Overwhelmed with what to do next and how to go about it, Wendy increased her chances for a successful, smooth transition by utilizing the services of a life coach. Together, they came up with a *statement of intent.* For Wendy, this included getting her own apartment and becoming financially independent. Next, they *outlined a game plan,* making a list of the specific steps she would have to take to get from here to there. Wendy's initial list looked like this:

Talk with Ken about her intention
Find an apartment
Buy necessary furniture and household items
Ask her father for a loan to cover the security deposit
Take stock of finances: assess financial obligations/income
Develop ways to increase her business visibility and revenues
Stay physically balanced throughout the process
Remain faithful to her practice of prayer and meditation

After writing these steps down, and knowing her tendency to procrastinate, Wendy put an approximate date beside those tasks that required it. Because the most difficult part of this plan was, of course, speaking with Ken, she made that the number one priority, giving herself only a week to accomplish this. She also felt certain that it would take a fair amount of time to find the appropriate apartment, so she needed to talk with Ken about this as well. Although naturally very upset at her decision to leave, he agreed to let her stay for as long as was necessary. This took the immediate pressure off Wendy.

Her next step was to *do her homework.* This included taking stock of her financial situation, an area in which Wendy always felt inadequate. She knew two truths about herself regarding finances: she spent much more than she needed to, and with a little effort, she could make more than she currently did. So, with the help of her coach, she made a game plan of how to make those changes happen. For her, this included a commitment to write down everything she spent on a daily basis for a month, just to get an idea of where her money went and how much she actually spent. At the same time, she hired an accountant to help obtain a realistic financial picture of her business. The good news was, things were actually better than she had thought.

Next, she put in the legwork of finding a suitable apartment. Safety and cost were her primary considerations, but she also wanted a place that reflected who she was. After determining what general location would work for her, she visited local real estate agencies, spoke with friends, looked in the papers, and researched the internet for apartments in her price range in that area. At the same time, she began working with the Small Business Administration and other professionals to find ways to promote and increase her business visibility.

Because Wendy already had many close friends, she didn't need to *develop a support system.* What she did do, though, was to make a point of informing those closest to her of her decision. Many of them had personally witnessed her struggles in this relationship over the years, and they affirmed and encouraged her in making this move.

Next, Wendy had to *put in today's effort.* This was not initially that easy. The decision to leave had been so traumatic that it made putting one foot in front of the other very difficult. Yet with the help of her friends, Wendy did what she needed to: she looked at apartments; went to yard sales for furniture; and packed up boxes, even though her heart wasn't always in it. Being responsible for reporting her weekly progress to her life coach was of immeasurable help in her *maintaining accountability* during this time of heightened vulnerability, insecurity, and depression.

Of course, it was when she found the "ideal" apartment that Ken tried to convince her to stay even though he confessed to still feeling incapable of committing to marriage. As tempted as Wendy was, she knew at this point that she needed to *remain vigilant for self-sabotage.* After all, if nothing changes, nothing changes. And nothing had changed.

Oddly enough, it was during this time of emotional upheaval that Wendy had a most profound dream. In this dream, she was driving down a wide open highway, feeling great. She loved the car she was in, and knew that the road she was on was the right one for her. After awhile, however, she became increasingly aware of a car following closely behind her. As she peered in the rear-view mirror, she thought the faces looked familiar. Did they need her for something, she wondered? Were they following her for a reason?

As she continued down the road, the car continued to follow. Slowly but steadily, she became more and more obsessed with its occupants. Who were those people in the car? What were they doing? Why were they following her? Little by little, her curiosity and attention began to shift from the road in front of her to the car in back of her. Eventually, she became so fully engrossed looking in the rearview mirror that she took her eyes completely off the road ahead. When she did this, she missed a pivotal turn, one which would have brought her to her desired destination.

This dream woke Wendy up to the realization that she had spent a lifetime doing one of two things: either putting a great deal of her attention in the wrong direction - on the road behind, the one of "no longer an option" - or going so fast through life that she failed to notice the many opportunities she had to change direction, opportunities to turn off the main road and take a less traveled road to authenticity and joy.

Motivated by the message behind this dream, Wendy redoubled her efforts at keeping her *attention on the intention.* Each time she felt tempted to fall back into the old longing, disappointment, and heartbreak, she made a conscious effort to shift her focus, hold her head high, and look straight ahead. By focusing on the road in front of her, Wendy dramatically increased her potential for encountering a multitude of marvelous prospects for her future. This is how positive change is made: by taking right action no matter what.

Dream Big

Many of us women have grown up learning to color within the lines and think within the box. Along the way, we have somehow absorbed the tendency to keep our expectations unrealistically high (and therefore unattainable) or amazing low. Either way, rather than give ourselves permission to pay attention to the value contained within our dreams and desires, we continue to find reasons to discount or deny how very much potential each one of us truly has.

Even when we do pay attention to our innermost hopes, our negative thinking often jumps in, trying to sabotage and prevent us from taking the necessary steps for making our dreams become our reality. We desire to write a book and then complain that everybody else has written what we wanted to write about. We desperately want to change careers but are terrified of giving up the security and benefits of the status quo. We want to move out of relationships that are no longer fulfilling, or in some cases, that are actually harmful, but we convince ourselves that bad breath is better than no breath. We want to go to college, but think we're too old or not smart enough to do so. We want to change the world in some small way, but do nothing because, after all, what can one person do?

The truth is, we each have our own particular set of gifts. Our challenge is to take actions that are in accordance with these gifts – to claim our gifts -- to celebrate them -- to live them. To ask ourselves, "What makes my heart glad?" and then to do the next right thing. If we take responsibility for the effort, we can be assured that God will take care of the outcome. Even if the results aren't what we expected, they will be the right ones if we continue to do our part by remaining balanced and staying spiritually connected.

There is a definite ripple effect of right action. When we bring new life to ourselves, it can't help but spill out over the world. Rather than continue with small aspirations or look for reasons why our dreams can't come true, we must begin to dream BIG -- and then step forward to take the right action to manifest our hopes and desires.

It might help for us to reflect upon these words written by the wonderful and gifted Marianne Williamson in her book, *A Return to Love:*

Our deepest fear is not that we are inadequate. Our deepest fear is that we are powerful beyond measure. It is our light, not our darkness which frightens us. We ask ourselves, who am I to be brilliant, gorgeous, talented and fabulous? Actually, who are you not to be? You are a child of God. Your playing small doesn't serve the world. There's nothing enlightened about shrinking so that other people won't feel insecure around you. We were born to manifest the glory of God within us. It's not just in some of us; it's in everyone. And as we let our own light shine, we unconsciously give other people permission to do the same. As we are liberated from our own fear, our presence automatically liberates others.

Suggestions for Taking Right Action

1. Are you having difficulty discerning what to do next? If so, prior to doing anything, examine the condition of your physical balance and spiritual connection. If necessary, go back and follow the suggestions of some of the previous chapters.

2. Consider that your life force is pure energy and take an inventory of the current energy exchanges in your life. Examine any relationships, jobs, or situations that consistently deplete your energy and enthusiasm. Think of some that add to your energy supply.

3. Are you presently in a period of "wait?" If so, find ways to make yourself comfortable during this time. Are there things you could be doing that you have put off for a rainy day? Use this time to do them gently and lovingly.

4. Do you habitually fail to follow through on your good ideas and intentions? Is lack of accountability a factor? If so, make yourself accountable to a life coach, a friend, or a specific group. Develop ways to maintain self-accountability.

5. Choose an area in which you feel ready to make a change. Write a statement of intention. Apply the eight steps for right action to this change. Remind yourself that you only have to put in today's effort.

6. Who supports your efforts for positive change? Look around to see who might be added to this list. Ask God for what you need in this area.

7. Go back and reread the words of Marianne Williamson on the previous page. Write them in your journal. Read them everyday until you believe them. Dare to dream big.

Visualization Meditation

Schedule an uninterrupted hour with yourself, making sure it is free of all possible distractions. Invite your Higher Power into this time and space. Use your breathing exercises or a meditation tape to quiet your mind and your body.

Once you feel calm and centered, imagine yourself one year from today. Where would you like to be in your life? What would you like to have accomplished? How do you want to look? To feel?

Picture your future physical health. Do you see a woman who is strong, vital, and healthy? What would it take to become this woman? Take a few moments to visualize yourself as healthy and whole.

Now imagine your future emotional self. Do you see a woman who people enjoy being around? A woman who is responsive rather than reactive? Positive instead of negative? Joyful rather than depressed? Spend a few moments visualizing yourself as emotionally balanced and serene.

In your imagination, one year from today, what do the relationships in your life look like? Are there people you would like to have in your life that you don't have now? Are there ones that you would rather be rid of? Visualize yourself with the relationships that you would wish for.

Where would you like to be in terms of your professional or creative self one year from now? Are there goals you would like to accomplish? Visualize what it would look like to have accomplished them.

If you can visualize it, it can happen. So dream big.

The Eighth Solution:
Live Consciously

Underlying Principle: Life is not about getting there, but about experiencing the joy in the journey.

We women have become so caught up in the momentum of our lives that we have lost our awareness of the moment. In our attempts to accomplish more, we miss out on the simplicity and serenity of less. In our quest to have it all, we end up empty. Mistakenly believing that life is about getting there, we fail to realize that we've already arrived. The Eighth Solution helps us bridge the gap between what appears to be important, and what really is. By showing us ways to stay awake, it provides the means for our lives to continue evolving along the underlying principles we have encountered thus far, and the spiritual truths that they promote. Learning to live consciously allows us to do more than simply endure or cope with our life's changes and crises; it enables us to weave both the difficult and the divine into the core and substance of who we really are. By making a decision to walk through life with our eyes wide open, we become empowered to fully embrace every dimension of our lives -- the reality of the known, the uncertainty of the unknown, and the marvelous mystery of the Unknowable.

With the First Solution, we began our pilgrimage through crisis and change by making a decision to accept ourselves under any and all circumstances. In the past, self-acceptance was a concept that created difficulty, primarily because we placed too much importance on how things looked, and consequently felt "less-than" when our unrealistic expectations or desires didn't materialize. Often, we were motivated by an insidious pursuit of perfection or immobilized by the opposite extreme of, "Who cares anyway?" Neither way promoted a healthy self-image.

We no longer need to travel down that difficult road. We have discovered a new path simply by our willingness to make a decision to accept ourselves *just as we are in this moment.* This, we have found, is our first giant step toward self-actualization, wholeness, and authentic change.

Our Second Solution highlighted the importance of maintaining personal balance in our daily lives. Despite all previous excuses for not taking care of ourselves, we now realize that lack of balance never contributes to a positive outcome. In fact, it usually carries a hefty price tag. Generally speaking, this can include feeling fragmented, unfulfilled, and anxious. Being out of balance also causes us to lose touch with our own true nature and to the incredible potential we carry within. However, the good news is, not only is every situation improved as we incorporate balance into our lives, but we also become empowered in the process, able to feel better about ourselves regardless of what's happening.

The Third Solution was undoubtedly our most challenging. By endorsing a spiritual approach to life, this chapter asked us to make a radical shift in our everyday, earth-bound consciousness. It gave us permission to dwell in the realm of possibilities and encouraged us to expand or reconsider our previous concepts of spirituality. In addition, this Third Solution offered specific guidelines for developing a living relationship with a Power Greater than ourselves, a partnership that works under any and all conditions, crises, or changes. If we have followed this chapter's lead, then we have experienced the freedom that is a direct result of coming to trust that the Higher Power is in charge. By getting out of God's chair, we no longer need to exhaust ourselves with anxiety and effort trying to make things happen. We can loosen our fear-based grip on that which we have previously struggled to control, and be confident in the outcome. Our fears can be kept in perspective, allowing us to live with comfort and hopefulness in the uncertainty of, "It remains to be seen."

Our Fourth Solution involved letting go. Rather than focus on the obvious sources of people, places, and things in which we undoubtedly need to make changes, this chapter gave us tools to look beneath the surface in order to engage in some much overdue emotional house-cleaning. It encouraged us to be curious rather than critical, as we explored the little acknowledged inner areas of our unrealistic illusions, energy-draining worries and fears, poisonous resentments and anger, and esteem-corroding guilt and shame. This Solution not only made it clear *why* we need to let go of these negative emotions, but also showed us *how.*

We next moved into the Fifth Solution, where our self-knowledge and awareness continued to deepen as we identified ourselves as members of the walking wounded. Some of us have unconsciously spent far too much energy trying to outrun, outwit, or ignore the fact that we have needed deep emotional healing. This chapter emphasized that healing is necessary for growth; it is a prerequisite to conscious living. And although we are powerless over the inevitability of future heartache, we now have permission, tools, and support for walking through today's sorrow while resolving any unhealed pain of yesterday.

Our Sixth Solution highlighted the more troublesome behavioral and emotional ruts to which we tend to fall victim, especially during a period of upset or transition. Stressing the fact that *what we don't know about ourselves can and does harm us,* this chapter helped us pinpoint the negative thoughts, behaviors, and attitudes that have hitherto kept us stuck in fear-based distractions and/or high anxiety. Through stories and examples, we were encouraged to listen to our own inner voice, and to pay attention to the glimpses that reveal the truth. Even though it was painful to identify things about ourselves that need changing, this awareness was our first giant step out of our denial and into the solution.

The Seventh Solution continued our progress by showing us how to take right action to promote positive change. By teaching us the wisdom of discernment, and then outlining eight specific steps for moving into right action, this chapter empowered us to suit up and show up for our lives, even to make changes that don't come easily. By learning to put one foot in front of the other in any and all conditions, we have been able to experience the satisfaction and fulfillment of having our dreams and goals materialize.

Together, these Solutions have guided, and will continue to guide us through all of our crises and changes. They have offered practical tools for coping successfully with the immediate stresses of our critical or transitional period, while providing a blueprint for growing along spiritual lines. If we have followed the suggestions as laid out, chances are that we have made an organic shift, getting over our *false* sense of selves in order to discover and love our own *true* selves. This transformation has involved moving out of our fear-based complacency into a stronger conviction of our own competency and self-worth, and then going one step further into a consciousness of, and dependency upon, a Power Greater than ourselves. What a journey this has been! If we were to graph our inner movement, it would look like this:

This organic shift has reunited us with that essential spiritual part of ourselves that we misplaced so long ago. In this reunion, an amazing thing has taken place. We have developed a whole new attitude about, and understanding of, what is *really* important. We have recovered our spiritual intuition, and our behaviors, attitudes, and choices are beginning to reflect this. We have come to viscerally understand that:

- Self-acceptance is the first positive step through crisis and change.
- Every situation is improved by self-care.
- A Spiritual Connection is our greatest resource.
- To embrace the new, we must let go of the old.
- Healing is essential for wholeness.
- We all have an inner voice that knows the truth.
- Right action promotes positive change.

These are the underlying principles that will continue to support and encourage our journeys. We will never master them completely, yet it is almost impossible to go back from whence we came. Even if we try to re-immerse our head in the sand or fall back into our old ruts, we'll never be able to do it with the same degree of oblivion as before. We have awakened. We are becoming increasingly authentic. We are learning to live our lives fully, deliberately, and radically alive. Consequently, we are realizing more and more that *life is not about getting there, but about experiencing the joy in the journey.*

The Simplicity of Less

Conscious living requires a willingness to pay attention to the details and the moments of our lives as they unfold. Consciousness insists that we keep our eyes wide open so as not to miss the multitude of opportunities that present themselves. It also implores us to keep our heart open wide so that it may become full of compassion and love for ourselves, while helping us to be fully available to the various people that God places in our path. Conscious living is what we've been working on throughout the pages of this book.

But sometimes, we feel frustrated in our attempts to live consciously. We work hard to pay attention, yet days, even weeks go by in which we have no conscious contact with ourselves, our lives, our Higher Power, or even the people who are most important to us. As hard as we think we're trying, we still can't seem to move out of the momentum and into the moments of our lives.

If this is our case, we might want to check and make sure that we're not overlooking the obvious. For many women, a common cause of drifting off and staying asleep to self, spirit, opportunity and relationship is closer at hand than we might know. In fact, it probably could be summed up in one word: clutter.

Face it – our lives are jammed full of belongings. Clutter, chaos, possessions, stuff: the things that we have been culturally conditioned into believing will bring us fulfillment and satisfaction; the universal remedy for all that ails us. Our rooms are cluttered, our storage bins packed, our closets overflowing, our cupboards and drawers bulging at the seams. If we're not busy buying stuff, we're unpacking it, trying to find a place for it, sorting through it, picking it up, having it cleaned, wondering what to do with it, stepping over it, or in many cases, just trying to find it amidst the rest of the stuff! No wonder we feel empty and exhausted! We have unconsciously allowed our relationship with "things" to usurp our relationship to soul and to one another. We're so busy guarding, taking care of, and acquiring more possessions, we have lost touch with the joy and serenity of being present to what is really important.

We must reverse this trend if we want to live consciously, and there is only one way to do it: we must be willing to de-clutter, to get rid of everything that isn't useful or beautiful. To simplify, simplify, simplify, eliminating anything that distracts us from the real. De-cluttering and simplifying our surroundings frees up our energy so that we can be available for more important things in our lives.

This act of simplifying our surroundings will not be as difficult as we might initially think. And we don't have to become raving lunatics or whirling dervishes in order to do it! On the contrary, de-cluttering is a task that we can not only learn to do, but also learn to perform mindfully and deliberately. We can even choose to make it a meditative discipline, one that will bring us more fully into the consciousness that we seek.

This was Katie's experience. Upon returning home with her husband and three young children from their summer beach house, she was immediately overwhelmed by the amount of "stuff" in their suburban residence. At the beach, they had lived so simply and peacefully. The summer cottage was sparsely furnished, containing only what they needed. Life there felt right-sized and manageable, in direct contrast to the way she felt in a house loaded to the rooftops. Katie was sick and tired of taking care of all this stuff! She felt like her whole life was spent moving things around or worse, looking for something. She was sick and tired of getting after her children to take care of their stuff, and of being angry at her husband for not taking care of his.

She knew it was time to reassess her relationship with the "things" of her life, but where was she to begin? In the past, she accomplished her goals only by sheer willpower and extremism. She certainly didn't want to resort to those old tactics. After all, she had just spent the summer getting her priorities in place, primarily working on personal balance, spiritual growth, and family values.

Still, she knew that the stuff in her life was a burden, one that caused her to be overwhelmed, anxious, and often cranky with her children and spouse. So with serenity as her long-range goal, she made a conscious decision to de-clutter – to get rid of the belongings that were just taking up room and making her life unmanageable. At the same time, she decided to go about de-cluttering in a different way than she was accustomed. Rather than *attack* the work, she would *address* it -- methodically and peacefully.

She began by assigning one hour every day to be used solely for the purpose of de-cluttering her house. Just one hour. In her case, it was between 6 and 7 in the morning, before anyone else was up. This was her time to sort, discriminate, toss out, and in some instances, save in a designated place. She decided the night before which drawer, box, or file she planned to address the following day and, in the silence of the early morning, she focused on nothing else but the task at hand. Knowing her propensity for distraction, she kept three boxes handy at all times so that she would not have to leave the particular spot in which she worked. One box was for stuff to be thrown out, one for things to be recycled or given away, and the third box for items to be put in their rightful place.

As the days passed, she began to look forward more and more to this morning ritual of sorting and discarding. It was a peaceful, almost meditative, hour each day in which she could be totally present and focused on what she was doing. The more she sifted and sorted, the easier it became. Eventually, her consciousness of "stuff" increased to such an extent that she paid closer attention to what she and her family members brought into the house. She became much more discriminating with purchases, buying only what they needed, not what they wanted in the moment. This eliminated a great deal of potential future clutter.

If we want conscious living, we, too, must get rid of anything that keeps us unconscious. We can free up our energy and de-muddle our mind by de-cluttering our home: step by step, drawer by drawer, little by little. Then, like Katie, we can begin to pay attention to everything that comes into our house. When shopping, we become clutter-conscious, asking ourselves, "Do I really need this, or will it just add to the clutter? Where will we put it? Do I already have three of them? Does it match anything or is it just a good buy?" After all, buying something just because it is a great deal is similar to finishing up everything on our plate just to keep from wasting it. Both ways, we end up with more than we want or need.

The important thing to remember about de-cluttering is that, once we begin, we must stay current or it won't be long before we are right back where we started. Therefore, on those occasions when we do buy something new, we can make room for it by getting rid of something old, either by throwing something out or giving it away. At the same time, we discipline ourselves to put things in their proper place on a regular basis. We hang them in the closet, file them away, or put them in the drawer. This de-cluttering of our immediate surroundings frees up our physical, mental, and spiritual energy. We will not only be more conscious, but not nearly as cranky and exhausted. When we are not overwhelmed with clutter, we are generally much better prepared to handle the circumstances of any given day.

The "simplicity of less" demands that we know when enough is enough. More is not, and never has been, necessarily better. Therefore, instead of having more, more, more of everything, we can choose to have only the best; instead of *doing* more, more, more, we can choose to do only the best. When we read, we can read the best. Rather than watch mindless television ad nauseam, we can only watch the best shows, those we have made a prior decision to watch. We can eat less by eating the best whole and real food, and by eating consciously rather than on the run, standing at the kitchen sink, or sitting in front of the computer. Instead of drinking the entire pot of coffee, we can choose to have a great cup of cappuccino at a time when we can sit and savor it. And how about choosing to cultivate our very best friendships, rather than running hither and yon trying to stay connected with everybody?

When it comes to simplifying our lives, we might all do well to take a page from the philosophy of an ancient Navajo Indian tribe. Their consciousness was a highly developed one that appreciated the fact that there was plenty to go around. Rather than push the other guy aside in their struggles to "get theirs," they were confident in the knowledge that there was enough to share. This spiritual enlightenment allowed them to embrace each moment of their earthly existence without undue anxiety, and to experience the daily joy of the journey. They were a people who "walked their talk" when it came to the following principles:

Only use/take what you need.
Provide for others.
Do not waste.

This, too, is our call. By bringing these principles into our everyday consciousness and putting them into action, we can move towards the simplicity -- and the joy -- of less. Therein lies our freedom.

What *Really* Matters?

In the same way that discernment is pivotal to our ability to take right action (as we learned in the previous chapter), it is also critical when it comes to conscious living. Daily, often on a moment to moment basis, we must determine between right choices or unhealthy ones, between motion and action, between hard work and struggle, care-taking or care-giving, between what *looks right* and what *is right.* We make these distinctions by keeping our core values and priorities in the limelight, so that our choices and decisions remain compatible with them. When we get off the beam, which we often and painfully do (after all, we have our human qualities), we must return over and over, again and again, to the basic question of, "What *really* matters?"

This is conscious discrimination at work, and we usually start developing it when we have experienced some sort of emotional catharsis in our lives. This turning point might be the result of a crisis or change; it might happen as a response to a glimpse or an awakening in our lives. It might be a byproduct of becoming older and wiser, or it might be the result of working the Solutions recommended in this book! Whatever triggers our turning point is of little consequence. What is important is that we remain true to our discriminating process.

For most of her adult life, Susan's primary concern was to get married, have a husband, and raise a family. This was her dream, and even though it is a common and appropriate one, in this particular case it was underscored by fear, primarily, the fear that there weren't enough men to go around, and that she wouldn't get hers.

Because of this underlying fear, Susan was not particularly discriminating when it came to choosing potential partners. Unwilling to risk being alone, time after time she would find herself in relationships with men whose interests in no way mirrored her own. More problematic than dissimilar interests, however, was the fact that their intrinsic values were in conflict. While there are many things in life over which we can compromise, we cannot compromise our values for long. We might chose to disagree about movies, friends, when and what to eat, even politics. But if we have a value of honesty and our partner is dishonest, this is a non-negotiable difference. If we value fidelity and our partner does not, this is also an area that does not lend itself to compromise.

After years of thwarted relationships, heartache, and disillusionment, Susan began to wake up to the fact that she needed to do things differently. Rather than look *for* a man, she decided to try something novel – to ask herself, "What exactly was she looking for *in* a man? What values was it essential for them to share? What was her bottom line on certain behaviors? What was she unwilling to compromise?"

As she began taking an inventory, Susan came to the realization that being healthy had always been one of her top priorities. For years she had taken good care of herself, eating right, working out, not smoking, imbibing in little alcohol, having regular checkups, taking yoga classes, and even meditating. She realized that it was important for her to have a mate who shared some of these holistic disciplines. Having children was also high on her list of priorities. And yet, because she had habitually operated from the perspective of not-enough-to-go-around, she had repeatedly ended up in relationships with men whose ideas of good health included smoking a pack a day or getting drunk on week-ends, and she frequently dated men who had children from previous marriages and who were unwilling to consider having another family.

It is amazing how seldom women ask ourselves what *we* want! The moment Susan began doing just this, her consciousness increased ten fold, and her choices became healthier as a result. Although the desire for marriage and family remained high on her list, she no longer found it necessary to stay in relationships that she knew would ultimately fail because of conflicting values. Instead, she continued to clarify for herself and others what she deemed important in a life partner. And strangely enough, when she clearly defined what she wanted and needed, the universe delivered, as it often does.

Keeping our values and priorities in the forefront and remaining faithful to them is how we live a conscious life of authenticity, fulfillment and integrity. Yet, because fear-based distractions are frequent and insidious, we must stay constantly vigilant lest things that matter most become buried beneath the chaff.

After being married for a year, Earl and Kelly decided to buy a home in the suburbs. At the time, he owned a house in the state where he had previously lived, and she owned a condo on Long Island where they had settled in as a married couple. If they sold both places, then they would have enough money to put a hefty down payment on a new house.

However, before they even listed their homes for sale, Kelly fell in love with a house in the next neighborhood. It was very expensive but exactly what she thought she wanted. So much so, that it became the center of her universe. Or rather, the fear that she wouldn't get what she wanted became the center of her universe. This fear quickly took over her core consciousness as she became caught in an obsession of "what ifs" that created sleepless nights, worrisome days, and frequent disagreements with her husband.

Fortunately, Kelly is generally quite conscious. All it took to move her out of this obsession and back into reality was a question from one of her closest friends. Knowing that Kelly places much value on family, spiritual growth, and serenity, the question the friend asked was profoundly simple. "Kelly, what is most important in your life?" That one question was all it took, in Kelly's words, to restore her to sanity.

Vigilance is the key to living a conscious life. After all, if we don't pay attention, it doesn't take much for us to fall right back into feeling anxious, discontented, unfulfilled, and downright irritable, a place where we feel certain that we're missing something vital. And the truth is, when we're unconscious, we are missing something -- pretty much everything that *really* matters.

Marcy's primary goal in life was *not* to miss anything. Because of this, she had a New Year's practice of outlining her goals and objectives for the upcoming year. During this day, she'd make decisions about what courses she wanted to take, what changes she desired to make in her body, lifestyle or friends, places to visit, people to see, and creative enterprises to explore. All of which were worthy goals, to be sure.

But at some deeper level of her being, Marcy generally felt more fragmented than fulfilled. Being continually over-booked and in a hurry had been the modus operandi for most of her life. So one New Year's Day, when her inner unrest was really getting her attention due to a relationship difficulty, she had her moment of truth. She was worn-out due to all her commitments, and sick and tired of feeling frazzled most of the time. So this particular year, rather than write her normal "what I want to do" list, she spent some serious time getting in touch with what was *really* important to her. In other words, what were her core values and priorities? What *really* mattered?

The first three words that came to mind when she seriously considered her priorities were peace, love, and service. This prompted her to ask some questions she had neglected to ask herself for many years. How peaceful was her life? Was she doing her part to promote harmony in her home, in her relationships, in the world? Did she feel fulfilled at the end of a day, or simply exhausted from a hectic pace of living? Was she living the moments of her life, or was she so totally caught up in the blur of the momentum that everything was experienced in a daze?

And what about love? When was the last time she spent a whole week-end with her mother? How often did she stay in touch with her siblings? When did she go out of her way for one of her friends? What sort of service did her life reflect? Was she generally helpful to others or to a Higher Cause, or were all of her energies consumed by satisfying her own desires?

By honestly answering these questions, Marcy became painfully aware of just how far she had strayed from the things that were most important to her. Fortunately, as soon as she became conscious of her innermost values and priorities, they became the reference point for her much revised 'to do' list. Marcy will be the first to tell you that, although she may accomplish fewer things these days, she is infinitely more fulfilled.

What *really* matters? This is the question that we need to vocalize on a regular basis lest we forget who we are and what really counts. It might increase our consciousness to think about the underlying message of the following tale adapted from the Brothers Grimm in *The Book of Virtues* (Simon and Schuster, 1993). It speaks volumes about keeping our priorities in place.

Once there was a feeble old woman whose husband died and left her all alone, so she went to live with her son and his wife and their own little daughter. Every day the old woman's sight dimmed and her hearing grew worse, and sometimes at dinner her hands trembled so badly the peas rolled off her spoon or the soup ran from her cup. The son and his wife could not help but be annoyed at the way she spilled her meal all over the table, and one day, after she knocked over a glass of milk, they told each other enough was enough.

They set up a small table for her in a corner next to the broom closet and made the old woman eat her meals there. She sat all alone, looking with tear-filled eyes across the room at the others. Sometimes they spoke to her while they ate, but usually it was to scold her for dropping a bowl or fork.

One evening just before dinner, the little girl was busy playing on the floor with her building blocks, and her father asked her what she was making. "I'm building a little table for you and Mother," she smiled, "so you can eat by yourselves in the corner someday when I get big."

Her parents sat staring at her for some time, and then suddenly both began to cry. That night at dinnertime, they led the old woman back to her place at the big table. From then on she ate with the rest of the family, and her son and his wife never seemed to mind a bit when she spilled something every now and then.

Consciousness is what enables us to keep our values and priorities in the limelight so that we can walk in the courage of our convictions. It is what paves the road for us to become fully ourselves: women who know what *really* matters.

Sensory Awareness

One of the major stumbling blocks to a woman's ability to be present in the moment is the fact that we are so good at multi-tasking. Instead of doing one thing at a time -- i.e. giving our undivided attention to the person, place, or task at hand -- our body engages in several activities at once while our mind is preoccupied elsewhere. Not only does this intensify our feelings of anxious-apartness and depletion, but it also contributes to "sense sedation." In other words, our God given senses of seeing, hearing, touching, tasting and smelling have become lethargic and jaded due to over-stimulation and under-appreciation.

One way to become fully conscious is to begin paying attention to, honoring, and valuing the multi-faceted and marvelous nature of these five senses. In their more practical function, our senses work like radar to warn us of impending doom and give us the means to stay safe and thus survive. We look before crossing a street, we listen for the sound of an intruder, we touch to feel if the burner is hot, we taste the bitter potion, we smell the smoke of a dangerous fire.

But the gift of our senses was intended for far more than keeping us safe. Our five senses are also the means by which we connect with our sensate nature, the direct line into our physical capacity for pleasure and joy. Unfortunately, we have frequently overused and abused this primary purpose of our wonderful senses. By attempting to have it all and do it all, and with lives overloaded with stimuli from every direction and on every front, we have become desensitized. We see and hear so much that we actually see and hear very little. We touch, taste, and smell on such an unconscious level, that our awareness of these senses is minimal as well. Periodically, we may try to shake our senses awake by seeking the sensational, but this only contributes to our missing out on the wonders of the ordinary.

If "moment consciousness" is what we seek, we must make a conscious decision to stop our frantic and fragmented busyness and put our full attention on the immediate task, activity, person, or moment at hand; if we are eating or drinking, to focus attentively on how things taste; if we are looking, to really see; to hear when listening, smell when smelling, to feel when touching. Rather than continually upping the ante on the sensate, conscious awareness is our solution for waking up and experiencing the fullness of each moment.

Our five senses were intended to help us do this. Yet how well do we utilize our senses to increase our capacity to enjoy the pleasure of moment consciousness? It might help for us to take a quick "senses inventory." When was the last time we actually tasted the food we eat? When did we linger over a meal, savoring every mouthful, chewing our food deliberately and mindfully, rather than eating in a hurry, in the car, or at our desk? When was the last time our taste buds actually exploded with pleasure? We would probably have much less of a problem with obesity in this country if our relationship with our sense of taste became a conscious one.

What about the way we listen? When someone is speaking to us, is our mind focused on what they are saying, or is it busy thinking up a response? Is our body physically present to the one doing the talking, or does it convey the message that we are impatient to move on? What about our heart? Is it open wide enough to hear the feelings beneath the spoken word, or is it hardened and closed?

How often do we listen to ourselves as we speak? Are we communicating to others clearly and honestly? Do we say what we mean, and mean what we say, but not say it meanly? Do our words reflect who we really are? Are they in keeping with our inner truths? If our values include that of peace and harmony, is this evidenced in our manner and countenance when speaking? Or do we lash out with a harsh tongue, even raising our voice to get a point across?

Active communication is not the only place where we would benefit from auditory mindfulness. Remembering that our senses were given to us to promote pleasure and joy, we might ask ourselves when we last connected with our deeper self by listening attentively and consciously to music that stirs the soul, a distant train rumbling through the night, surf gently lapping the shore, rain playing a symphony upon the roof, wind whipping through the trees, the steady sweet breathing of our child, or the hum of bees in a field of wildflowers?

What about our sense of sight? When was the last time we really looked at this marvelous creation called life or the bounteous beauty of the world around us? When did we notice, beyond a passing glance, the magnificence of a sunrise, the perfection of a snowflake, the crinkle lines on our smiling grandmother's face, or the look of sweet success from our two-year-old? When did we last take a long, loving look at the autumn sky, the sparkling stars at night, or our lover's eyes?

How long has it been since we actually looked at our neighbor, or at a family member? Did we really notice our child as he grew those last two inches? What about our own reflection staring back from the mirror? If our eyes are the windows to our soul, do we take the time and attention to look deep within ours?

What would an inventory tell us about our sense of smell? Have our poor olfactory glands become so saturated with manufactured scents that we have lost touch with the natural and real? Can we recall the last time we smelled the sweet air of the sea, a wood fire burning in the distance, our youngster's skin as we tucked them in at night, or sheets that have been line dried?

Scents have a lot to tell us when we pay attention to them. Some remind us of memories long past. Some caution us what to avoid. Others tell us what we might like. Several scents simply please.

Each morning, Sonya takes the bus into the city to go to work. Normally, it is full of commuters reading their papers, drinking their coffee, and eating bagels and donuts. But Sonya, having always been rather health conscious, doesn't bring coffee and donuts for her morning commute. Instead, every morning, she brings a big, juicy orange. About halfway to her destination, she takes it out and slowly peels it. Within seconds, the entire bus fills with its wonderful aroma. There is hardly a person there who doesn't momentarily enjoy the smell of that orange. In fact, many of them probably think, "What a great idea. I'm going to bring an orange tomorrow instead of a donut." Of course, when the next day comes, they have fallen asleep again and end up doing the very same thing they did the day before.

Last, but certainly not least, let us take an inventory of our relationship to touch. What can we tell ourselves about touch? Have we forgotten the simple pleasure of stroking, patting, fondling, or caressing? What do we touch that brings us into the conscious moment, instead of out of it? Do we touch everything lightly, knowing it is fragile and temporary, or do we grab and horde the things of life? And what place does reverence have in relationship to our sense of touch? Have we lost "touch" with that?

If this sense inventory has revealed that our tendency is to undervalue and neglect our individual senses, we might want to try an experiment to help us get out of the momentum and into the moment. Actually, sensory awareness is as close as the hand in front of us. All we have to do is take five minutes in the midst of any busy day, stop everything, and then, beginning with our thumb, go through our five senses individually, giving total and due attention to each one in the moment. Wherever we are, no matter what we're doing, we can stop and take five minutes to smell, hear, taste, touch, and see whatever is in the moment we presently occupy.

Our sensory consciousness can also be increased by making small changes in the way we habitually do things. For instance, we could walk around the block instead of driving, allowing us to see, smell, and hear things we would never experience while in our car. Placing ourselves in a different chair during mealtimes allows us to see the individuals we share the table with in a new light. We could sit and sip our morning coffee consciously, instead of making it mobile. We could spend five minutes practicing touching things lightly.

Sensory awareness is all about bringing us back into the moments of our lives that we so often and quickly step out of. By giving us five great and diverse ways to experience the *now*, our senses are bound to increase our capacity for pleasure, serenity, and consciousness. Isn't one moment of consciousness worth more than a day of its opposite? After all, as Hugh Mulligan quotes, "What we do with today is important because we're exchanging a day of our lives for it." If we want to *experience* our lives instead of simply drifting through them, consciousness must be our choice. Because *life is not about getting there, but about experiencing the joy in the journey.*

Soul Satisfaction

God not only gave us the ability to see, taste, smell, hear, and touch, but also graced us with a sixth sense, one that could be likened to having an inner eye. This inner eye knows everything and sees all. It goes by the name of Soul. Soul – spirit, psyche, true being, vital force, higher consciousness. Soul arrived with us when we were born and will transition with us when we depart this earthly manifestation called life. Soul is, has been, and always will be our connecting link. It connects us to our authentic selves, it makes possible our deepest connections to special others along the path, and it keeps us mindful that we are part and parcel of something Greater than ourselves. According to Ralph Waldo Emerson, "The only thing in the world of value is the active soul."

Our soul/spirit knows the Truth, and when we live our lives in accordance with this truth, we are able to embody what we truly seek: authentic connection and genuine fulfillment. Yet, in many ways, we are even more out of touch with this inner eye than we are with our other five senses. So, just as we took an inventory of those senses, it behooves us to do the same regarding the state of our soul and our relationship to it.

We might begin by trying to envision our soul. If we could see our spirit, what would it look like? Would it be light and open, with wings ready to fly, feet eager to skip, and a heart bursting with song? Or would it, instead, have slumped shoulders from neglect, feet buried in murky despair, and contain the unsung melodies of a lifetime?

If we could paint our psyche, what colors would it reflect back to us? Would it pulsate with a vibrant red or passionate purple? Would it manifest serenity in the color of peaceful blue or glow with the iridescent purity of a newborn star? Or would it, instead, fade into the shadows as a gray unseen child in grief?

If we could sing out our vital force, what would the words and melody sound like? Would they consist of alleluias unending in their praise and gratitude? Or would they be, instead, the sour notes and hoarse discord of apathy and cynicism?

Does our soul have a feel-good boldness that comes from knowing itself? Does it overflow with joyful expectation of what remains to be seen? Does it eagerly participate in seeking other souls? Or does it shy away from connection, a stranger to itself and others, doubting the reality of true communion?

These are the questions we must ask ourselves in order to live consciously. Because:

We are soul -- in need of a spiritual awakening.
We are soul -- in need of being discovered, uncovered, and recovered.
We are soul -- in need of a shaking out and dusting off.
We are soul -- desirous of divine and human attention.
We are soul -- worthy of our own consideration.
We are soul -- knowing what fulfills us.
We are soul -- deserving to have our needs satisfied.

We have already spoken of several ways to experience this soul satisfaction. They all involve being mindful, taking the time to tune into our senses, paying attention to what is directly in front of us. Anytime we luxuriate in moment consciousness, we satisfy our soul. And once our soul gets a taste of attention, it entreats us to make these moments more the norm than the exception. This requires a radical shift in our priorities. *Primarily, it involves changing our focus from solely satisfying our desires, to desiring to satisfy our soul.* In other words, if we want to experience soul satisfaction, we must make soul satisfaction our priority.

One way we can work on soul satisfaction is by learning to identify and then to follow our bliss. Bliss is a byproduct of being with people and being involved in circumstances that energize and feed us, that make our heart sing, and that bring us joy and delight. The only way we can experience this bliss in our lives is by waking up and asking ourselves some pertinent questions. What sets us on fire? When do we become totally engrossed in what we're doing or speaking about? When do we feel more fully ourselves and alive than at any other time? If the answer is still, "I don't know," once again, who should we ask?

Nobody knows better than we do about what sparks our soul and makes us tingle. Regardless of our apathy/denial, we truly do know under what circumstances and with whom we feel more ourselves than at other times. The problem is, we don't always acknowledge and honor this inner truth. When we don't follow our soul's lead, our passions becomes dulled. Instead of leading us onward into what stimulates and fulfills, our misdirected passion turns into depression, frustration, and anger. Passion gone astray and left unexpressed is what eventually creates bitter old women.

Sometimes we attempt to placate our inner clamors for more of the authentic by promising them future fulfillment. That was Marie's case for years. Working as a sales rep for a huge manufacturing company, she felt more fatigued than fulfilled on any given day. However, she kept telling herself that by the time she turned fifty, she would have enough financial security to really begin living her life. Unfortunately, due to pancreatic cancer, Marie never made it to fifty.

We cannot postpone until tomorrow what our soul cries out for today. Still, it doesn't have to be all or nothing. Few of us are in the position of being able to quit everything we're presently doing to totally follow our bliss. That was certainly Colleen's case. As a single mother of three, she needed her full time job in order to put food on the table and provide her family with health benefits. Yet it had always been her dream to write. When sharing this desire with a close friend, she was asked how much time she presently spent writing. The answer was, of course, none at all. After all, she was waiting to quit her full-time job in order to write the great American novel. It had never occurred to her to begin following her bliss in a less dramatic and more balanced fashion.

Upon the advice of her friend, Colleen began looking for smaller and more practical ways to explore her desire for writing. She ended up by showing her children how to do the weekly laundry, and then giving them this Saturday morning chore so that she could devote this time slot to her writing. She also decided to become right-sized. Rather than attempt a novel, she began by working on a short story about her very flamboyant mother. The process of writing this story satisfied her soul at a very deep level. To her increased delight, a local magazine published her story and more publications followed.

Once we begin following our bliss, it is amazing how the universe conspires to help us. Individual and invisible hands come forth to assist us, often in surprising and unexpected ways. People are put in our path, doors open all by themselves, support comes in the way we need it most, when we need it most. We call such things coincidental and serendipitous, but at this point, we are probably beginning to recognize that coincidence is God's way of remaining anonymous.

It is important to note that following our bliss is not about hedonism or self-centeredness. Although it encourages putting our "shoulds" to the side, the process of satisfying our soul is almost always involved with sharing or giving something away. If we are feeling unfulfilled in our heart space, this might be a sign that we need to be of some service in the world. This is not about selling our soul, but about digging deep into our soul, claiming our gifts and passion, and offering them up to the universe in a way that will benefit others as well as ourselves. We all have gifts, and if we've been doing the previous work of these Solutions, we have undoubtedly resurrected some old ones and uncovered some new ones.

This was Sandy's case. After years of owning her own photography business, she realized that her heart and soul had long ago vacated her work. Taking school pictures of sports teams no longer fulfilled her. Even though she was providing a service, most days her motivation came from a sense of duty rather than desire. Underlying everything was her biggest fear -- she might end up just like her mother, stoic in her responsibilities but totally lacking in the joy of living.

In her frustration and desire for change, Sandy joined a meditation group that met twice a week in her neighborhood. Good things began to happen right from the beginning. The practice of slowing herself down enabled her to give up smoking, a habit she had struggled with for years. She even lost weight in the process! It was also during a deep meditation that an idea came to her of how she might use her gifts in a way that would re-energize her passion for photography, and be of service to others at the same time. This vision involved teaching female inmates at the local prisons how to take pictures. After all, she had always wanted to do something to help women restore their self-esteem and confidence. Photography would be a wonderful medium to facilitate this. Not only that, but she also had many contacts in the business world who would help supply her with the necessary equipment.

The more she meditated on this possibility, the more excited and passionate she became. And wasn't it coincidental that she just happened to run into the woman in charge of prison affairs at the local library? After more red tape than she would have liked, Sandy taught her first photography class to a small group of five female prisoners. Her soul felt engaged and satisfied as never before. Not only was her energy restored, but it also spilled into her day job in which she began to take renewed interest. When we bring new life to the world, we bring new life to ourselves and visa versa.

If our spirit is feeling unfulfilled, it is probably a sign that we need to be of service *somewhere.* Once again, this is not about trying to be all things to all people. It is about listening for our soul's lead and then following it. We all have gifts that are longing to be shared. It might be as simple as lending a listening ear to a nursing home patient, driving a neighbor to a chemotherapy appointment, arranging the flowers for the altar, organizing the fund drive, or teaching our art through continuing education. Taking never makes us feel as alive as giving does.

But if take we must, then let's take a stand! We can take a stand for breast cancer, for an environmental concern, for the rights of women or children, or to help promote our political candidate. We can look around and find one cause, one committee, or one commitment that shakes, rattles and rolls our soul. We can be alert for opportunities that resonate with our highest ideals and then give to them fully and freely, joyfully and selflessly. If we don't think one person can effect lasting change, we might want to remember Rosa Parks' contribution to the Civil Rights Movement.

We are not living consciously if our life does not include service. Women who find ways to express and share their passion live longer and feel better while doing so. We must listen to the urging of our soul, find a cause that is in keeping with our passion, and jump into it wholeheartedly. The good news is, according to Julia Cameron in her best selling *The Artist's Way*, "What we are seeking is also seeking us." And when that connection is made, our soul will not only be satisfied, it will be delighted.

Celebrate Mystery

As we conclude our journey through crisis and change on the path of conscious living, we might want to revisit the promises laid out in the beginning of the book to see how well they apply to our lives today. If we have been taking the suggestions as outlined in these chapters (rather than just reading or giving them lip service), chances are that some, if not all, of the following have come true in our lives.

- We have developed a greater compassion for the women we were and a deeper love for the women we are.
- Our inner security is not contingent upon the outer circumstances of our lives.
- We are no longer paralyzed by fear of the unknown.
- We have tools to cope with our insecurities and our circumstances as they arise.
- Our inner wounds have been uncovered, salved, and healed.
- Our lives are lived purposefully, not randomly.
- We no longer feel isolated and alone.
- We put our energy into the solution, rather than the problem.
- We feel confident that our needs can be used as God's opportunity.
- We have experienced first-hand the words expressed by Thomas Merton. "When we find our own true selves, we find God; and when we find God, we find our own true selves."

These promises have put us on the path to right living. Yet, we cannot rest on our laurels. We must continue to keep our eyes wide open, remaining vigilant for the first sign of one of our greatest enemies, one who walks just one step behind us at all times. His name is Indifference, and he is a killer when it comes to living consciously. He kills spirits, souls, energy, passion, and even hope. Our indifference comes in many guises, including self-sabotage and disregard towards ourselves, lack of concern for the needs and feelings of others, and spiritual apathy. While our Solutions have given us the tools to wake up and take action, they are not intended to be simply studied once and then put away. Indeed, these Solutions are to become a new way of life, one that allows us not only to cope with, but also to embrace the reality of the known, the uncertainty of the unknown, and the mystery of the Unknowable.

It is this marvelous mystery that we are encouraged to celebrate. Because when all is said and done, life is mystery. We are mystery, God is mystery, all is mystery. Life events happen with and without our permission or design. Circumstances shock and surprise us, disappoint, delight, and distress us. People and things are painfully removed from our lives; others are placed in our path unexpectedly. None of it makes much sense and, in truth, most things "remain to be seen." Therefore, rather than continue to fear, dread, or try to figure life out, we can make a conscious decision to trust, appreciate, and celebrate the marvelous mystery of it all.

Celebrating mystery is about living in active awe, wonder, reverence, and respect. It suggests practicing what Joseph Campbell, world-renowned author and lecturer on comparative religions and mythology, referred to as "Thou Consciousness." This is where, rather than view the world and its occupants as he, she, and it, we look upon everyone and everything as "thou." This heightened consciousness inspires a profound inner respect that is similar to that practiced by the early Southwestern Native Americans who regarded everything as sacred, from the lizard under the rock to the Great Sun God overhead.

When practiced on a consistent basis, this consciousness has tremendous potential to transform us. Seeing everything as being sacred awakens us to the magnificent mystery known as life, and empowers us to celebrate our part in it. After all, we don't have to look very hard to realize that our lives are filled with awesomeness. It is nothing short of a miracle that we have all these complicated body parts that somehow work in unison to perform the most complex of tasks. Think about the awesome mystery surrounding our orbiting earth: the miracle of sunrises and sunsets; the regularity of the tides; the migration cycle of birds; the changing of the seasons. Even though scientists try and explain the facts behind these occurrences, most of them remain a mystery. If we really want to live consciously, we need to not only take time out to appreciate these everyday miracles of life, but to also put ourselves into as many places as possible to celebrate their sacredness.

Communing with nature in any form is a great way to promote our sense of wonder, awe, and reverence. We might visit a canyon, walk upon a beach in the midst of a storm, spend a night camping on top of a mountain, catch an early morning sunrise, or simply pay attention to how Nature/God plays among the dancing clouds, dances upon the mighty waves, or sings in harmony with the frolicking wind.

Gratitude is another place in which to cultivate awe and wonder, a place that is easily accessible. We don't have to move a muscle to enter into it, only change a thought. An attitude of gratitude has more power to move us out of the negative and into the positive than practically anything else. The more we can learn to express our gratitude in thought, word, and deed, the more aware and appreciative we will be of the simple joys in life that we so often overlook or take for granted. Gratitude goes hand in hand with reverence. And if we want to practice reverence, all we need to do is s*low down, open our eyes, and honor whatever we find in front of us.* We surely don't need to wait until we are given a cancer diagnosis or lose a loved one before doing this.

As great as nature and gratitude are to inspire our reverence, nothing has more potential to nurture our sense of mystery than the place of silence – solitude, quiet, peacefulness, serenity. The more willing and committed we can become to put ourselves in these places, the greater our chances are for both living consciously and celebrating mystery, because the two cannot be separated.

There are several ways to enter the silence. On a daily basis, as discussed in our Third Solution on Growing Spiritually, we can book-end our individual days with prayer and meditation. During the day, when feeling overwhelmed with fatigue or emotional excess, we can make a conscious decision to stop, breathe ourselves back into the moment at hand, become clear about our priorities, and then take a moment to glance around at, or think about, the mystery of it all.

On a weekly basis, we can assign one full day for leisure, a concept on which the generations before us placed far more importance. Without the distractions of modern conveniences and shopping centers open at all hours, they understood the value of taking the time just to be. Perhaps they even used this time to reflect upon their many blessings, or upon the miracle of life itself. Indeed, we have had many role models over the years who have demonstrated the significance of taking time off from regular duties and routines; even God took a day off!

If we really want to live consciously and celebrate mystery, we could even go one step further by making a commitment to take at least one week-end each year for a spiritual tune-up; to go away on a retreat, a place where we can reflect, refresh, rejoice, and renew our relationship with spirit/soul. Consciousness thrives upon these self-designated times of *"soulitude*."

And if we want to increase our chances of being transformed even more, we could really jump in the fire by deciding to go on a longer retreat every few years – one that lasts a week or more. Not a vacation, but time devoted entirely to entering into the stillness, into the illuminating silence of God's universe, into the place that our own true selves can be found. If we dare to do this, and if we have the patience to sit quietly in the stillness, it is guaranteed that there will come the moment when we will hear God's voice as it softly calls us by name, invites us into deeper relationship, and gently whispers in our ear the wisdom of all ages: "Life is not about getting there, but about experiencing the joy in the journey."

Living Consciously

There are no suggestions or meditation for this final chapter of *The Joy is in the Journey.* It is the author's hope that you, the reader, will be able to take it from here; that you will be at a place in your own spiritual journey where you intuitively know what to do next; that you will have discovered the pure joy and serenity that comes from standing tall, taking responsibility for your actions as well as your reactions, and living life consciously. In other words, it is hoped that you have done more than learned to survive, but that you have experienced the simple delight of taking a long, loving, look at the marvelous-ness within you and around you.

If you are having difficulty with how to meditate, perhaps you can take time to simply sit and reflect upon the fact that somebody who doesn't even know you has spent over six years of her life writing this book, in the hopes that it might enable you to cope better with the particulars of your critical or transitional period, and to help you find a little more of yourself and the God of your understanding in the process.

You might spend some time thinking about all the women who have shared bits and pieces of their lives throughout this book with the hope that you will identify with their stories and their feelings and know that you are not alone. You might reflect upon just how it happened that this book found its way into your hands in the first place. And, most importantly, you might give some serious thought to the fact that regardless of what has happened to you or in your life, you are lovable, just as you are; you are worthy, just as you are; and you matter to a Power Greater than yourself more than you will ever know.

About The Author

In addition to being an author, Betty Hill Crowson is a Personal Life Coach, Retreat Director, and Licensed Social Worker who has spent over two decades working in the areas of crisis intervention, grief counseling, addictive behaviors, and spirituality. Her women's spiritual retreats, workshops, and in-service training under the trademark of The Joy is in the Journey® are highly in demand and reviewed as "life changing" by participants. Betty is a popular and charismatic speaker/writer/teacher with an unusual ability to synthesize traditional and current wisdom-knowledge into an easily understood and practical form. More information about her work can be obtained by visiting www.thejoyisinthejourney.com.

Made in the USA
Middletown, DE
01 August 2018